URBAN ECONOMIES
Analysis and Policy

URBAN ECONOMIES

Analysis and Policy

R. W. VICKERMAN

Senior Lecturer in Economics
The University of Kent at Canterbury

Philip Allan

First published 1984 by

PHILIP ALLAN PUBLISHERS LTD
MARKET PLACE
DEDDINGTON
OXFORD OX5 4SE

British Library Cataloguing in Publication Data

Vickerman, R. W.
Urban economies.
1. Urban economies 2. Great Britain——
Economic conditions——1945–
I. Title
330.941′0858 HC256.5

ISBN 0-86003-057-1
ISBN 0-86003-152-7 Pbk

Typeset by Activity Ltd., Salisbury, Wilts
Printed and bound in Great Britain by
Billing and Sons Ltd., Worcester

To Stephen and Jennifer

Contents

Preface

The aim of this book is to provide a rigorous and consistent introduction to the economic analysis of urban areas and to place into context recent research in this general field. It is also a book about urban economic policy and the analysis of specific policies affecting urban economies. It is principally aimed at students taking courses at advanced undergraduate level in urban or regional economics; parts of the book may also be of value to students of transport, housing or public finance. However, the more technical sections of the book are largely self-contained; the general argument is presented in a way which non-specialist economists can follow. All that is required is a basic training in economic principles. The subject matter of the book should be of interest to geographers, planners and students of urban society generally.

The book is based on a course in Urban Economics which I have given to third-year students of economics and urban studies at Kent. This encourages students to use other literature as a supplement to textbooks and I have included guides to further reading at the end of each main chapter. These both consolidate and extend the discussion of the chapter. No attempt has been made to provide a totally exhaustive bibliography of the subject but key developments and pieces of evidence are referenced in the text.

The book is also about policy and concentrates on issues of current concern. This limits the effective discussion to Britain to ensure a consistent treatment of the subject and avoid unnecessary comparisons. However, I believe that examination of recent and current British policy in this area is of relevance to students of urban economic problems in other countries, and although the treatment of policy is not exhaustive, I hope that it will serve as a useful introduction to British urban policy for those in other countries.

Any writer of a textbook is indebted to those whose works he has read and digested. I hope that all representations made in this book are fair, but final responsibility for all views expressed lies with the author. I am also deeply indebted to my colleague, Ian Gordon, for the time he has spent in discussing the ideas in this book and in reading drafts of the manuscript. Without his insightful comments it would have been much less perfect, but he is not implicated in any imperfections which remain as a result of my failure to take his advice.

Once again my wife, Chris, has worked wonders in producing immaculate typescript in the far too little time I have given her. This book is dedicated to Stephen and Jennifer who have too often been shouted at for disturbing my thoughts. My hope is that understanding of the contents of this book may make a better world in which they may live.

Roger Vickerman
Canterbury, December 1983.

PART ONE

Analysis of the Urban Economy

1
Urban Economics and the Urban Economy

Much of recent economics has been plagued by a rather artificial distinction between what are usually called microeconomics and macroeconomics. The problems of the behaviour of individual consumers or firms and their interaction in markets tend to be analysed quite separately from the behaviour of economic aggregates and the performance of the national economy as a whole. There exists, however, an important range of problems between these two extremes which has required the consideration of a more integrated view of these approaches: the economic problems of local economies, regions and urban areas. Because of the smaller spatial scale of the economy, the relationships between aggregates and the components of those aggregates in terms of the economic decisions of firms and other residents of the economy are much more immediate and this leads to a necessary consideration of such relationships in an explicit manner. Even here, however, there have grown up rather different traditions which have distinguished between *urban* economics and *regional* economics. What this book sets out to do is to establish a more integrated and rigorous basis for the study of the economies of urban areas in all their dimensions and to try to cut across some of the divides.

Regional economics in Britain has traditionally concerned itself with the behaviour of macroeconomic aggregates at a spatial level below that of the national economy. The approach has essentially followed a typical income–expenditure view of an economy, examining both the static and dynamic properties and concentrating particularly on the sources of regional divergence within an otherwise unified economy. The principal rationale for regional economics has been the need to provide policy advice and to provide a theoretical underpinning for the infrastructure of regional policy which has developed in the post-war period.

Urban economics has a somewhat different history, but one which is rather more firmly rooted in microeconomics. There are essentially three strands of interest which have come together in modern urban economics. One is common to urban and regional economics: an interest in location theory, and particularly in industrial location, as a means of explaining why some economic activities are located in different places. The second is the gradual development of a theory of land-use and urban land rents which has a series of different origins: in nineteenth-century agricultural economics, in the economics of real property, and in geographical theories of urban structure. The third strand of interest, and the most recent, is a concern with the welfare economics problems posed by the growth of urban areas in the latter half of the twentieth century. Problems of dealing with congestion, pollution, housing provision, public transport and, more recently, urban unemployment, as well as concentrations of deprived families in inner urban areas, have dominated much of the discussion and the development of the subject.

Parallel to these developments in regional and urban economics has been the growth of regional science, tackling the same problems and often using the same techniques, but with a rather different philosophy. Regional science has developed out of the principal interest in location and has dealt with the general difficulty of incorporating spatial aspects into traditional economic theories by the use of mathematical programming techniques to simulate the organisation and behaviour of a local spatial economy. Because of the advantages of using such models as planning tools, regional science has increasingly formed the basis of regional planning.

In recent years there has been renewed interest among economists in the more fundamental problems of a spatially organised economy and this has manifested itself in a new branch of the subject, appropriately (though perhaps inaccurately) called the 'new urban economics'. The primary objective of this new development has been to demonstrate, first, that it is possible to derive consistent general equilibrium models of cities from basic principles of economic behaviour and secondly, that such models provide a better basis for economic policy assessment and evaluation. These general equilibrium models use the basic tools of economic analysis, notions of utility and production functions and markets (but with spatial dimensions and transport sectors) to provide insights into the allocation of land to different uses, levels of rents, the total size of the city in terms of area or population and the level and distribution of economic welfare. In contrast to the regional science type of model, the new urban economics aims to produce analytically-determined solutions rather than just simulations of cities, and hence to be able to answer questions about optimality. The great drawback to the new urban economics approach is its dependence on equilibrium solutions when it would often appear that urban problems arise specifically because of disequilibrium. Also, in order to provide tractable analytical solutions, it must often rely on certain very restrictive assumptions in certain aspects (a typical one is the concentration of all production in a single area at the city centre) which, although they do not alter the structure of the model or its solution, render it less useful as a practical application for policy purposes.

This book sets out to provide a structure for the study of the entire economies of urban areas in all their dimensions, and to make an assessment of recent urban policies in Britain in the light of this analysis. In order to distinguish it from the traditional approach of urban economics it has been titled *Urban Economies*. This is not just semantics: it draws attention to the fact that the book needs to draw on a much wider range of theoretical background than just that which is provided by urban economics of either traditional or new persuasions. However, this is a book essentially about economics and not about regional or urban planning. Our interest in the location of activity and the use of land is from the standpoint of understanding what effect it will have on the economic aggregates of the city—income, employment, etc.—and the welfare of its residents. It is also necessary to consider the relationships between different urban economies, and most particularly between the national economy and the local economy.

The book is divided into two principal parts. In Part I, Chapters 2 to 4, we shall concentrate on the development of an analytical framework, drawn from the various sources of the subject discussed above. This is not abstract analysis, however: the development of the framework is illustrated by evidence drawn from recent British experience. Part II, Chapters 5 to 8, discusses the development of policy in both a general sense and in certain key sectoral areas—transport, housing, labour markets and industrial development. A major theme of this is the nature of the relationship between central and local governments, both over these specific policies and in a more general way through the control of expenditure and the general fiscal relationship. This need to develop a total picture of policy relationships has, however, necessitated what may seem to be an excessively parochial view of the world. Except for the discussion of evidence for other countries (when this supports or refutes an argument about British experiences), we shall concentrate entirely on British data and experience. The reader should, however, gain a fairly comprehensive picture of the way in which a particular set of urban economies works and of the problems inherent in developing a coherent urban policy for these economies.

Structure of the Book

The principal emphasis of the book is on understanding the main economic linkages at work in an urban economy. It is thought, therefore, that the traditional division of texts on urban economics into clear compartments—land-use, transport, housing, public finance, etc.—is not conducive to the building-up of a total picture of an integrated economy. In the analysis section of this book we look at the economic rationale for the existence of cities and then try to build up a simple economic model showing the key relationships in the economy.

Chapter 2, therefore, discusses the basic issues in urban economies, the role of agglomeration and urbanisation economies and the way in which industrial structure has related to economic performance; it also provides a background to the development of a theoretical approach.

Chapter 3 concentrates on the internal structure of the urban economy and integrates the two basic dimensions of this: the industrial or *economic* structure and the land use or *spatial* structure. This chapter also draws attention to the links between structure and overall performance which operate through the trade of the city with other areas and to the role of an implicit urban balance of trade and payments in the context of its macroeconomic structure.

Whilst Chapter 3 is concerned essentially with the static analysis of the economy, Chapter 4 explores the dynamic processes within it. A number of alternative approaches to explaining growth and decline are outlined, including a consideration of the relationships between growth in the individual city, in other cities and in the economy as a whole.

In the second part of the book we look at different sectors in turn, essentially in the context of the different sorts of policy instrument which may be available. This recognises that it is impossible to give adequate coverage to all the issues involved in such important areas as transport, housing, the labour market or local industry. What we need to identify is the critical issue from the point of view of the operation of the overall urban economy. Considerable reliance is placed on an introduction to sources of further detailed reading.

Chapter 5 discusses the general issues of determining welfare and the possibilities for public sector intervention in the urban economy. Chapter 6 tackles the question of pricing and investment in urban infrastructure in the context of the transport and housing sectors. Particular emphasis is placed on the determination of optimal prices in the context of the city as a whole and on the analysis of subsidies, together with a review of recent policy. Chapter 7 considers factor markets and industrial investment. There are detailed considerations of unemployment and mobility and of recent urban aids to industry. Chapter 8 concludes this section with a detailed study of the basis of local fiscal relations and policy.

Neither part of the book is intended to produce complete economic models of the working of a city economy purporting to explain every aspect. Instead, a series of consistent and interrelated economic models is presented and used to analyse policy options and assess aspects of current policy. A detailed technical knowledge of economics is not necessary for understanding these; although more technical treatments of some aspects are included, especially in Chapters 3, 4 and 6, these can be omitted without any serious loss of understanding of the main arguments, as they are included in separate sections.

The Policy Context

This is a book about the economic analysis of the problems which beset urban areas in a modern economy and the way in which a better understanding of such analysis has implications for policy guidance. The second part of the book contains detailed discussions of both the rationale for local economic policies and examples of applications in relevant sectors. The book cannot hope to give a complete history of all the various aspects of government policy affecting urban areas, since this would encompass virtually the whole of central government policy. The intention has rather been to select specific aspects of policy which reflect different analytical issues: price subsidies in transport, tax subsidies in housing; policies towards retraining and mobility in the labour market; direct provision of industrial infrastructure for economic development—these are particular examples. A second aim has been to show ways in which different policies can interrelate or conflict.

Certain aspects of economic policy affecting urban areas, especially the larger cities in Britain, have been at the centre of attention in the immediate past, principally because of conflicts between perceived local and national interests. This has led to the appearance of a number of proposals for fairly radical restructuring of some aspects of central–local government relations. An attempt has been made to assess the basis and significance of some of these. The final chapter, Chapter 9, discusses the possible future of urban policy in Britain and draws attention to some of the wider aspects of this in the context of national economic growth and of Britain's place in the European Economic Community. The basic message is, in some respects, a bleak one. Persistent failure to understand the real basis of urban economic problems, and the way the various parts of these interrelate, has led to a set of inconsistent policies at both local and national levels. Recent attempts to force local government to conform more closely to national policy objectives have done little to ensure greater consistency of treatment, either within a single city or between different urban areas.

2

Basic Issues in the Urban Economy

Some 40 per cent of the world's population lives in urban areas. In Western and Northern Europe nearly 30 per cent of the population lives in cities of more than 100,000 people and 75 per cent in areas classified as urban. An even higher proportion lives in areas within or dependent on metropolitan areas. It is more difficult to ascribe production to urban and rural areas, but since urban populations in modern developed countries are typically more highly paid and have higher productivity than rural populations, it is reasonable to assume that output is even more heavily concentrated in urban areas. The most basic question we have to answer is why is this so.

2.1 Specialisation, Agglomeration and Urbanisation

The rationale for the existence of cities derives initially from the economies arising from specialisation. Economies of scale accrue to firms and external economies arise out of the increasing specialisation of the local labour force. Further economies can arise from agglomeration. Agglomeration economies comprise both those economies that are external to the firm but internal to the industry and, more importantly, economies external to the industry which arise through the coincident location of the centres of a number of market areas for different products. There is a further sort of agglomeration economy which is associated with the process of urbanisation itself: economies arise in the provision of infrastructure and social overhead capital in the urban area (houses, transport, etc.).

There are, of course, limits to the extent of such economies: most economic activities eventually run into the problem of diminishing returns. Inefficiencies in both production and in the organisation of production in an urban area which produce both internal and external diseconomies (the latter through congestion and pollution, in particular) will eventually occur. Furthermore, some of the benefits from agglomeration and urbanisation may be diverted away from the residents of the city in general through the growth of monopoly and other restraints on free exchange.

Essentially, however, cities exist because they are more sucessful in attracting resources due to higher productivity and higher returns and this advantage is a cumulative one which encourages settlements at some locations to grow at the expense of others. Growth implies both the attracting of new firms taking advantage of larger markets and pools of labour and capital, and the in-migration of population attracted by the advantage (pecuniary and otherwise) of urban living. When cities lose this advantage, the cumulative nature of the specialisation-agglomeration-urbanisation process can also work in reverse and lead to a continuing decline in fortunes.

This very simplistic overview of the rationale for the existence of cities contains a number of features which we shall need to examine in greater detail. Decisions about location of both firms and individuals will be critical. The siting of production in one location rather than another will depend on the existing competitive characteristics of that location, and will typically alter those characteristics by adding to or subtracting from the competitive advantage. Similarly, individuals' decisions about where to live will depend on employment opportunities and other advantages—the availability of housing, schools, cultural facilities, and so on. However, the total competitive advantage of a city is not just a simple sum of its parts and the impact of a marginal location decision on the city is not equal to the impact on the individual because of the externalities of agglomeration and urbanisation involved. The total impact may be greater or smaller when we take these external or social effects into account. This can be done in two ways: one is just to examine how aggregate output or city income responds to increasing city size to see if there are scale economies associated with size (this implies that an aggregate production function for the city can be defined). The second, more complex, way is to look at the internal organisation of the city. This organisation, or structure, of the city economy involves two different but related concerns which we can term economic structure and spatial structure.

The economic structure of the city involves examination not just of the degree of specialisation in city functions, but also of the amount of linkage between different activities. This has both microeconomic and macroeconomic implications in that it can determine the competitive advantage of individual plants, firms or industries and the economic performance of the city as a whole. The spatial structure also has a number of dimensions. The absolute size of the city will determine both the size of the immediate market area and the total transport costs involved in transporting labour and finished products around the city. The internal allocation of land use will depend on the structure of land rents, and this is a component of costs to both production and individual residents. Furthermore, land rents in total are a measure of the surplus from the productive sector of the economy—they represent the extent to which the city can provide urban public services without reducing the competitive advantage enjoyed by resident firms.

We shall examine each of these aspects of structure in more detail in Chapter 3. We turn in the rest of this chapter to an examination of evidence on the economic structure and performance of local economies in order to set in context the more formal theoretical analysis of Chapters 3 and 4. This will also enable some insight to be gained into the nature and extent of the urban economic problem.

2.2 Structure of Employment and Output

We have identified the critical aspects of the economic structure of the local economy to be the degree of specialisation and the extent of agglomeration and urbanisation economies. As we shall see more formally later, each of these has both positive and negative aspects. Specialisation brings economies, but also brings vulnerability to external changes in demand or loss of competitiveness through changes in the effective terms of trade. Agglomeration and urbanisation can ultimately lead to diseconomies. The incidence of an 'optimal' city size is not at the same point for all industries and hence a trade-off will need to occur. Practically, output measures are difficult to obtain for small areas, especially disaggregated to an industry level, as are reliable measures of capital inputs. We must rely initially, therefore, on measures of the structure of employment in given areas and, more particularly, on examining the way in which changes in employment (and unemployment) in a local economy can be related to its structure as opposed to more dynamic forces in the economy.

Measuring Structural Effects

Economists working on the problems of local economies have always been aware of the importance of their structure. Structure can usually only be understood in the context of the effects of changes in structure through time, though this is typically only obtained through a comparative statics analysis. In particular, attempts have been made to associate deviations in the performance of a particular local economy from that of the national economy with specific variations in industrial structure. Hence, given that different industries grow at a different rate nationally, regions with a different balance of industries will have different overall growth rates. However, it is also true that any given industry may display different growth propensities in a different location, both because of spatial variations in demand and spatial variations in production costs.

Shift-share analysis attempts to divide the total change in output or employment in an area in a given time period into three effective components: a national component, a structural or share component, and a differential or shift component. The national component applies the national growth rate over all relevant industries to the area's total employment, regardless of its actual structure or performance—it simply predicts what would have happened if the area had grown at the national aggregate rate of growth. National components are constant in proportional terms over all areas. The structural component measures the extent to which any deviation from the national rate of growth can be attributed to the deviation from the national structure of employment. It attempts to assess how much of the change is due to over- or under-representation of particular industries in the area, industries which are growing nationally at different rates from the aggregate. This component predicts what would happen if each industry in an area were to grow at its national rate of growth. The differential component measures the differential growth rate of each industry in the local economy from its national rate of growth. This is measured as the residual from the total change in employment after accounting for the first two components.

Whilst the approach is conceptually fairly straightforward, there are some difficulties in applying it in practice. Bishop and Simpson (1972) have noted that certain formulations can lead to the ascribing of some of the national component to the structural component so that, when aggregated, the structural effects fail to add up to zero at the national level. They suggest that any differential growth in an industry at the national level should be ascribed to the national component and deducted from the structural component. However, when formulated at an industry level, this approach can lead to other problems since it implies intra- as well as inter-industry structural effects, making the structural component dependent on the level of industrial aggregation used. In this case, it is the aggregation over industry groups which does not add up.

The sensitivity of the results to variations in the degree of industrial disaggregation or the period of analysis has led to criticism of the method itself by some writers (Brown 1972; Richardson 1978). Different relative component sizes can be identified for short- and long-run analyses and even changing starting and finishing dates for a particular analysis could lead to rather different results. The accumulation of longer runs of data for consistent levels of aggregation has, however, produced more consistent sets of results (Fothergill and Gudgin 1979a). However, there is a more fundamental criticism of shift-share type approaches in that whilst they can provide consistent descriptions of changes in industrial structures, they are not based on a rigorous theoretical foundation and therefore do not provide a good guide to policy options. If one finds that a lagging region's performance is mainly attributable to its structure, it is not sufficient simply to conclude that if only it had a different structure it would perform better. A change in the structure of one region is likely to affect other regions and the national economy and therefore change the parameters of the underlying economic model. Furthermore, the measurement of the differential component as a residual divorces it from any objective evidence of differential performance.

The most consistent evidence on the performance of local

economies in Britain has been collected by the Department of Applied Economics at Cambridge and the principal conclusion of its research has been that structural factors, while accounting for the differential performance of some regions, have played very little part in the performance of others (Fothergill and Gudgin 1982). Interestingly, there are no cases where a region suffers badly because of a very adverse structure (high proportion of lagging industries) and a very adverse differential performance; rather are there cases where a favourable structure (high proportion of growing industries) is counterbalanced by adverse performance (West Midlands and the South-east), or an adverse structure is compensated for by a better performance, although only to a rather lesser extent (Yorkshire and Humberside and Northern Ireland). In two other regions, Scotland and the North-west, there is both an adverse structure and a rather poor differential performance, but the impact of the latter is not large.

What is of more relevance here: Fothergill and Gudgin's work has also been extended to consider urban areas of different sizes. This suggests that structure has been virtually insignificant in contributing to the markedly different recent histories of such areas. London, as would be expected given the result for the South-east, has a very favourable industrial structure which would have implied a growth in manufacturing employment of the order of 8 per cent in the period 1959–75, whereas the actual outcome was a decline of nearly 38 per cent. Even in the other conurbations which generally had adverse industrial structures, only just over a quarter of the employment loss can be attributed to structure—rather less than that attributable to national changes. Conversely, in areas with favourable industrial structures, such as the major non-conurbation cities or county towns, that structure accounted for only 20 per cent and under 5 per cent respectively of the actual growth from 1959 to 1975 (Table 2.1). Narrowing down the area to the worst-off areas of cities (the inner areas of the major conurbations) suggests that over an even longer period (1951–76), when manufacturing employment in these areas declined by between 26 per cent in Tyneside and 56 per cent in London, the industrial structures of these areas were actually favourable in every case but that of Glasgow, where the adverse structure accounted for a loss of just 0.4 per cent. Only in the case of Glasgow (to a very marginal extent) and of London was the structural factor more favourable to industry

Table 2.1 Components of Employment Change by Type of Area, 1959–75 (% Change on 1959 Manufacturing Employment)

	Actual change	*National component*	*Structural component*	*Differential shift*		
				Total	Industrial movement	Indigenous performance
London	−37.8	−5.3	+8.3	−40.8	−12.1	−28.7
Conurbations	−15.9	−5.3	−4.2	−6.3	+1.5	−7.8
Cities	+4.8	−5.3	+1.0	+9.1	+1.1	+7.9
Industrial towns	+16.3	−5.3	−0.4	+21.9	+4.2	+17.7
County towns	+28.8	−5.3	+1.3	+32.8	+7.3	+25.5
Rural areas	+77.2	−5.3	−1.6	+84.1	+29.4	+54.7

Source: Fothergill and Gudgin (1982)

Table 2.2 Sectoral Employment in Urban Areas in the United Kingdom, 1981 (%)

	Manufacturing industry	*Distributive trades*	*Transport & communication*	*Services*
Greater London	19.0	19.1	9.6	42.6
Inner London	16.2	19.1	9.6	45.9
Outer London	20.7	19.1	9.7	40.8
Conurbations				
Greater Manchester	32.7	19.8	6.2	30.9
Merseyside	27.2	18.5	8.5	36.0
South Yorkshire	30.2	17.7	5.1	28.7
Tyne and Wear	27.8	18.4	6.1	33.9
West Midlands	41.2	18.2	4.7	27.5
West Yorkshire	32.8	19.9	5.3	29.8
Glasgow	25.0	19.1	6.9	35.7
Cities				
Aberdeen	17.0	24.0	7.4	35.3
Bournemouth & Poole	24.8	24.8	5.9	33.7
Brighton & Hove	17.2	23.2	8.7	40.4
Bristol	26.9	19.8	8.5	35.3
Cardiff	17.2	20.8	8.5	43.0
Derby	43.2	16.5	6.6	25.2
Edinburgh	16.8	13.8	7.4	47.0
Hull	30.5	21.8	9.7	27.9
Leicester	44.1	18.5	4.6	24.5

as a whole than to manufacturing which suggests that the popular story of inner cities declining because of adverse structures of old manufacturing industry and the squeezing-out effect that industries moving in may have is not particularly accurate.

These results are confirmed by the study of the conurbations by Danson *et al.* (1980) which goes further to identify separately inner and outer areas, again without finding any significant structural basis for differing performance.

Table 2.2 (cont.)

	Manufacturing industry	*Distributive trades*	*Transport & communication*	*Services*
Medway & Gillingham	28.2	17.6	6.8	33.2
Nottingham	34.9	20.4	5.5	27.3
Plymouth	21.4	19.3	5.8	44.2
Portsmouth	22.3	19.4	5.9	43.7
Southampton	24.7	20.9	12.4	32.0
Stoke-on-Trent	45.3	17.0	4.9	19.2
Towns				
Bath	24.3	20.7	4.4	47.3
Blackburn	42.3	18.2	5.0	26.6
Cambridge	17.2	19.5	6.0	48.1
Carlisle	22.0	21.6	7.9	32.8
Exeter	13.2	23.9	7.4	43.4
Gloucester	32.4	20.4	5.8	32.0
Ipswich	27.8	20.0	9.9	31.2
Lincoln	28.9	21.4	6.6	32.8
Luton	43.8	17.2	6.4	23.7
Northampton	31.3	21.9	5.7	31.4
Norwich	28.1	21.2	6.1	33.7
Oxford	17.0	15.4	3.5	39.0
Preston	28.9	23.1	6.8	36.0
Reading	24.2	20.8	8.1	37.2
York	28.3	20.6	10.2	31.6

Source: Census (1981)

Urban Industrial Structures in Britain

Even if industrial structure is not the major explanatory factor in determining the relative economic performance of a local economy, there may be other implications of structure which are relevant to an understanding of the spatial structure of the economy and indeed to determining the differential shifts which, as we have seen, are the main explainers of performance. In doing this we need to examine not just the industrial structure in terms of the mix of industries present in the area, but also the structure of production in other dimensions: the technology used (especially the land requirements for different processes), the size of firms and the age of firms. But first, let us examine the basic industrial structure of the typical urban area, or rather of a range of urban areas of different sizes.

In Table 2.2 we can see the diversity of employment structures of the major urban areas in Britain in 1981. The main general sectors for all urban areas are manufacturing industry and services, but the relative balance of these shows some wide variations. It would appear, therefore, that there is neither a simple relationship between overall city size and the importance of one sector, nor a stable underlying relationship between manufacturing industry (as the urban base) and the service sector (as secondary industry) which transcends city size.

If we disaggregate employment further into separate manufacturing and service industries, it is even more difficult to observe any coherent pattern. We must conclude, therefore, that the observed economic structure of a city is usually the result of a unique combination of circumstances which apply to that city.

There may, however, be some more specific relationships between size or economic structure and the role of certain key urban sectors such as transport or other individual urban services. The role of manufacturing industry does tend to be rather less marked in proportional terms in towns and small cities than in large cities or metropolitan areas, but this ignores the diversity found: many small cities have manufacturing sectors as large as, or, in relative terms larger than, some very large cities. Similarly, despite the diversity service sector employment becomes rather more important in small towns than in large cities or metropolitan areas (excepting London). To a lesser extent this would also be true of the distributive trades. Transport, on the other hand, is most important as a source of employment in the large cities and, with the exception of London, the metropolitan areas have a lower level of employment per head of population in transport and communication than even the small cities and towns. What we may be seeing here is a more general notion of relative efficiency and urban size: small towns need rather more service employment per head and large cities have a high *per capita* transport requirement, but metropolitan areas up to a certain size can gain greater economies in both these areas.

Of course, it is not clear from this cursory look at employment structures whether these differences are exactly reflected in output since productivity may differ between areas for many reasons: scale, local efficiency, and so forth. We must also take care not to assume that, by observing manufacturing industry set against various non-manufacturing industries, we are observing the roles of basic and non-basic industries in the sense that the former produce for 'export' as well for the 'home' market and the latter are restricted to the 'home' market. Many of the individual towns and cities which have abnormally high scores for distributive trades, transport and service employment, are those which serve either as a market centre for a much wider hinterland (and hence their economies are built on the export of such services) or which provide transport services for more than just the support of the local economy (as in the case of major ports). It becomes very difficult, therefore, even with disaggregated data, to identify the way in which the economic structure of the town may be reduced to a basic/non-basic form.

There are, however, some further factors at the more disaggregated level which need consideration: the degree of dependence on single industries or even single employers (especially in the more basic sectors) and the degree of linkage which can be identified between those industries which do exist. These are important for the macroeconomic issues which we have been concerned with so far in this chapter (in that they might indicate the degree of vulnerability of the local economy to a changing economic structure) and for the microeconomic issues of the internal organisation of the local economy in both a spatial and non-spatial way. Unfortunately, there is no way in which we can hope to provide an overall picture of urban economies as a whole here: the evidence depends on the work which has been done in great detail on individual urban economies and on attempts to draw some general conclusions from the performance of, for example, a limited number of similar areas, such as Inner Cities or New Towns.

Dominant Industries

The distributive trades actually form the leading sector by employment for many of the large cities in Britain. It is only in a few specialised centres that an individual manufacturing industry reaches a level of having 15 to 20 per cent of the working population in a single order industry. Outstanding examples of those that have are cities such as Coventry (with 33 per cent in the vehicle industry in 1971) or Stoke-on-Trent (with over 27 per cent in the bricks, pottery, glass and cement sector in 1971). Even leading textile towns such as Bradford (18.5 per cent) or Leicester (13.9 per cent) cannot match such a degree of dependence. In one of the most comprehensive studies of dominance in Britain, Lever (1978, 1979) looked at non-tertiary employment in 301 labour market areas and, taking a benchmark of 12.5 per cent of the workforce in a single industry or plant as a definition of the dominance of that labour market, concluded that as many as 95 local labour markets were plant dominated in that they had at least one plant controlling 12.5 per cent of employment (three of the 95 had more than one such plant) and a further 34 local labour markets were dominated by one industrial sector. Plant domination occurred most typically in mining and the heavier, mass production type of industrial sectors. Industry domination without plant domination occurred more particularly in the case of textiles and footwear. The effect of such domination on one economy has been reviewed for the case of Coventry by Morris and Jepson (1981).

Fear of domination, either by plants or industries, is one of the dynamic consequences on the local economy of relying on a single economic area for a large part of economic activity so that the local economy as a whole is very sensitive to upswings and downswings of that key sector. Whilst the evidence is largely against purely structural effects influencing the long-term economic performance of regions or metropolitan areas, there is clearly a greater danger of this at a more local level (although the consequences may be less serious if contiguous labour market areas are not dominated by the same industry). In Lever's study an attempt was made to analyse the effects on the local labour market of the degree of dominance which showed that there was indeed a greater vulnerability of unemployment rates to cyclical swings in the dominated labour markets (Lever 1980). However, there may be some partial compensation in that dominated labour markets are more efficient in their matching of the unemployed to vacancies, thereby reducing structural and frictional unemployment. This does seem to happen in industry-dominated labour markets—but rather less clearly so when the dominance is that of the single plant. We shall return to this issue of the operation of local labour markets in much more detail in Chapter 7.

Industrial Linkages

We have also noted that industrial linkage may be important. This is not simply a question of industry mix in the area but one of identifying the precise linkages which exist between industries: the extent to which they form demands or provide supplies for each other; the implications for trading with other local economies of such linkages; and the implications for the urban non-basic industries such as transport and financial and other services. The basic tool for the economist in these circumstances is the input–output table which provides a matrix of accounts of the production, sales and purchases of each industrial sector and which can be used as a planning tool both to identify the total effect of a change in, for example, final demand for one industry's output on all industries in the economy and on its 'imports', and to assess what might be the best mix of industries for future development in order to promote self-sustaining growth of a local economy. This latter point has been shown to be of particular significance in regional economic planning through the so-called growth pole or industrial complex analysis policies employed in a number of countries and first analysed by François Perroux (1955). However, it has also been recognised that, realistically, input–output analysis as a complete accounting matrix is only possible at a regional or large metropolitan level. Whilst the recording of the information necessary for an input–output table as part of a national income-accounting exercise is extremely difficult at the level of a local economy (partly because of problems of data confidentiality and partly because the exercise is probably not cost-effective), it is possible to build up some detail of the input–output matrix from survey methods (see, for example, the work of Morrison 1973). For certain key parts of an economy the linkages can be examined individually. The latter approach was followed in earlier studies by Lever (1972, 1974). The conclusions are interesting in that they suggest that linkages are a critical factor in industrial location and agglomeration but that, despite close local linkages, many industries purchase most of their inputs from outside the local economy.

Even though the practice of input–output analysis may not be particularly easily applied in urban economies, it does provide a useful conceptual framework from which to develop dynamic models of the urban economy; and even at a static level it draws attention to the key role of exchange within the economy. This has been developed on a general level by Parry Lewis (1979) who has attempted to extend the basic notion of a sectoral set of accounts to one of a household series of accounts which exist in parallel, since households provide labour and/or capital to one set of sectors, purchase goods from another set, exchange between each other in the purchase of housing, etc. What Parry Lewis particularly tries to show is that the many different roles which individuals play in a society as suppliers of labour, consumers, members of voluntary societies, voters, ratepayers, etc. defy any simple accounting framework and, more particularly, defy any simple categorisation of individuals, since the same person appears in different hats according to the emphasis one wishes to place on the problem. The decision-making framework of the local economy, the decisions taken, must reflect this.

2.3 The Organisation of Production

Analysing Differential Performance

It is not proposed to examine in great detail the technical characteristics of production processes in different urban economies. We know from the discussion in Section 2.2 that a large part of the differences in overall performance between local economies can be attributed to differences in the performance of individual industries between those economies and not just to industry mix. The differential component of the shift-share analysis can itself be thought of as the sum of two separate effects (Bishop and Simpson 1972; Danson *et al.* 1980) which can be termed the competitive effect and the allocative effect.

The competitive effect attempts to measure the extent to which the local economy is becoming more attractive as a location in that employment is growing faster than nationally in each industry through the attracting in of new firms, or higher-than-average rates of investment, assuming that the area has the expected structure of industry based on national structure. The allocative effect attempts to measure the extent to which such differential rates of growth are compounded by an initial structural advantage or disadvantage; for example, where an advantageous structure leads to higher rates of growth of the over-represented industries because of scale effects or other initial locational advantages. In their work on the British conurbations, Danson *et al.* (1980) found that the competitive effect typically swamped the allocative effect in terms of size, the latter often being insignificant; but there were some instances in outer conurbation areas where the benefits of a positive competitive effect were reduced to some extent by a negative allocational effect. This is important because it suggests that it is the more dynamic aspects embodied in the competitive effect which dominate the more static allocational notions of the production function. This would imply that we should look rather less at factor supplies and the simple choice of technology on the basis of factor availability and price, and rather more at such factors as the age and size of firms in an area and their propensities to invest.

Firm Size and Age

This view is also supported by studies of location and industrial movement which show that changes in manufacturing employment are much more likely to be caused by the birth and death or shrinkage of firms than by any process of relocation because of changing advantages in local economies (Keeble 1976; Gripaios 1977; Dennis 1978; Lloyd 1979). In a comprehensive study undertaken at the sub-regional level Fothergill and Gudgin (1979b, 1982) also identified the important role of new firms in areas showing above-average rates of employment growth. The importance of the age of firms has a deeper significance, too, since it will also reflect something of the age of the technology employed: new firms may typically apply new technologies which lead to greater efficiency and lower costs and hence gain potential comparative advantages. New firms may also be better able to adopt new working practices than older firms and thus be more flexible to changing economic environments. Although age and size are not necessarily related, there is a tendency for new firms to be smaller. This introduces a further dimension to their role: although they may be more efficient through having lower overhead costs, they may also be less likely to be able to employ capital intensive techniques of production. Hence the typical use of an input measure—employment—as a measure of an area's economic performance is potentially misleading if used as a policy objective: to introduce small firms in order to boost the area's economy.

Small firms are also more dependent on the economies of agglomeration and the availability of an efficient local infrastructure. It was long maintained that the economy of the typical metropolitan area was based on the activities of small firms located in central areas where they made efficient and intensive use of land and could benefit most from their proximity to each other in the provision and enjoyment of common services. As firms grew, they would tend to become more independent and self-sufficient and could move out to new locations outside central areas. This so-called incubator hypothesis of the role of central cities has been tested recently by Nicholson *et al.* (1981) following work in the United States by Leone and Struyk (1976) and Struyk and James (1975) and found to be not very convincing once the process of sorting out the differences between new firms and branch firms has been carried out. If anything, it is market-oriented firms which have a higher propensity to set up in inner areas than those seeking production-side economies (e.g. printing, clothing and similar industries): a finding also true of work in Glasgow by Cameron (1980b). The only real evidence of a supply side effect was identified by Fagg (1980) in a study of a large city (Leicester) which has a highly dominated manufacturing industry, rather than of a metropolitan area. Here it was a highly specific effect— that of the availability of premises—which advantaged inner locations. Nicholson *et al.* also found particular evidence of the role of old cheap premises in inner areas providing attractive locations for new firms setting up, but concluded that this would provide little basis for substantive programmes of urban regeneration.

There may also be a cumulative effect on industrial costs which is set in motion by any differential in that out-movement of firms and population imposes higher costs on those remaining, especially fiscal costs (Eversley 1972): a point to which we shall need to return in a more dynamic context later.

The theme of land availability in general is also taken up in detail by Fothergill and Gudgin (1982) who make it a central premise of their theory of the decline of old industrial regions to the benefit of newer, less urbanised regions. The emphasis is placed on the way in which it is the lack of suitable sites at the right price that forces manufacturing industry (particularly in modern sectors which require relatively large capital inputs relative to labour and relatively spacious premises in which to accommodate the machinery) either to grow at a slower rate, or to develop outside traditional urban locations. This reintroduces a key element in traditional urban economic analysis: that of land use and location.

Whilst there is the obvious dynamic influence of new and small plants benefitting the growth of those areas where they establish and no real evidence that such firms do either better or worse by being located in central city areas where agglomeration effects are strongest, there is also a minus side to this in that small new plants also have rather low survival rates (Storey 1982). This is true whether we are talking about the establishment of new firms or the establishment of branch plants. As well as producing by far the largest source of growth in employment, small plants also produce a very substantial part of the contribution to decline through closure. The potential instability which this causes has been a major source of concern. This has been the case particularly with branch plants which may be seen as peripheral to a firm's operations in one sense, although reflecting its dynamism and expansion in another: in some cases it is difficult to decide whether the 'branch' or new plant or the 'main' original is the more vulnerable.

Contrasts between main and branch plants, when coupled with the role of the size distribution of plants, lead to considerations of corporate structure as a source of possible differences in performance. Despite the interest of some writers in the role of capitalist development in the unequal development of different local economies (Broadbent 1977) and the attempts to relate the process of job creation and destruction to this aspect of the organisation of production (Massey and Meegan 1982), there is little substantial evidence that types of corporate structure (local, national or multinational), single or multiple plant, single or multiple product have a significant effect on the performance of an individual economy in terms of employment change. Small single-plant firms may show a greater dynamism than multi-plant multinationals, but it is also the case that more of the differential between areas is determined by the better performance of all plants regardless of the corporate structure in one area than in another. We are back to the need to look for what may be thought of as ubiquitous advantages possessed by one area which can accrue to any plant, in any firm, in any industry.

2.4 Infrastructure and Relative Performance

The effect of infrastructure on an economy's performance is much more difficult to assess, partly because of measurement problems. There has been a long-standing debate about the role of transport infrastructure in regional economic development, namely, that it is the relative inaccessibility of a region which must be overcome by the provision of better transport links to that region (Gwilliam 1979; Sharp 1980). The evidence, such as it is, suggests rather ambivalent results for this. The provision of improved infrastructure in the form of, for example, motorways, has the dual effect of improving the centre's access to a peripheral region's markets as much as it improves the periphery's access to centre markets, and it is the already developed industry in the centre which is best able to benefit from this. Hence, transport improvements may benefit one peripheral region at the expense of another, but very rarely at the expense of a more developed region. Very little consideration has been given at the empirical level to the role of infrastructure within the local economy. We know that the importance of transport costs in total industrial costs varies from industry to industry. Edwards (1970) has estimated a range of costs as a proportion of net output for British industries, with the highest typically being in the primary sector, but with considerable regional variations being identified (Edwards 1975). Gudgin (1978) has suggested that for manufacturing industry transport costs are typically less than 5 per cent of gross output, although Chisholm (1971) and Gwilliam (1979) have agreed that such variations as do occur may be critical because of their role in determining levels of profit.

Whilst transport costs may not affect costs significantly, they do affect location. Hence the possibility of securing a reduction in total industrial costs will depend on the industrial structure of the local economy and on the degree of 'domestic' self-sufficiency. Whilst at a regional level this may not lead to great variations between regions, at the level of the more varied urban economy variations in access to the national transport network may lead to significant variations in industrial costs. Those marketing the new and expanding towns certainly believe in the importance of easy access to motorways as a major incentive to firms considering relocation. There is a further aspect to costs at the urban level: for many industries, labour costs are amongst the most significant and these may also be closely related to variations in urban transport efficiency and provision. First, there may be some relationship between local wage levels and the costs of transport: not just because very high local transport costs may lead to increased wage claims, but also because a more efficient transport system may widen the effective labour market search areas for both employers and potential employees, leading to greater competition. Whilst this may not be directly reflected in lower wage rates, it may be reflected in improved productivity and hence lower unit labour costs.

In addition to the transport system, such features as housing, sewage disposal and energy provision (and less tangible infrastructures such as health care, education, cultural and leisure provision) need to be borne by the city's economy. If there are important economies in the provision of such services accruing to cities of a certain size, then the burden of provision is less on those cities (on a *per capita* basis) and they gain a productive cost advantage (or more public services). In practice it is generally argued that there are economies of scale up to a certain size, but that cities larger than that size suffer major diseconomies from congestion, pollution and administrative inefficiencies. There is no general agreement on what that size is: figures ranging from 100,000 through 250,000 up to one-third of a million have been suggested (Richardson 1973b). The main problem is that the most efficient size differs for different infrastructures, and so the aggregate most efficient size depends on some prior choice of the desired bundle of infrastructures and the weight given to each. A city with a heavy weight attached to culture might need to be a very different size from a city worried only about getting people to and from work.

A number of writers have attempted to provide some estimate of the total scale economies attributable to urbanisation by estimating aggregate production functions for cities. Such an approach involves relating total output, measured for example by the incomes of residents, to inputs such as labour (city population) and capital (although estimates of the latter are more difficult to obtain). The results of such studies can only provide an indication of the nature and extent of any economies of scale. The early attempts of Ullman (1962) and Hoch (1972) concentrated on incomes and found some evidence of incomes increasing with city size. Shefer (1973) identified marginally increasing returns to scale in output, with output increasing by 1.14 times any given increase in population. Sveikausas (1975) estimated that a doubling of city size led to a 6.4 per cent increase in labour productivity. In a model which also included some capital stock estimates, Segal (1976) found that scale economies were only present in the largest cities, and then only in a minor way. Some recent evidence suggests that older and larger cities have tended to display lagging growth or decline and in an attempt to capture this effect Carlino (1982) has suggested that the models of Sveikausas and Segal were at fault for concentrating only on measuring agglomeration economies through the constant term in the production function. Carlino estimates a returns to scale parameter in the actual production process and finds this is significantly related to population in U.S. cities (positively to population, and negatively to population squared). This captures both the slower growth rates and the higher rates of decentralisation characteristic of large old cities (Watkins 1980).

2.5 Urbanisation, Suburbanisation and De-urbanisation

We have noted throughout the discussion in this chapter that the understanding of the working of urban economies requires us to take a more dynamic view of the development process. Cities do not just tend to an equilibrium size but they grow, spread and often decline. Some consideration of these patterns of development in an aggregated way and a more detailed look at the main processes involved in recent years are an essential part of our overview of the issues to be analysed.

Patterns of Urban Change

It is clear from much of the work on the historical development of cities (see Hall *et al.* 1973 and Hall and Hay 1980, for useful statistical summaries) that distinct phases of development can be identified. There is a period of rapid growth in which the city grows at the expense of rural hinterlands (and sometimes at the expense of other, declining, cities). This is the period in which the comparative advantage of the city is greatest and can be exploited through the increasing returns available in the form of agglomeration economies. Secondly, there is a period of declining growth in which the comparative advantage becomes less marked: agglomeration economies decline in importance as the external costs of congestion and servicing the large city come to the fore, but the physical size of the city increases as a period of suburbanisation begins. During suburbanisation there is a restructuring of the land use within the city with greater decentralisation, and this is closely associated with greater use of private transport and a more varied spatial pattern of urban activity. Subsequently, the cumulative forces of increasing costs overcome the agglomeration economies and begin to undermine the comparative advantage of the city. This leads to a movement of economic activity totally beyond the city and towards a new generation of urban areas. The declining city then faces a cumulative decline of its position. Some have looked further than this to a situation of re-urbanisation following the sort of policy response necessary to cope with the problems emanating from de-urbanisation, not just at the local level but also at the national level (Klaassen *et al*. 1981).

It is clear, however, that this sort of typology does require some rather careful definitions if consistent evidence is to be presented. We need to start once again from the basic question: what is an urban area? Hall and Hay (1980) note that there are three possible meanings: the obvious physical definition of built-up areas and associated recreational open spaces; the functional view of the town in terms of its size, economic activity, population density and travel-to-work area; and the administrative view of the town in terms of often arbitrary divisions of government. According to the definition adopted, the answer may be very different, and without some sort of international standard, international comparisons of the type attempted by Hall and Hay (1980) become highly unreliable. As they point out, it is difficult to make comparisons with European countries which lack the very detailed information available in, for example, the United States, Britain or even Japan. What is involved is the rather laborious building up of what is sometimes referred to as 'daily urban systems' from information on residential location, density and commuting patterns. This is then converted into data for three types of areas: the core metropolitan areas, the outer rings of metropolitan areas and non-metropolitan areas. The core is typically defined, on the basis of employment concentration, as an area with a minimum workforce of twenty thousand or, in agglomerations, as contiguous areas with at least five workers per acre (3,200 per square mile). The rings have both inner and outer elements defined on the basis of the proportion of the population commuting daily into the core. The core and rings combined are defined as a Metropolitan Economic Labour Area (MELA). Non-metropolitan areas are the remaining areas of the country which do not have a clearly defined core as outlined above, but which can be regionalised on the basis of daily commuting flows (Smart 1974). Table 2.3 presents data taken from Hall and Hay (1980). It illustrates the patterns of change for Britain, and for some other countries for comparison, in terms of both total population change and employment change. This confirms very clearly the pattern of phases of development outlined at the beginning of this section.

A rather different analysis based on employment data for different types of urban area produced by the Cambridge Economic Policy Group highlights very similar trends in terms of the slowing down and then decline in both conurbation centres and large towns, and the more recent rise in the growth of small towns and rural areas as employment centres: see Table 2.4.

Whilst it is possible to describe the pattern of change which has occurred, it is rather more difficult to produce a consistent set of explanations as to why that pattern has occurred. Why, for example, does the conventional balancing force of the neoclassical model not come into play leading to stabilisation of growth rates and/or income levels in various types of area? Simplistic answers to this could be that market imperfections prevent a full adjustment of resources through mobility, or that government policies designed to control divergences in the performance of individual regions actually have a destabilising effect. Hall and Hay (1980) attempted a very crude aggregate analysis of both population and employment changes in terms of the most obvious independent variables: size, density and concentration within the core of both population and employment, age of the city, location relative to the capital city, and latitude. None of these provides a totally satisfactory explanation of performance, and certainly cannot capture either the cumulative

Table 2.3 Urbanisation Trends in Western Europe, 1950–70 (% Changes)

	Core		*Ring*		*Non-metropolitan*	
	1950–60	*1960–70*	*1950–60*	*1960–70*	*1950–60*	*1960–70*
Population change						
Great Britain	+1.95	−2.52	+9.18	+14.52	−1.57	+5.44
West Germany	+20.91	+4.25	+3.67	+12.25	–	–
France	+21.24	+19.96	+2.61	+6.50	+1.62	+4.18
Netherlands	+9.91	+1.12	+18.73	+24.64	+10.44	+12.50
Belgium & Luxembourg	+4.12	−0.57	+10.38	+6.94	+3.81	+0.70
Italy	+22.68	+15.03	+0.27	+6.12	−3.73	−0.12
Sweden	+17.16	+11.08	−0.52	+10.56	+1.44	+0.24
Employment change						
Great Britain	+6.46	−2.80	+2.88	+10.38	−2.97	+3.21
West Germany	+25.91	+3.50	−9.98	−0.19	–	–
France	n.a.	n.a.	n.a.	n.a.	n.a.	n.a.
Netherlands	+14.94	+0.03	+7.52	+4.26	+0.44	−2.52
Belgium & Luxembourg	n.a.	+3.20	n.a.	+14.20	n.a.	−4.32
Italy	n.a.	+8.19	n.a.	−3.18	n.a.	−11.10
Sweden	n.a.	+11.85	n.a.	−7.82	n.a.	−4.25

Source: Hall and Hay (1980)
Note: n.a. = not available

Table 2.4 Population, Employment and Commuting by Area (1976 as % of 1951)

	Conurbations		*Cities*	*Towns and rural areas*
	Inner areas	*Outer areas*		
Population of working age	72	68	98	120
Employment	79	108	109	122
Net inward commuting	128	71	224	274
Employment less commuting	67	101	100	128

Source: *Cambridge Economic Policy Review*, December 1982

nature of the process of change or the reason for turning points in a city's economic performance. To obtain a more detailed picture it will be necessary to look at some features of the recent performance of a single urban economy.

Detailed Evidence for London

London displays in an extreme form the recent history of most British metropolitan areas. Greater London, the area covered since 1964 by the Greater London Council, showed rapid population growth up to 1931 (Table 2.5), a slower growth from 1931 to 1951; since then there has been an accelerating decline in population, so that by 1981 the total population was the same as that in 1901. The downturn came a little earlier for London than for other cities. The West Midlands conurbation continued to grow until 1971 and West Yorkshire was continuing to grow thereafter, although the downturn had occurred by the late 1970s; most of the large free-standing cities in Britain peaked in terms of population in the 1960s or early 1970s. The pattern was slightly different for inner and outer areas of the conurbations with growth continuing in the outer areas up to about 1971 in most conurbations. Over the conurbation as a whole, therefore, population densities declined.

Table 2.5 Population Growth in Selected Areas, 1891–1981 (% Change in Period)

	1891–1911	*1911–31*	*1931–51*	*1951–61*	*1961–71*	*1971–81*
Greater London	+28.51	+13.27	+1.07	−2.49	−6.76	−9.92
Greater Manchester	+22.40	+3.37	−0.40	+0.14	+0.33	−4.88
Merseyside	+27.80	+15.15	+4.80	+3.34	−3.59	−8.73
South Yorkshire	+45.35	+21.75	+6.83	+4.03	+1.47	−1.40
Tyne and Wear	+38.25	+8.65	+0.04	+3.53	−2.59	−5.70
West Midlands	+31.26	+20.40	+18.83	+7.28	+2.25	−5.17
West Yorkshire	+15.87	+4.68	+2.41	+1.00	+3.10	−1.47
All metropolitan districts	–	–	–	–	+0.5	−4.6
All non-metropolitan districts	–	–	–	–	+11.8	+5.3
Large cities	–	–	–	–	−1.5	−5.2
Small cities	–	–	–	–	+1.9	−3.5
Rural areas	–	–	–	–	+17.0	+9.9

Source: Census (1981) *Selected Reports*

It is tempting simply to conclude that there was a movement out of cities, and indeed analysis of net migration suggests that. Between 1966 and 1971 London lost a net 400,000 residents to the South-east region with over three times as many out-migrants as in-migrants, and a further 73,000 to the rest of the country, although here gross losses were only some 40 per cent greater than gains. Between 1971 and 1981 Greater London lost nearly 10 per cent of its 1971 population, whilst the OMA gained nearly 5 per cent and the Outer South-east 8 per cent. Ten-year migration figures are not available, but in the year preceding the 1981 Census Greater London lost a net 41,000 residents to the South-east region and gained a net 3,000 from the rest of Great Britain. Some recent work has suggested that aggregate figures of net migration may be hiding some important differences in the actual nature of the movement taking place. As we shall discuss in more detail in Chapter 7, it is possible to view migration in terms of national, regional and local flows which roughly correspond to moves made in response to employment factors, to a mixture of environmental and housing factors, and to housing factors alone (Gordon and Vickerman 1982). Table 2.6 illustrates the migration patterns following this disaggregation for London in the 1966–71 period for males aged 15–65. From this we can see the way in which, despite considerable net losses for largely housing and environmental reasons, London, and particularly Inner London, was still able to attract quite large gross inflows of mobile people for employment reasons but these attracted in-migrants who were themselves also more likely to move out in subsequent periods.

Turning to changes in employment we have already encountered the problems of assessing the extent to which such changes are cause or effect of other changes in the local economy. Reference to Table 2.4 demonstrates in terms of crude aggregates the sort of changes taking place and Table 2.7 illustrates the sectoral shifts which have occurred in London in recent years. Within the overall decline in employment there has been a disproportional decline in manufacturing industries, and despite an overall decline in service employment there has been a slight increase in certain sectors such as financial and miscellaneous services. It is interesting that to some extent there has been a net transfer of employment into the South-east region, especially in the service sectors, but also in the key electrical engineering sector. Against national trends, however,

Table 2.6 Migration Flows, London Region, 1966–71 (in 000s)

To / From	*Stream*	*Inner London*	*Outer London*	*Outer Metropolitan Area*	*Rest of Great Britain*	*Total*
Inner London (group A boroughs)	N	8.6	11.1	15.4	43.4	78.5
	R	0.0	7.6	29.2	19.3	56.1
	L	256.5	88.3	6.0	0.0	350.8
Outer London (group B boroughs)	N	14.8	16.6	24.8	70.2	126.4
	R	0.0	8.1	46.5	31.1	85.7
	L	14.2	293.7	22.9	0.1	330.9
Outer Metropolitan Area	N	14.2	17.1	24.0	72.2	127.5
	R	0.0	1.5	32.6	41.8	75.9
	L	0.2	6.4	283.6	9.1	299.3
Rest of Great Britain	N	40.0	48.3	73.0	–	161.3
	R	0.0	0.1	7.0	–	7.1
	L	0.0	0.0	0.9	–	0.9
Total	N	77.6	93.1	137.2	185.8	493.7
	R	0.0	17.3	115.3	92.2	224.8
	L	270.9	388.4	313.4	9.2	981.9

Source: Gordon and Vickerman (1982)
Notes: a) N = national stream; R = regional stream; L = local stream.
b) All intra-zonal flows have been attributed to the local stream.

the steepness of the decline in manufacturing is less pronounced in London than in the country as a whole. This suggests that the finding of Fothergill and Gudgin (1982) that London had lagged

Table 2.7 Changes in Employment by Sector, 1978–81 (%)

	Greater London	*Rest of South-east*	*Great Britain*
Agriculture	–	+1.3	−0.5
Mining	–	−0.2	−4.8
Food and drink	−14.8	−7.0	−7.8
Coal and petroleum	−40.0	−12.5	−30.0
Chemicals	−10.0	−9.1	−8.0
Metal manufacture	−20.0	−5.6	−31.4
Mechanical engineering	−12.8	−12.3	−16.9
Instrument engineering	−15.4	−4.4	−10.1
Electrical engineering	−10.2	+0.6	−10.1
Shipbuilding	−75.0	−16.7	−16.3
Vehicles	−19.6	−19.6	−20.7
Metal goods n.e.s	−19.6	−3.1	−17.3
Textiles	−30.0	−10.0	−31.5
Leather etc.	−20.0	−33.3	−21.0
Clothing and footwear	−36.7	−16.0	−26.4
Bricks and pottery	−16.7	−8.3	−17.8
Timber, furniture, etc.	−26.3	−11.5	−14.3
Paper, printing, etc.	−0.8	−3.5	−4.9
Other manufacturing	−28.9	−20.3	−22.1
Construction	−7.4	−6.5	−11.0
Gas, electricity, water	−4.3	+11.3	+2.4
Transport and communication	−4.8	+4.9	−2.9
Distribution	−4.4	+4.7	−0.2
Insurance, banking, etc.	+5.7	+15.9	+10.8
Professional services	−2.4	+3.7	+0.1
Miscellaneous services	+4.2	+10.7	+7.2
Public administration	−6.3	+0.4	−2.4

Source: Census of Employment (1983) *Department of Employment Gazette*, February.

behind the nation during periods of employment growth does not apply at times of falling employment, when its manufacturing industry has declined to a lesser degree.

We have, therefore, a number of phenomena to explain: the rate of growth of a city in terms of both population and employment; the changing nature of economic activity within that overall growth; the relationship of the city to other cities and non-urban areas within the national economy in terms of both its relative growth and its pattern of resource flows with other areas; and, finally, the changing internal structure of the urban area as people change residence in response to other phenomena such as housing or a changing environment.

Further Reading

Richardson (1973b) provides a good starting point to the basic issues involved in urban size; Segal (1977), in Chapter 4, has a useful summary of the basic city size models. The best review of the structural question and differential economic performance is in the work of Fothergill and Gudgin (1979b; 1982); and see the complementary work on British conurbations by Danson *et al.* (1980). Armstrong and Taylor (1978) provide a valuable background to the regional question in Britain. For a more detailed discussion of changing urban patterns, see Hall *et al.* (1973) and Hall and Hay (1980).

3
The Structure of the Urban Economy

It was suggested in Chapter 2 that structure consists of two different but related concerns: economic structure and spatial structure. That discussion has established an agenda of issues for which we now need to develop an analytical framework. This chapter is concerned with what we can term the static equilibrium issues. These can be conveniently divided into three broad areas of concern: industrial location decisions and spatial competition, land use and rent structure within the city, and the macroeconomic and trading structure of the city. However, the basic aim will be to explore the links between these structural elements as a means of trying to integrate the various dimensions.

3.1 Location Theory and Spatial Competition

The location of economic activity is the central concern of spatial economics and hence forms a key part of any discussion of a local economy such as that of a town or region. Theories of location set out to achieve two goals. Firstly, they need to provide some account of where a given economic activity will locate, given an existing spatial structure of the economy in question. Secondly, there is the market equilibrium problem of what sort of equilibrium spatial structure will emerge from a complete set of individual but interdependent location decisions. There are various dimensions to this market: there is the spatial structure of firms or plants in a given industry (the market area structure we have already met); there is the structure of land use within a given area (the spatial organisation of the individual city or region); and there is the degree of spatial specialisation or competition within the economy as a whole—the mixture of industrialisation and urbanisation which emerges from an interplay of the first two sets of market operations.

Location and Market Areas

Early writers on urbanisation and location began essentially with a pre-industrial situation. Ths starting point was to consider the location of service industries on the classic flat featureless plain which figures so strongly in locational geography, based on the early work of von Thünen (1966) and which reached its culmination in the work of Christaller (1966). If resources and population are evenly distributed, the critical factor will be the optimal size of market areas for the various products. The main determinant of market area size will be the cost of transport and hence with a constant transport rate per unit of distance, market areas will vary in size. High-cost products will have smaller market areas than low-cost products but, for any given product, assuming a structure of perfect competition, market areas will be regular. There will be an even distribution of production points and these can easily be shown to be most efficiently mapped as a network of regular hexagons.

Although the pattern for any one product is regular there is little relationship between the market areas for different products. Overlaying of market areas for different products can produce situations in which the market centres for those different products coincide at certain locations. Where the market centres for several products happen to coincide there is the basis for the founding of a city. However, given the initial premise about the ubiquitous uniform plain, it can be seen that any geographical distribution of market centres would be feasible; only the regularity and size of the grid of market areas is determined by economic forces, principally transport costs. That one particular point should become a market centre is often a case of geographical accident. Once a town is established it is easy to show how the market areas develop around that point, but it is less easy to make the development of the market centre itself an endogenous part of that process.

The Weberian Model

Traditional industrial location analysis derives from the original work of Weber (1929) and concentrates on defining the spatial input to the production process in terms of the costs of transport incurred by producing a given output, by a given production technology, at different locations. Transport costs are incurred in the acquisition of inputs and in the marketing of finished products. The space-cost curve, the relationship between total costs of production (including all transport costs) and location, will depend on the transport rates and the amount of materials to be transported to and from each location. Certain industries are clearly tied either to a specific input or to the market in that the total transport costs of transporting one of the materials, or the finished product, are prohibitively high, so that the minimum space-cost occurs at the source of the input or at the market. The majority of industries are not so tied and therefore can choose a location somewhere between the various sources of inputs and the market centre.

If the transport rates are assumed to be related primarily to the weight or bulk of the material being transported, processes involving a loss of weight or bulk in manufacture will tend to have least costs nearer to input sources, while those involving a gain will gravitate towards the market centre. Hence it has been common to classify industries according to a materials index which indicates the relative importance of these conflicting pulls.

There are a number of problems with this approach. First, the treatment of the market is rather limited. It is assumed that it can be represented by a single point which could be interpreted as a market centre. This may be appropriate for small-scale local or regional industries, but much less relevant for large national or transnational concerns. This problem also applies to the important labour input which cannot be viewed as single sourced and indeed, since many industries depend on the input of intermediate products from other industries, they may specifically wish to avoid being tied to a single source. Secondly, transport rates are much less uniform and constant per unit distance than typically assumed. Large firms may be in a position to manipulate transport rates to their advantage regardless of location—especially, as we have already seen, since these usually represent a fairly small proportion of costs.

The most important limitation, however, is the assumption that production and location decisions are essentially independent: that there is no trade-off between location and the technology used (the relative demands for various inputs) and that there is no influence of location on output through the ability to capture larger markets.

Trade-Offs in Spatial Production

Despite attempts to develop a deterministic theory of location based on cost minimisation (carried to its ultimate condition in the work of Isard 1956) and despite attempts to introduce some discussion of markets into the analysis (see Lösch 1954), these theories all failed to integrate location into a theory of production. Following an outline by Predöhl (1928) the next attempt at a formal statement of a genuine spatial theory of production was by Moses (1958).

What Moses demonstrated was that Isard's basic conclusion was inadequate. Not only could firms substitute between transport as an input and any other input according to relative costs at different locations, which would produce a situation where there was always an optimal location, but the other inputs could be substituted for each other and, moreover, the scale of output could be changed. The essential feature of the Moses analysis is captured in Figure 3.1 which demonstrates that if we assume just two alternative locations and two factor inputs, since the effective prices of the inputs differ in the two locations there will be a kink in the isocost line facing the firm. This shows that for any given level of total costs the firm can either purchase relatively more of one factor—say capital—which is relatively cheap at location *A*, or relatively more of the other which is cheaper at location *B*. At any point on the steeper part of the isocost line location *A* is preferable and at any point on the flatter part location *B* is preferable. If we assume that the production technology available is the same at both locations, there will be a single set of isoquants determined by the production function. The point of tangency will determine both the optimal input combination and the optimal location.

It can easily be seen from the diagram that two additional outcomes are possible to the single optimal location result suggested by Isard: first, at some outputs a producer may be indifferent to location in that there is a double tangency (although he will choose different input proportions at the two locations); secondly, expansion of output may lead to the optimal location

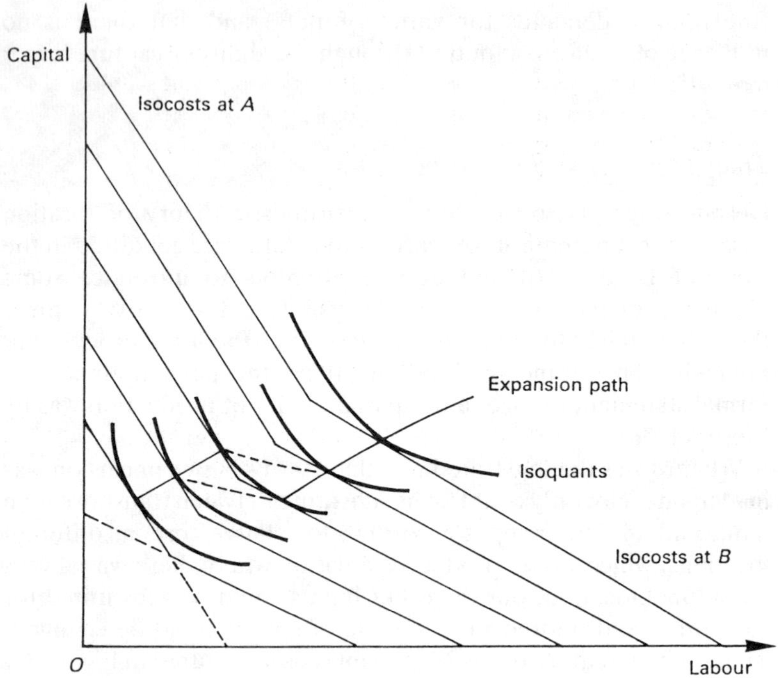

Figure 3.1 Optimal Production and Location Decisions

changing beyond a certain level of output. Of course, changes in the prices of factor inputs will lead to possible changes in optimal location as well as changes in input combinations or output scale. If we think of raw material inputs, the relevant price at each location is the delivered price and hence changes in transport costs which affect different locations differentially will also affect the slopes of the isocosts, for example through the improvement of transport facilities when a new motorway is opened.

Competition and Spatial Production

Moses' contribution demonstrates clearly the relationship between locational and other production decisions and also between these and market conditions. It is implicit in the most basic theories of market areas that it is in a firm's interest to locate as optimally as possible with respect to the market which is being served. If the firm charges a delivered price for its output, it will locate so as to minimise the transport costs of delivering that output. If it charges a mill or factory gate price so that the consumer has to bear the transport costs, then, assuming that consumers have a conventional downward sloping demand curve for the delivered good including delivery charges, it will still be in the firm's interest to minimise total transport costs of delivery since this will maximise total demand for output. This result will of course be modified by any variation in mill prices to reflect differing costs of production in differing locations.

Under these conditions, the optimal location for a firm could also produce a socially optimal distribution of firms to the extent that the location minimises the total transport costs involved in producing a given level of output. This was the principal objective of the analysis of market areas developed by Lösch (1954). However, such a solution depended on the assumption of perfect competition, and in particular of free entry, so that a firm at a given location could not earn profits above normal without a new firm entering and reducing the size of the existing firm's market area—and hence its profits. Prior to Lösch's comprehensive analysis of such a situation, it had been recognised that spatial monopoly was an important source of monopoly power. Under conditions of limited competition it was fairly easy to show that the desire to prevent loss of market area would lead to a socially sub-optimal distribution of firms, and to greater concentrations of locations. The most famous example was Hotelling's (1929) analogy of the location of ice-cream salesmen on a linear beach always tending to the centre. Later extensions under a variety of competitive assumptions were made by Lerner and Singer (1939) and Smithies (1941) which suggested that equilibrium locations may actually be unstable.

More recently, however, Eaton and Lipsey (1978) have shown that even under assumptions of free entry, as long as there is a range of falling long-run average costs, there will be a minimum plant size which a potential new entrant must be able to achieve to warrant entry. This confers some effective protection on existing firms, enabling them to grow and consolidate their spatial market position even without needing to assume imperfections in competition.

The key result of this analysis is that production is likely to be more highly concentrated than would otherwise be the case, for reasons implicit in the production function. However, changing production and market conditions would add to the inherent tendency of oligopolistic markets to have unstable locational equilibria, suggesting that firms may have strong incentives to be mobile.

Empirical Evidence on Location

Evidence on the relative mobility of firms and on the factors taken into account by firms when deciding on location comes from two sorts of study. In the one, the way in which patterns of industrial location at the regional or sub-regional level change over time is examined and the possible causal factors are analysed (Keeble 1976; Fothergill and Gudgin 1982). In the other, micro-behavioural studies of firms actually moving are undertaken to assess the specific factors influencing that decision (Sant 1975; Townroe 1973).

The pattern of industrial location at a particular time is not likely to be an equilibrium pattern to the extent that many existing firms in the area may be at the point where they are considering either moving to a new and preferred location, or closing down altogether, whilst other firms are on the point of moving in or setting up for the first time. We are, of course, not only interested in the birth, death or movement of firms or plants but in their size, and especially in the level of employment. This means that we need to introduce a further dimension to change through time: the growth or decline of existing non-mobile firms or plants. In fact, the available evidence suggests that the bulk of employment growth or decline in an area is due to the expansion or contraction of non-mobile plants and not to a great deal of actual movement of plants (Fothergill and Gudgin 1982). Although in the aggregate this does seem to be true, there is also some evidence (Keeble 1976) that the mobile firms are, on the whole, the most dynamic and display average growth rates in excess of those displayed by growing indigenous firms. Thus a city which can prove more attractive than its rivals to migrant firms is likely to have a faster growth rate of employment than one which simply tries to promote the growth rate of indigenous firms.

The study of migrant firm behaviour is typically concerned with the way in which micro-behavioural studies of location decisions have been carried out. The latter are somewhat limited in that they may ignore some of the more important dynamic elements present in non-migrant firms: it is the location of productive capacity and not just of firms as units which is the more important consideration. Nevertheless, the results of such studies are broadly confirmatory of the range of factors which are implicit in the more aggregate studies such as that of Keeble.

One consistent theme which has run through many of these studies is that factor availability has often been the critical factor in a choice between locations. Apart from the obvious constraints imposed by raw material inputs, labour availability has often been perceived as a problem (Department of Trade and Industry 1973) together with the constraint of inadequate premises and lack of space for expansion. It has also been argued that personal preference factors are a critical ultimate determinant of location; and that decision makers tend to choose locations in which they would like to live. Indeed, Keeble (1976) found some evidence that aggregate changes in industrial location patterns were consistent with measures of the attractiveness of residental areas. The more recent work of Fothergill and Gudgin tends to play down these elements as explanations of aggregate changes except for entrepreneurship and the critical factor of land availability. To some exent this may reflect a change in economic environment: earlier work on location was conducted in an environment of a basically growing national economy (up to the early 1970s) whereas Fothergill and Gudgin's work incorporates the movement into decline of the 1970s. However, their results are also consistent over a longer period of time and suggest that, although specific attractiveness and factor availability issues may play some part in major relocation decisions, the bulk of change in the location of productive capacity comes, as we have seen, through changes in existing firms and such factors, except for land availability which is the one completely immobile factor, cannot operate here. Interestingly, Keeble's later work (1980) also fails to find any significant association with attractiveness in a later period.

In the light of the more theoretical models of location discussed earlier, it is interesting that very little empirical evidence has emerged on the role of price variations. National wage agreements and the integration of capital markets on a national level mean that the only real spatial variations in nominal prices of these factors are those caused by government intervention through investment grants and allowances or through measures such as the regional employment premium. Real unit labour costs may vary rather more because of productivity differences, but it is difficult to ascribe these to the individual factor and a study of strike activity in different regions (Smith *et al.* 1978) could find no consistent pattern which might explain different rates of change in employment. The evidence for land availability is rather different, however, partly because of a consistent trend to changing factor proportions in manufacturing industry. Fothergill and Gudgin estimate that the capital requirement per worker was increasing throughout the period from 1952 and at a rate which increased. At the same time there was a rising requirement of floor space per worker which, at least over the period 1966–75 (for which data are available), was increasing faster than that for the capital requirement. This reinforces the more traditional view in urban economics that we need to understand the allocation of land to activities and the implicit price of land in that allocation, not only to understand the structure of the city, but also to understand its dynamic properties.

3.2 Location and Land Use within the City

We have now identified that a key component of the production function for urban economic activity is the use of land, its availability and cost, within the city. This brings us to one of the core aspects of urban economics: the mechanism by which land within an urban area is allocated to different uses—not just to different production activities but also between productive uses and infrastructure (particularly transport) and between productive uses and housing. Since allocation is likely to involve a market in urban land, this also involves the determination of urban land rents which themselves are an important input to the costs of the various urban activities. It is, of course, not only a question of the determination of *relative* rents for land in different parts of the city, but also of the determination of the absolute *level* of rents in one city relative to another and hence of the influence that this will have on inter-urban as well as intra-urban location. The level of rents and the rate at which rents change with location within the city relative to the location with the highest rents will together help to determine the size of the city in terms of area. The reason for this is that the marginal rent paid for urban usage of the land cannot fall below what that land could command in a non-urban usage. If there is a clear relationship between economic activity, population and area, the size of the city in terms of area will also help to determine the population and the density of urban development. It is this set of inter-relationships which provides the pivotal linkage between the various dimensions of the urban economy.

A Simple Theory of the Urban Land Market

The simplest models of the structure of land rents within a city have taken an essentially von Thünen approach. This assumes that all productive activity within the city takes place at the centre of the city (equivalent to von Thünen's market centre) and that the edge of the city is marked by the price of agricultural land (which is generally assumed to have uniform quality and a uniform price). Since the city is assumed to be regular in shape, the preferred location for all activity is the city centre since this has the best accessibility to all other locations within the city. Hence for a productive activity which depends on the urban market the profitability, before allowing for rents, is greatest at the centre. For 'exporting' industries the centre is assumed to be the market place and transport focus through which goods must be shipped. For the individual city resident all relevant activity (and in most simple models this means just work) is concentrated in the city centre and hence, since travel is assumed to be a disutility, he, too, will wish to locate as close to the centre as possible. Since all activity cannot be at the same location there will be competition for the use of land which we shall assume to be uniformly suitable for any purpose (i.e. no topographical features and no zoning or planning restrictions) and to be available always and immediately to the highest bidder (i.e. no irreversible investment in buildings on the land and no speculation). In such a situation it is clear that a simple trade-off of rent payable against distance from the centre will emerge, as formalised by Alonso (1964).

Alonso's theory of the urban land market was in many ways just a development of a tradition dating back to early writings on urban land values (Ratcliffe 1949; Hurd 1903) and the models of the social structure of cities developed by such writers as Park, Burgess and MacKenzie (1925). The key element in the Alonso model is that of the bid-rent function: the maximum rent that a potential user of land is prepared to pay for a particular activity at a given location in order to keep himself just as well off in terms of, say, profit or utility as at any other location. Since profits or utility have been assumed to be highest at the centre, potential land users can naturally bid the highest level of rent at that location. The maximum rent they can bid is the total profit obtainable from their operations at the location. At any other location, firms suffer from poorer accessibility and this implies a need for transport to gain access to the centre. The transport cost per unit of distance can be used as a measure of the rate at which the maximum bid-rent must fall to maintain profits at a constant level. Hence we can depict the family of bid-rent curves shown in Figure 3.2 for a given activity. If activities have different land requirements because of differing production techniques, as discussed earlier in this chapter, the maximum rent which can be bid per unit of land will be less per £ of profit in activities with higher land requirements than in those which require much less land.

The structure of land rents in the city as a whole can then be built

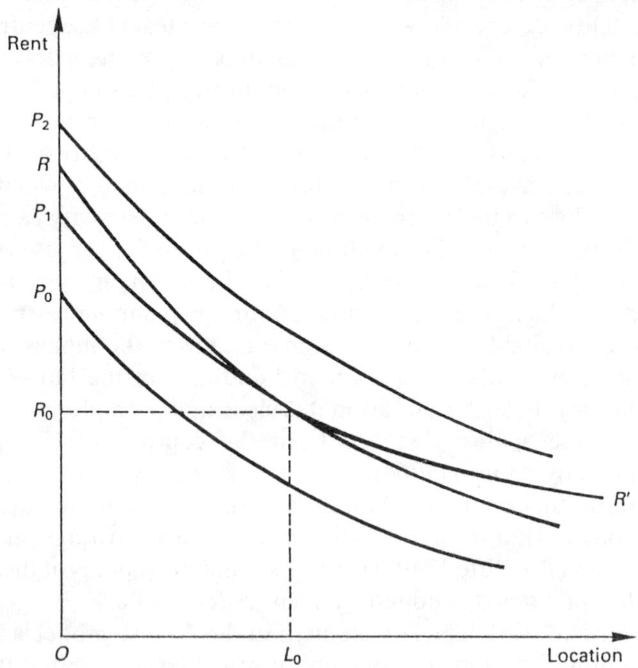

Figure 3.2

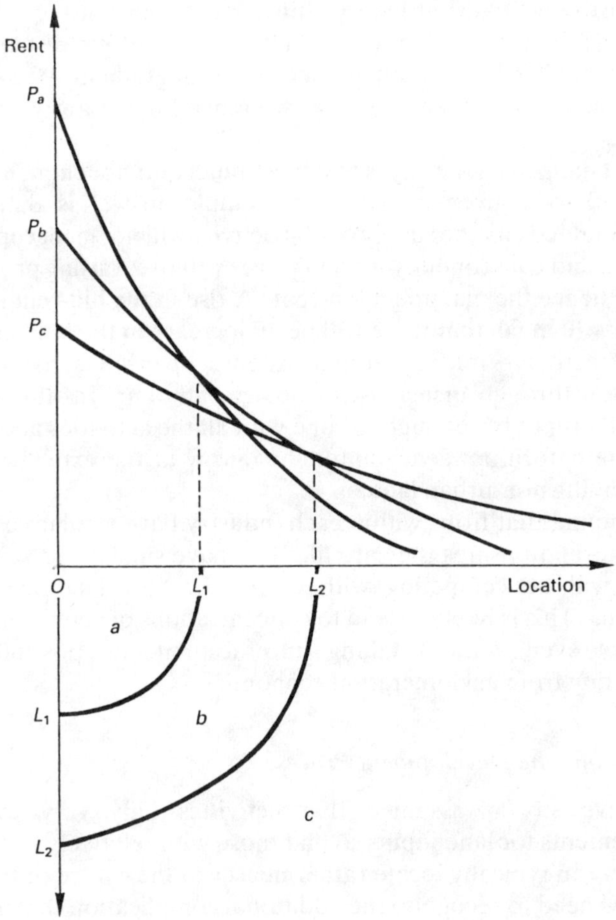

Figure 3.3

up from the bid-rent curves for all activities competing for the use of land in the rather simplistic way shown in Figure 3.3. Activities which can generate a high profit per unit of land will be able to bid higher rents for the use of land nearer to the centre, pushing out activities with lower profitability or higher land requirements (or both) to locations further out. We must also remember that the supply of land at a given location relative to the centre of the city increases as we move further out. In a regular circular city there is only just over 3 km^2 of land within 1 km of the centre, nearly 10 km^2 of land at 1 to 2 km, and 60 km^2 at 9 to 10 km distant. This helps to explain the flattening out of the rent gradient—the overall rent structure which emerges—as we move further away from the centre.

What happens if the city is not big enough or if not enough land is allocated to a given activity? The simple answer is that for a self-contained city the supply of that activity will not meet consumer demand and consequently market prices will rise, raising profitability and hence the maximum bid-rent. A rise in the bid-rent for one activity will mean that there will be an increase in the land devoted to that activity—initially at the expense of other activities, but ultimately through an increase in the size of the city. In other words, if the city is not big enough to cope with all the activities necessary, then the natural tendency is for it to grow at the expense of the surrounding non-urban land.

Assuming that firms within each industry have similar cost-and-demand relationships they are likely to have similar bid-rents and hence will be competing with each other for land in similar locations. This is likely to lead to concentrations of activities within the city even without taking into account the possibility of benefitting from agglomeration economies.

Density and the Development Process

We have so far assumed that activities only vary in their requirements for land inputs so that those with relatively little need for land can typically locate rather nearer to the centre of the city. We now need to recognise the additional complication that units of land can be developed at different densities, in consequence of which more than one user or more than one activity can be accommodated on a single unit area of land. This raises two issues. One is that some activities, particularly in heavier manufacturing industry, are discriminated against because not only is their demand for space larger, but it is less amenable to concentration in, for example, multi-storeyed developments. Thus we get the phenomenon that in central city districts, where rents are highest, there is a concentration of service-sector employment and small-scale manufacturing which can be highly concentrated in small workshops (the clothing and jewellery trades being classic examples of this). In addition, of course, these are the activities which typically require a much closer contact with the ultimate consumer and hence have the greatest need for a central accessible location. The other issue, and one with considerable consequences, is the notion that land is developed not by the final user but by an intermediary, the developer, who conditions the use of the land by the nature of the (often speculative) develoment of buildings on the land.

The introduction of the notion of development itself raises two sorts of issue. First, we can no longer assume that land supply is fixed and known—developers can vary the effective supply of land both by the nature of the development and by the possibility of withholding or releasing land on to the market as part of a speculative process. Secondly, the intervention of the middleman, although in one sense it may aid the smooth running of the land market and the exchange of land between different uses, also distorts the relationship between the bid-rent (the value of the land to the user) and the true opportunity cost of the land. The practical outcome of this is the need to consider the question of the taxation of the gains from land when these are no longer pure economic rent.

This raises the question of the price of land in relationship to its rental value. In a perfect market the current market price of a unit of land will be determined as the capitalised sum of future rental payments, so that it makes no difference to talk in terms of prices or rentals since these can be resolved to be the same thing. When the market is not perfect, however, the current price of land may reflect other factors. It is against this background that the debates about land value and development gains taxes and the process of development have taken place (Rose 1973; Neutze 1974; Foster and Glaister 1975; Evans 1982). The outcome has been inconclusive since the taxes may both discourage developers, for cost reasons, and encourage the granting of development permission, for local authority revenue reasons. Evans (1983) has suggested a rather different approach to the problem, recognising the importance of consumer surplus accruing to an occupier over and above the exchange value of the land. An existing occupier typically values land more than a would-be purchaser, especially one with a different use for the land—a fact often discovered in attempts to value land for compulsory purchase. Any tax falls on this consumer's surplus and is hence not neutral in its effects since it will reduce supply and raise the market price of land.

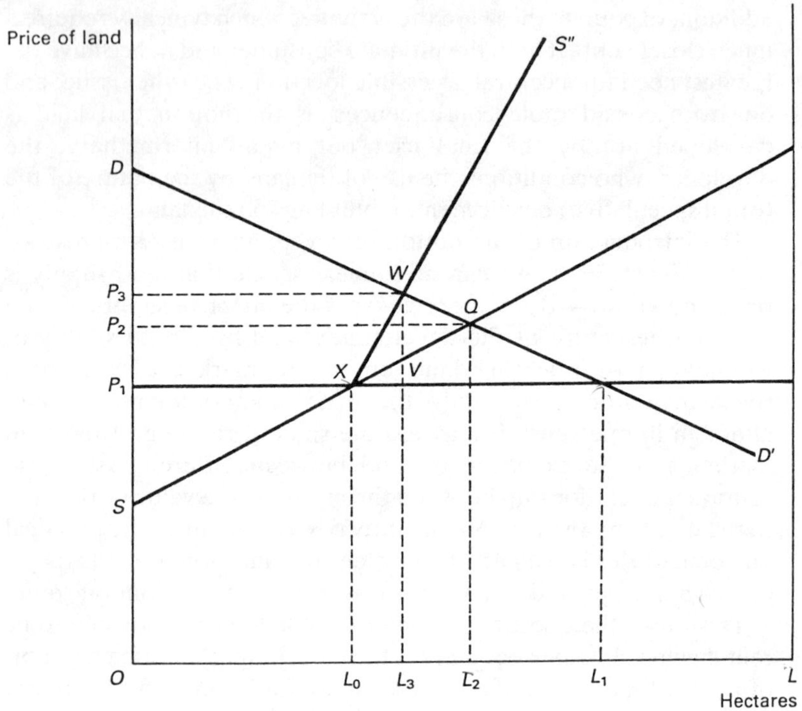

Figure 3.4

Let us examine development taking place at the urban fringe, on agricultural land with an opportunity cost in the market of OP_1 in Figure 3.4, and assume there is OL land available at such a location. If we superimpose a demand schedule for development into housing on this of DD' we would expect OL_1 land to be developed. Suppose that there is also a supply schedule SS' which takes into account the consumers' surplus of existing land owners. From this we can see that at a price of OP_1 only OL_0 hectares would be developed; hence, to satisfy development demand, price will be bid up to OP_2, above the opportunity cost, at which price OL_2 hectares will be developed. If a tax is imposed on any excess of sale price above opportunity cost, this will change the supply curve to SXS'' reducing land supplied to OL_3 and raising price to OP_3. The tax taxes VW of this price and the net benefit to the land owner is still less than at Q. The higher the tax rate, the steeper is

XS'' and hence the higher the price necessary to secure land releases greater than OL_0.

Taxation is not the only way in which government will interfere in the land market. Possibly of greater importance is the role of government in the zoning of land: its allocation to specific uses primarily to avoid external conflicts between adjacent users, and controls on density to reduce the external costs of congestion and pollution. Principally, zoning is an administrative reinforcement of the effective zoning which is likely to come about as a result of the sort of market forces discussed above, but it does then tend to limit the amount of exchange which can take place at the edges of zones as well as hindering change and leading to speculative problems. Speculation here comes about as a result of the expectation that changes to the zoning will become necessary as a result of market pressures on changing structure of land uses within the city.

We can see, therefore, that it will be exceedingly difficult to consider adequately both the use of land and the price for the use of land in a static framework since the nature of land development itself means that considerable speculation about future changes in use must take place; that the possible rental value of the land over a long time period will be relevant to determining the capitalised price of land; and that the risks associated with land development are considerable so that a substantial risk premium will be involved in any determined market price.

Housing Markets

So far, we have only looked at the use of land for rather abstract 'activities', recognising that some of these are productive and others mainly consumption-oriented (the use of land for residential housing). The literature in the Alonso tradition has recognised that many of the most interesting aspects of land allocation occur within the housing market, partly because housing occupies such a large part of the land area of most cities, and partly because housing shelters the population of the city which comprises its workforce. The growth of a city typically implies a need to attract population in order to supply the increasing demand for labour which is not met by natural rates of increase. Conversely, in a declining city, many of the problems are caused by the inability of the city to lose population as fast as its economic base declines.

The first thing to note is that we cannot regard housing as a homogeneous commodity, a single activity. Houses themselves are of many different types, particularly in terms of their size, and residents of the city will also be extremely varied in their characteristics. The most important of these characteristics is income, and even early theories of city structure (Burgess 1925) attempted to distinguish between areas of rich and poor housing. Implicit in these early theories was a dynamic structure of housing location and use such that as the city grew the areas devoted to housing the rich and the poor would change. The rich would seek the development of new and more spacious areas on the fringes of the built-up area, whilst the poor would be confined to high-density living in inner areas. Paradoxically, therefore, the poor tended to live on the highest valued land with the best accessibility, necessary because of their lack of private transport. In order to be able to afford the land costs meant, first, that densities had to be much higher (to share out the land cost amongst more households) and, secondly, that the buildings used were often those vacated by previous richer residents. These buildings, to become affordable, would need to be depreciated rapidly which could be achieved by subdivision into smaller units and undermaintenance, both of which features fairly quickly produced slum conditions and, depending on the social and ethnic mixes within the city, the potential problem of ghettos. This 'filtering' theory of urban housing was principally propounded by Hoyt (1939), developed by Grigsby (1963) and in a series of subsequent analyses, as reviewed by Maclennan (1982).

A second major problem with any view of the housing market is that it is not just a question of a series of separate but related sub-markets: cutting across the various size and quality categories there is the question of tenure—whether the house is owned or rented by the occupant (and hence the extent to which there is an investment as well as a consumption aspect to the housing decision) and, if rented, from whom (noting in particular the contrast between public and private rentals and the implications that this has for housing investment and pricing). The interest in the tenure question arises because of the possibility of decisions about tenure affecting decisions about both the amount of housing to be consumed and the location of that housing. Whilst some writers have thought that this was the logical ordering of the decision, it is not clear that potential residents do take an unconditional view about tenure and some may find that only one tenure is available given definite ideas about the size, quality and location of the housing required. We shall need to look rather more closely at this critical aspect of housing demand and choice in Chapter 6, placing it in the wider context of decisions about workplaces and transport choice (Vickerman 1984).

The Access-Space Trade-Off Model

For the present, we need to develop a little more formally the model of the household choice of housing location as a sort of demand side analogue for living in the urban economy to the production function of economic activity. Following the outlining of the main issues of any residential location choice model developed so far, we can see that the primary concern of the model will be to formalise the question of choice between accessibility and the quality of housing as measured in part by the space consumed by any particular house. The typical form of this so-called access-space trade-off model depends on a utility function for urban dwellers which incorporates as arguments the consumption of goods x, the size of the site occupied at location i, s_i, and the distance from the central area d_i (assuming typically that all employment and other activity is concentrated at that location). The utility function is maximised subject to a budget constraint which measures the total expenditure on goods, land and travel. Hence we get the basic Alonso model of the form:

$$\max U = U(x, s, d) \qquad (3.1)$$

subject to

$$Y = px + r_i s + t_i d \qquad (3.2)$$

where p, r_i, t_i are the unit prices of goods, land (rent) and travel respectively. This model of Alonso was an improvement on some earlier attempts, such as that by Wingo (1961) which worked on the assumption that the trade-off was an exact one between land and location in that $(r_i s_i + t_i d_i)$ was a constant and equal to transport costs at the city boundary where land rents would fall to the opportunity cost of land and hence r_i would be interpreted as the purely urban rental of land. In Alonso's model it was possible for people to trade off either or both of these spatial elements against the non-spatial elements in individual utility.

From equations 3.1 and 3.2 we derive the most basic result about urban land rents and allocation. The condition for an optimum in terms of marginal rates of substitution can be written as:

$$\frac{U_d}{U_x} = \frac{1}{p}\left[s.\frac{dr}{dd} + \frac{d(td)}{dd}\right] \qquad 3.3$$

This tells us that the rate at which we are prepared to substitute travel for goods as we move outwards is given by the net change in the cost of that movement in terms of the total paid for land and the change in commuting costs. Since normally transport costs are positive and increase with distance (even if at a declining rate) and since the size of the plot occupied must be positive, it is clear that the term *dr/dd* must be negative and this can be interpreted as the bid-rent for any particular location.

From this rather basic formulation has stemmed a whole series of refinements and complications, some of which have been concerned just with the improvement of the land allocation model for residential purposes, but many of which have seen this as one part of a more complete and elaborate general equilibrium model of an urban system in which not just the allocation of land, but also the size of the city itself can be determined endogenously. The major landmarks in this series of improvements are the models of Muth (1969), Evans (1973) and MacDonald (1979). Each of these advances essentially involves a refinement of the specification of the utility function in a way that enables a more realistic interpretation of the implications of the model to be drawn.

Muth (1969) tried to specify the housing element in the model more precisely, rather than just rely on units of space as the measure of housing consumption. Muth concentrated on the trade-off between goods and housing by viewing commuting costs in any location as given and therefore to be deducted from income before a consumer could consider the allocation of his disposable income. In moving to a more distant location, increased commuting costs lead to a reduction in the household's disposable income which means that, unless the price of a unit of housing falls, the household will be worse off. The substitution effect of the fall in the price of a unit of housing is, however, likely to mean that consumers buy more housing at the more distant location, where housing is cheaper. Muth, therefore, demonstrates both the requirement that house costs per unit should fall with increasing distance from the centre of the city, and the commonly observed fact that housing consumption increases with distance from the city. The model rests on the key definition of a standard unit of housing service as a means of avoiding the problem of heterogeneity in housing as a good. Since the amount of money available for commuting expenditure will increase with income (given a particular price structure for housing) and since it is to be expected that the marginal cost of commuting decreases with distance (given the structure of most transport rates), Muth then demonstrates that the condition for a *stable* spatial equilibrium in his model demands both that the marginal saving in housing costs at a given point (for consuming a given level of housing) equals the marginal incremental commuting costs at that point, and that the former is decreasing faster than the latter.

This is shown in Figure 3.5 by the intersection between the housing and marginal commuting cost functions at d_1. Any increase in household income will lead to an outward movement in both of these functions on the basis that the income elasticities of demand for both housing and transport are positive. For increasing income to result in a movement outwards is clearly shown by this simple model to require that the income elasticity of demand for housing is greater than that for transport to ensure that d_2 lies to the right of d_1.

Whilst Muth concentrated on income relationships, Evans (1973) incorporated the developments in consumer theory due to Becker (1965) and Lancaster (1966) to demonstrate that understanding of patterns of urban location required greater understanding of the *activities* which people undertake and not just the *goods* they consume. The key feature of a spatial economy is that to engage in any activity, whether production- or consumption-oriented, people must expend time as well as money (and in many cases time is both the more important and the more binding constraint on people's activities). Evans retains the simplicity of the central area workplace hypothesis and decomposes housing just to the space occupied so that in terms of the formulation of the Alonso model of equations (3.1) and (3.2) above we now have:

$$U = U(A, s, d, h) \tag{3.4}$$

where A is a vector of activities undertaken by the household, s is the space occupied as before, d is the distance to the central area

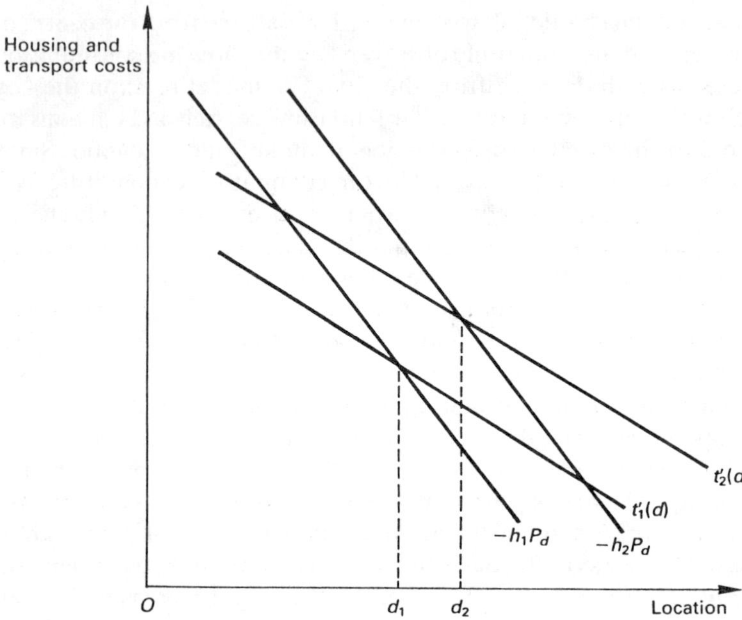

Key: h_1 and h_2 are levels of housing consumption;
p_d is the price of housing at location d;
$t_1'(d)$, $t_2'(d)$ are marginal commuting costs for a given level of housing consumption.

Figure 3.5 Income and Location

(but now measured in terms of time rather than physical distance) and h is the number of hours worked. There are two resource constraints. First, there is a financial constraint:

$$wh = r_i s + t_i d + \sum_j p_j a_j \tag{3.5}$$

where w is the hourly wage rate, r_i and t_i are the unit costs of land and transport at location i, and p_j is the price (per hour) of undertaking activity a_j. The time constraint for any given time period, H, is then:

$$H = h + d + \sum_j a_j \tag{3.6}$$

This model leads to fundamentally the same result as the Alonso model in terms of an equilibrium in which rental savings and incremental travel costs are equated.

MacDonald (1979) has gone a little further in trying to incorporate a more satisfactory treatment of housing and separate the goods and time elements in non-housing consumption. MacDonald's model therefore incorporates a housing production function for the household which includes house and locational variables as well as household time inputs. The MacDonald model is thus of the form:

$$\max U = U(X, Q, L, C, H) \tag{3.7}$$

where the arguments of the utility function are respectively vectors of non-housing consumption goods, housing and associated locational services, leisure time, commuting time and work time. The housing vector, Q, is produced by a function of the form:

$$Q_n = Q_n(Z, E) \tag{3.8}$$

where Z is a vector of the housing and locational attributes of a dwelling and E is the associated vector of time inputs. The constraints faced by the household are again income and time constraints:

$$\sum_j w_j h_j + G = X + \sum_m r^i_m z^i_m + \sum_j t^i_j c^i_j \tag{3.9}$$

$$E^i_j = \sum_n E_{jn} + L_j + C_j + H_j \tag{3.10}$$

where w_j is the wage rate of the jth person in the household, G is non-wage income of the household, X is the expenditure on non-housing consumption, $r_m z_m$ is the expenditure on the mth housing characteristics (at a specific location, i) and $t_j c_j$ represents the jth person's commuting costs at that location. The time constraint is shown just for person j as the sum of j's contribution to the nth characteristic and time devoted to leisure, commuting and work. Whilst this produces a model of excessive complexity for any simple tractable solutions, it does demonstrate the way in which a more complex and realistic model incorporating most of the elements of urban life can be defined which does not differ fundamentally from the basic underlying structure and predictions of the simple model.

Testing the Theory

Theoretical urban land allocation models may have a logical place in the development of a microeconomic theory of the urban space, but do they have any really useful function in helping us to understand some of the patterns and processes which we face in a real-world city? First, we have to note that these models are all demand side based: they ignore, or treat as given, the supply of land within the city and at any given location in a way which we have already suggested is misleading. Secondly, there is an assumption running throughout the models that individuals can adjust into equilibrium instantaneously, or at least that any failure to do so will not be destabilising. Moreover, it is assumed that individuals can make these adjustments simultaneously in all the markets in which they operate—housing, job, transport—as well as in the markets for non-housing goods, whereas we know that in all of these there are forces at work which prevent such adjustment—sometimes for the very reason that we are dealing with a spatial world and hence that market information is not perfect. For a discussion of these points, see Maclennan (1982, Chapter 1) and Vickerman (1980, Chapters 4, 5 and 7) and the discussion in Chapter 7 below.

Despite these problems of determining how and when equilibrium might occur and enable a valid testing of the hypotheses, Evans (1973) and MacDonald (1979) (among a number of authors) have tried to test the implication of their models on real cities, London and Chicago respectively. In general, these empirical applications suggest that the broad tenets of the model do hold, that rental gradients do exist which conform to the expected pattern (as do density gradients) and that the pattern of housing developments and the incomes of residents are not inconsistent with at least a fairly liberal interpretation of the model. Of course, real cities do not sit on flat featureless plains, they do not have spaceless central areas in which all employment activity is concentrated, and metropolitan areas consist of complex overlays of numerous spatial structures superimposed on top of one another. However, none of these features entirely undermines the basic presumptions of the most basic of the models. The latter might not be able to reproduce real cities, but they may nevertheless be able to simulate the sort of changes which might emanate from some fundamental changes in certain key parameters in the allocation process. In subsequent sections of this book we shall be concerned with some more detailed investigations of certain of those parameters and, as we shall see, it is necessary at all times to keep in mind some overall framework of the way the various bits of a city fit together.

We have now completed the basic microeconomic pieces of the allocation process. We have discussed the production relations for activities within the city in terms of both the technology and the organisation of production. We have examined a system of market allocation of land to different activities and considered in detail the allocation of land to the key input of labour for housing. We have two further tasks in this chapter before we can consider the dynamics of the urban economy. First of all, we need to consider the possibility of a general equilibrium model of allocation in the city and then, in the final section of this chapter, we shall provide a brief overview of the macroeconomic and trade accounts of the economy.

General Equilibrium in Land Use

The search for a general equilibrium model of the urban economy is an obvious corollary to the discussions of this chapter. Early attempts to find a solution emanated from inherently practical problems, namely, that as cities grew larger, more and more of their precious land resources had to be turned over to the essentially unproductive use of transport, whilst at the same time insufficient land was being allocated to this use so that congestion, which was a severe external cost to the city economy, increased (Solow 1973). Since we have a production function for urban activity and a utility function for city residents, both of which include some element of land use, it is possible to derive expressions for a general equilibrium allocation of land and the total size of the city. The model is only determined if closed from outside, either by fixing total population or physical size exogenously, or, in an even more general form, by considering a nationally determined level of utility to provide a limit to the acceptable city size (Mirrlees 1972). This has the advantage of setting one city within a national context and admits the possibility of an optimal urban geography. Fuller development of such models is beyond the scope of this book but some of the implications are considered in more detail in Vickerman (1980, Chapter 6).

3.3 Macroeconomic Structure and the Urban Balance of Payments

So far we have concentrated on the microeconomic aspects of the structure of the urban economy in terms of industry mix, the organisation of production and the spatial structure of land use. The macroeconomics of urban economies have tended to be either ignored or treated only at a very superficial level in much writing on the subject, partly because they appeared not to have any genuine spatial implications and partly because they did not appear to have any real policy implications. Cities have been assumed to exist within the overall macroeconomic framework of the national, or to a lesser extent the regional, economy. The collapse of manufacturing industry in recent years and its relatively worse performance in large urban areas than nationally has led to renewed interest in the possibilities of a real economic policy operating at the local level. It is clear that we cannot use conventional closed economy macroeconomics for economies which are typically small and open and this therefore means that we need to take a much closer look at the structure of the trade and balance of payments aspects of the model.

Input–Output Accounting

The most conventional starting point for considering the macroeconomic structure in terms of the techniques discussed so far is through the input–output framework. We are dealing here essentially with an accounting exercise which can be used to illustrate the structure of the economy, but the way in which the structure is formulated will influence our interpretation of its performance and the likely effects of policy. As well as providing information on the linkages between various industrial sectors within the economy, the input–output framework gives us details of the destinations of final output in terms of the consumer sector, investment sector or government sector within the economy, or destinations outside the local economy; and it shows the varying extent to which each sector, including the consumption, investment and government sectors, is dependent on imports from outside the local economy to satisfy final demand. A schematic version of an input–output table is shown in Figure 3.6.

For a typical national economy the trade sector represents a relatively small part of total output. In Britain exports have averaged 28 per cent of national GDP and imports 28 per cent over the period 1971–81 and Britain has historically had a relatively high dependence on trade. In such circumstances it has not normally been necessary to look in any great detail at the

From \ To	*Sectors* 1	*j*	*n*	*Domestic final demand*: *Household consumption*	*Investment*	*Government expenditure*	*Exports*	*Gross output*
Sectors	E_{11}	E_{1j}	E_{1n}	C_1	I_1	G_1	X_1	E_1
⋮	⋮	⋮	⋮					
i	E_{i1}	E_{ij}	E_{in}	C_i	I_i	G_i	X_i	E_i
⋮	⋮	⋮	⋮					
n	E_{n1}	E_{nj}	E_{nn}	C_n	I_n	G_n	X_n	E_n
Labour input	L_1	L_j	L_n	L_C	L_I	L_G	L_X	L
Other value added	V_1	V_j	V_n	V_C	V_I	V_G	V_X	V
Imports	M_1	M_j	M_n	M_C	M_I	M_G	–	M
Gross expenditure	E_1	E_j	E_n	C	I	G	X	E

$$E_i = \sum_j E_{ij} + C_i + I_i + G_i + X_i = \sum_j E_{ji} + L_j + V_j + M_j$$

$$E = \sum_i \sum_j E_{ij} + C + I + G + X = \sum_i \sum_j E_{ji} + L + V + M$$

$$L + V = Y = C + I + G + X - M$$

Figure 3.6 Schematic Input–Output Table for Single Region

composition of that trade, either in terms of the geography of the trading relationships or the types of commodities traded. However, as we have seen at a national level since Britain's entry to the EEC, being part of a single trading group, with no effective restraints on import penetration and no ability to assist industries wishing to export to other members of the group, does pose problems of needing to know what changes in the trading pattern are taking place. As has also frequently been discussed in the context of EEC membership, such problems are compounded if the economies involved become part of a common currency area with no controls on the flow of capital or other financial funds. In these circumstances, what is ideally required is a series of linked input–output tables for the various economies trading together so that both the geographical and the sectoral origins and destinations of trade are made clear. The outline table of Figure 3.6 is thus one element of a matrix of tables; the tables along the principal diagonal represent internal trading in each economy and the off-diagonal tables represent flows of goods between economies.

In practice the possibility of having available such comprehensive information even for one local economy at the urban level, let alone for a series of such economies (especially as it would need regular updating) is rather limited. All users of input-output analysis at any level have to resign themselves to this fact, but it does not render the technique useless since simply considering the structure of the economy in this way highlights the critical information which is needed to understand the working of the economy.

Even a cursory consideration of the table in Figure 3.6 will show that the key features in an input–output presentation of an economy are the so-called technical coefficients which detail the linkages between the various sectors in terms of the requirements placed on each sector for production of a unit of output from any one sector. In an expanded inter-regional input–output framework we need to know not just the technical relationships between sectors *i* and *j*, but the geographical trading relationships between those sectors so that we have information on the import and export propensities of each sector. It is, of course, possible to have sketchy information on trade coefficients without a full linking of tables but this would then assume that total trade relationships were independent of the geographical direction of trade. Such an assumption may be more acceptable (though potentially dangerous) when dealing with a less open economy in which trade is a fairly small proportion of total output. Here trade with any one other economy is a very small part of total trade. However, it is likely to be a very dangerous assumption for small open economies where there may be considerable variation in the nature of trading relationships with different partners and where often one other economy is a dominant trading partner. Such a situation is often found in small national economies neighbouring much larger ones (Austria, the Netherlands and Denmark are such examples) and is very typical of the situation of most urban economies in their relationships with both the hinterland and neighbouring urban areas. As we have already seen in this chapter, local economies can vary substantially in both structure and performance and this will be reflected in the values of both internal and trade technical coefficients.

There is a close link between the input–output framework and the notion of the urban base model since the latter is essentially a two-sector input–output model of the economy. The input–output matrix can be a very useful tool in assessing which industries fall within the base: those for which external final demands dominate output. It can also be a useful guide to the critical linkages within the economy which can be used as the basis of industrial complex analysis to design a self-sustaining 'package' of industries with high local linkages and low leakages to outside economies. Such analysis suggests that it is not just a question of finding export-based industries but also necessary to provide the right mix of secondary and supply industries within the local economy to avoid an 'enclave' effect where all the inputs for the export industry are imported.

One of the most detailed input–output models of an urban economy was developed for Peterborough by Morrison (1973). It is a worthwhile exercise to look at some of the main features of the results of this study to get a feel of the nature of the overall structure of a 'real' urban economy. Table 3.1 summarises the composition of input to each sector in terms of payments made to other local industries, to households and for 'imports', and the properties of total sales going in 'exports'. This demonstrates the variety of sectoral structure, even between quite closely related sectors such as the various elements of the retail trade. However, the clear distinction between manufacturing industry and the service sector (especially the government sectors) does emerge. All manufacturing industry sells a higher proportion of sales to export than it buys inputs from imports, despite substantial variations in the import contents. Note also the very high trade surplus (in proportional terms) generated by the financial and professional service sectors—and this in a not very large city. The linkage effects of purchases from other local sectors are strongest in the retail distribution sector.

The Components of Aggregate Demand

We have, so far, only considered the input–output framework as an accounting matrix. We must now turn to look behind this matrix at the factors which lead to the particular structure of the accounts

Table 3.1 Input–Output Components for Peterborough

Sector	Distribution of sectoral expenditure (%) *Local purchases from other sectors* ($\sum_j E_{ji}$)	*Payments to households* ($L_i + V_i$)	*Imports* (M_i)	*Total Sales to Exports* (%) (X_i)
Food and drink	3	7	75	100
Chemicals etc.	2	10	55	100
Metal manufacture	13	15	56	73
Mechanical engineering	3	20	49	100
Electrical engineering	6	21	53	99
Vehicles	2	12	61	100
Other metal goods	10	28	35	99
Clothing	1	16	76	100
Bricks etc.	16	25	24	98
Timber	11	21	51	89
Paper, publishing	9	15	51	82
Other manufacture	11	23	46	100
Construction	7	15	59	75
Gas & electricity	5	7	60	43
Transport	1	46	30	42
Communications	18	27	38	79
Wholesale distribution	18	28	11	50
Retail:				
grocery	45	29	3	16
other food	26	33	11	24
confectionery etc.	49	35	5	6
clothing	27	29	24	23
household goods	17	33	4	21
other non-food	15	22	17	11
general store	16	41	17	40
Coal, oil, builders' merchants	15	35	18	48
Other industrial materials	15	32	9	37
Insurance, banking, etc.	7	5	6	46
Professional & scientific services	9	43	30	68
Miscellaneous services	8	18	39	21
Local government:				
public services	17	15	28	8
social services	6	2	5	22
planning etc.	8	10	11	–
general purposes	8	53	33	26
delegated education	18	46	32	20
delegated health	27	45	21	–
other	14	29	24	14
National government (local)	2	98	–	100
Households	43	–	37	23

Source: Morrison (1973)

observed. This is typically done by examining the various elements of expenditure by consumers, investors, government, external purchasers, etc. separately, as in a conventional income–expenditure framework of macroeconomics. We shall just attempt to identify the urban peculiarities. In so doing we shall also point to areas where specific local estimates of relationships will be necessary rather than just assuming, as is so often done for lack of data, that estimates made at a national level can be applied to a similar function at the local level.

The consumption sector can be dealt with in a fairly conventional manner, with a consumption function relating consumer expenditure to disposable income. It should be remembered that this will refer to total consumer expenditure by residents of the economy —we shall need to specify carefully the import component of local consumers' expenditure and the amount of local expenditure by non-residents (both commuters and shoppers from out of town) when dealing with the balance of payments aspects. As far as the application of aggregate consumption functions is concerned, we must remember that the composition of the population in terms of income groups (and in many urban economies today the proportion of non-earning consumers) can be a key determinant of the aggregate marginal propensity to consume (for some discussion of this point in a very simple model of a metropolitan economy see Madden and Batey 1983).

In a static model, investment also is not too difficult to deal with in the aggregate: again, standard presentations representing investment as a function of the level of aggregate income in the local economy and the rate of interest are a reasonable first approximation. However, we must bear in mind that to the extent that decisions about investment may not be taken locally (because of national or multinational firms operating through branch plants in an area) and that there may be no independent local market for loanable funds, a closed economy model of investment may have serious limitations. This latter problem again parallels the issue raised by Common Market membership, where capital benefits most from the freeing of constraints on its mobility and funds tend to flow towards areas of the highest return. The *relative* rate of return on local investments may thus be more important than its absolute level. The structure of financial institutions may also be very important for channelling local savings into local investments.

Historically, it is clear that local banks were deeply involved in the economic development of their local economies. The trend to national banks, and now to banks operating internationally, militates against this in a way which we shall consider in greater detail in Chapter 7. The structure of interregional financial flows will thus be a key feature of the investment sector of the model.

The government sector—both its consumption and investment expenditure—does require a rather more fundamental reappraisal in the context of an urban economy. The principal reason for this is in the need to deal with different levels of government, each taking essentially independent decisions about both its own levels of expenditure and its policy towards influencing or controlling the expenditure decisions of the non-government sector by means of taxation, subsidy or direct intervention. Yet these decisions will ultimately be interrelated through some overall national government control on the level of public sector activity and the method of financing that activity. The question of finance is complicated here by the existence of inter-governmental transfers of resources through grants to allow for the inequalities in resources which exist between different local economies and to allow for the greatly differing needs of different local economies trying to meet certain nationally agreed minimum levels of provision of certain services. There is, therefore, a potential conflict between the independence of the local government sector in its decision making and the availability of resources and the demands placed on those resources. There will be substantial flows of resources out of the local economy into the (national) government sector in the form of taxes paid by local residents and substantial flows in through the various grants paid by central government to local government, as well as direct internal transfers through local taxes and individual grants and subsidies. However, none of these can be treated as independent factors nor aggregated with other flows. Clearly, the detailed operations of the government sector, and in particular the public finance aspects of it, need a much more comprehensive analysis which we shall delay until Chapter 8.

Trade and the Urban Balance of Payments

The trade sector is the most difficult to analyse empirically because of the lack of trade flow data at such a level of disaggregation. Even at a regional level it has not been possible to give full justice to the importance of the trade sector in Britain. Nevertheless, it is important to understand something of the determinants of exports and imports since the size of the trade sector relative to that of the economy as a whole tends to be inversely related to the economy's actual size. Thus, the smaller the city, the more important will exports be as a component of aggregate demand and imports as a source of leakage out of the economy.

The demands for exports and imports will both be determined by similar variables—income and prices. The relevant income will be that of the 'rest of the world' and the city respectively. The relevant prices will be the relative prices of 'domestically' produced goods and goods produced elsewhere. The importance of income is that it relates to the structure of output within the city, both as cause and effect. If the city produces a high proportion of goods with high income elasticities of demand, then both external and internal income growth will have advantageous balance of payments effects by increasing exports and not increasing imports as fast. This leads to the possibility of a faster growth in incomes within the city than in the rest of the world. If the output is mainly of goods with low income elasticities of demand, then the reverse will be true. However, regardless of such structural effects, the relative competitiveness of the output will be important. Individual cities are likely to be relatively small producers of most industrial products and hence open to considerable competition.

Price competitiveness is not just a question of variations in direct production costs arising from variations in input prices or economic efficiency in production. The degree of competition in the local market may affect mark-ups and hence competitiveness in the wider market. Several goods and services which are not traded across economy boundaries, such as urban transport and land, may be an important element in production costs. Their non-trading situation means that larger inter-urban disparities can arise in their prices, affecting the competitiveness of local industries using them as inputs. Capacity utilisation can also affect costs. Local shortages of capital and, more particularly, of labour of specific types (either real or perceived) have often been identified as critical factors in producers' decisions (Keeble 1976, Chapter 4).

In a national context, export and import issues are not independent, but link through the balance of payments and its effect on exchange rates. Whilst formal balance of payments and exchange rate problems do not arise, local economies do face effective balance of payments constraints on their performance since the rate of return on local investments will fall, resulting in capital and other resource outflows (see, for example, Thirlwall 1980b).

Equilibrium and Comparative Statics in the Urban Economy Model

We have now built up the elements of a fairly comprehensive model of the local economy out of the basic input–output framework with which we started. This framework can be used to demonstrate two basic effects. First, we can use the structure to derive the equilibrium level of income for the local economy in terms of the various exogenous variables and parameters which relate these to the endogenous variables such as consumption, imports, etc. Secondly, we can use the framework to demonstrate comparative static effects of a change in one of the exogenous variables or one of the parameters on the level of income. This latter relationship is the multiplier effect. The tendency will be for each increase in income to induce further increases in expenditure which induce further increases in income and so on, but at a declining rate since at each 'round' there will be a leakage out of the economy in the form of savings, expenditure on imports, tax payments and so forth. This relationship is an important concept in any economy: it demonstrates the relative efficiency of using different policy variables within the structure of the economy to generate a given policy objective as well as giving a quantitative indication of the size of change in the policy variable needed to achieve the given change in income and hence in employment.

What this structure which we have developed so far does not allow for is genuinely dynamic effects in the local economy. The presumption is that the economy will always return to a stable equilibrium level of income, albeit at a different level, after each change. In the context of several economies within a national economy it also carries with it an essentially neoclassical notion of balance and convergence. An economy which becomes depressed as the result of, say, falling exports will suffer an outflow of funds and a reduction in income relative to the national average. Since resources are free to move, both capital and labour will tend to move away from low income areas and towards higher income areas. The higher income areas will suffer the congestion effects which will eventually make them relatively less competitive, whilst the low income areas will now have lower levels of expenditure and lower imports but less congestion and, implicitly, higher levels of marginal productivity of the remaining factors. Hence the low income areas will benefit from a faster growth of income producing a convergent pattern of interregional incomes and the restoration of income equilibria. This model of interregional growth and development was developed initially in the United States by Borts and Stein (1964). What we now need to investigate is whether such a simple process is ever likely to occur. We shall look more closely in the next chapter at the way in which the various factors we have discussed in this chapter relate together in a dynamic system. Before turning to this, we shall outline the formal structure of our model of the local economy for completeness since we shall need to refer to the basic relationships in this at frequent intervals throughout the remainder of this book.

The Urban Income–Expenditure Model

The most basic model of income and expenditure in an urban economy, a, without a government sector can be written as:

$$Y_a = C_a + I_a + X_a - M_a \tag{3.11}$$

where Y is income, C, I, X and M represent consumption expenditure, investment, 'exports' and 'imports' respectively. The first two expenditure items represent expenditure within the city by its residents, and the last two flows of expenditure into and out of the city respectively. For the moment, we shall assume I_a is given exogenously ($\bar{I}_a$) to simplify the model without losing any real understanding of its working. Consumption consists of an autonomous element and an induced element dependent on income:

$$C_a = \bar{C}_a + c_a(Y_a) \tag{3.12}$$

Imports consist of an autonomous component and a series of induced elements, dependent on the (different) import propensities of each category of expenditure, remembering that import expenditures will be relatively high in an open city economy:

$$M_a = \bar{M}_a + m_{\bar{c}a}\bar{C}_a + m_{ca}c_aY_a + m_{ia}\bar{I}_a + m_{xa}X_a \tag{3.13}$$

Exports depend on the aggregate import propensities of all other regions within the country and outside. If, again for simplicity, we assume that these can be aggregated into a single 'rest of the world' region, b, with known import propensities from a, we can write the export function for a as:

$$X_a = \bar{X}_a + m_{\bar{c}b}\bar{C}_b + m_{cb}c_bY_b + m_{ib}\bar{I}_b + m_{xb}X_b \qquad (3.14)$$

In this formulation we are assuming that the import content of autonomous and induced consumption does vary, because of the rather different nature of the goods and services included in these elements, but we have not made any such adjustment for the other components of aggregate expenditure. However, it should be noted that this differs from a common formulation of the import function in that it treats imports as dependent on *expenditure* and not directly on *income* (see Thirlwall 1980a, Chapter 4 for a summary of such a model in a national context. In the urban case it is even more necessary since these export and import flows are typically of direct consumer expenditures, and not just flows of imported and exported goods, given that a large part of exports will consist of direct expenditure in local shops by non-residents and a large part of imports of similar direct expenditures by residents in other cities.

With this simple specification we can now set out two simple results: the condition for equilibrium and the implied multipliers relating changes in the autonomous components of expenditure to changes in income. If we substitute equations 3.12 and 3.13 into 3.11 and assume for the moment that $X_a = \bar{X}_a$, we have:

$$Y_a = (1 - m_{\bar{c}a})\bar{C}_a + c_a(1 - m_{ca})Y_a + (1 - m_{ia})\bar{I}_a + (1 - m_{xa})\bar{X}_a - \bar{M}_a \qquad (3.15)$$

and hence

$$Y_a = \frac{(1 - m_{\bar{c}a})\bar{C}_a + (1 - m_{ia})\bar{I}_a + (1 - m_{xa})\bar{X}_a - \bar{M}_a}{1 - c_a(1 - m_{ca})} \qquad (3.16)$$

from which, for example, an investment multiplier would be

$$\frac{\Delta Y_a}{\Delta \bar{I}_a} = \frac{1 - m_{ia}}{1 - c_a(1 - m_{ca})} \qquad (3.17)$$

This tells us that the multiplier value of any change in an autonomous element of expenditure depends on the import content of that expenditure as well as on the marginal propensity to consume and the import content of that consumption. Some care has to be taken in using simple multiplier formulations of the above type, especially in small open economies, because there is evidence that the 'leakages' in different rounds of the multiplier process are not of the same order. In the simple model above, where all investment expenditure is autonomous, the implied leakage in the numerator does allow for this. It may also be the case that some of the induced expenditure from that investment, for example expenditure by those employed on construction involved in the investment, may have different leakage rates from normal expenditure by city residents. This would apply in the case of large construction projects which employ large numbers of transient workers who remit large parts of their wages to another region (see Sinclair and Sutcliffe 1978; 1982, for a detailed discussion of this problem).

We now need to allow for the interaction between the city and other regions implied by the export function in equation 3.14. Assume that $m_{\bar{c}a} = m_{ca}$ and $m_{\bar{c}b} = m_{cb}$, simply to reduce the dimensions of the problem, and we can then derive expressions for the simultaneous achievement of income–expenditure equilibrium in both a and b from which a representative investment multiplier can be derived as:

$$\frac{\Delta Y_a}{\Delta \bar{I}_a} = \frac{(1 - m_{ia}) - \left[\dfrac{(m_{xa} - m_{ia})m_{xb} + c_b(m_{cb} - m_{xb})}{1 - c_b(1 - m_{cb})}\right]}{1 - c_a(1 - m_{ca}) - \left[\dfrac{m_{xa} + c_a(m_{ca} - m_{xa})m_{xb} + c_b(m_{cb} - m_{xb})}{1 - c_b(1 - m_{cb})}\right]} \tag{3.18}$$

The key elements in this formulation are the different marginal import contents of exports in the two 'regions', m_{xa} and m_{xb}, and the different marginal import contents of different elements of expenditure within each region, e.g. $(m_{xa} - m_{ia})$ and $(m_{cb} - m_{xb})$. If the latter were to be equal then the second term of the numerator of equation 3.18 reduces to zero and the final term in the denominator reduces to

$$\frac{m_{xa}m_{xb}}{1 - c_b(1 - m_{cb})}$$

i.e. the product of the import contents of exports reduced by the leakages from consumption in the trading partner. Of course, in a two-region world, b's imports are a's exports and therefore the product term $m_{xa}m_{xb}$ is rather like the product rule of import and export elasticities. In a multi-region world this simple reciprocity is lost since the import propensities become directional: m_{ca} is not constant for all countries. For example, m^b_{ca}, the propensity to import from b, may be greater than m^z_{ca}, the propensity to import from z, whilst m^z_{cb} is greater than m^a_{cb}. The effects of an initial injection in a, therefore, get spread indirectly through other regions' trade as well as directly through its own trade.

In the model we have so far assumed exogenous investment and no government sector. The first of these is not inherently difficult to adjust to allow for induced investment; the multiplier becomes accordingly more complex, but remains of the same nature. A simple government sector requires us to examine both expenditure and revenue implications. Thus, if we define government expenditure by

$$G_a = \bar{G}_a + g_a Y_a \tag{3.19}$$

and then add the following term to equation 3.13

$$m_{\bar{g}a} + m_{ga} g_a Y_a \tag{3.20}$$

whilst deducting the necessary tax payments from Y_a, the consumption function of equation 3.12 becomes:

$$C_a = \bar{C}_a + c_a(Y_a - t_a Y_a)$$

Ignoring the trade repercussions through induced exports, the multiplier of equation 3.17 now becomes:

$$\frac{\Delta Y_a}{\Delta I_a} = \frac{1 - m_{ia}}{1 - c_a(1 - m_{ca})(1 - t_a) - g_a(1 - m_{ga})} \tag{3.21}$$

Hence there is an additional leakage through taxation and an additional injection through the government's own marginal propensity to consume (net of the import content of its marginal expenditure).

However, the government sector is more complex because of the need to distinguish between local and national government expenditures and taxation which respond rather differently.

National government involvement in the local economy may be best treated as exogenous direct expenditure financed by taxation proportional to income. There is no reason to suppose that the national government's budget in the local economy balances—in fact, exactly the opposite is more likely because of the national government's involvement in nationwide redistribution and stabilisation and in providing public goods without reference to the local population's specific preferences. The local government sector is rather different. Its revenue will come from both local taxes (which will typically relate rather imperfectly to local incomes) and from national government grants, which to a large extent are designed to compensate for an inadequacy in the local tax base to support a given level of expenditure. Local government expenditure may be influenced by opposing forces. Some may relate positively to local income, simply reflecting greater local fiscal capacity. A large element may relate negatively to local income since many local public goods are compensatory for failures of the private sector (or the national government) to provide sufficient output. The budgetary balance is also rather difficult. Local government authority is less likely than a national government to engage in deficit financing for its economic effects. However, to the extent that it regards its expenditure as largely exogenously determined and its local fiscal capacity limited, then to the extent that central government grants fail to make up any deficit automatically the budget will not balance. One further impact is that the import content of local and national expenditures may also differ.

The conclusion from this discussion is that a simple treatment of the government sector is not a reasonable approach. We shall need to examine the various elements discussed above in rather more detail in Chapters 5 to 8. It will then become clear that a simple static equilibrium model of the urban economy is itself inadequate. The first modification we need to make is to introduce some dynamics, which we do in Chapter 4.

Further Reading

The classic geographical texts are those of von Thünen (1966) and Christaller (1966) which are well summarised by Lloyd and Dicken (1977). The basic model of von Thünen has been reassessed by Samuelson (1983). Early location theories are summarised and developed by Isard (1956) and comprehensively reviewed by Smith (1971). A useful discussion of the present state of industrial location analysis is in Keeble (1976); see also Greenhut (1956; 1963; 1975) and the reworking of the standard analysis of the firm by Eaton and Lipsey (1977). For a more detailed discussion of spatial economics in general, see Vickerman (1980); and for more elaborate and fully developed models, Paelinck (1982).

All serious students of urban structure should look at Alonso (1964). Evans (1973) and Maclennan (1982) attempt to apply versions of a basic model to British cities. The most analysed individual city is probably Chicago which featured in the early studies of Park, Burgess and MacKenzie (1925) and is the basis of both Muth (1969) and MacDonald (1979). Some study of the so-called New Urban Economics can be rewarding: three key papers are by Solow (1973), Mirrlees (1972), and Dixit (1973); see also the discussion in Richardson (1977), Vickerman (1980) and Paelinck (1982).

Discussion of urban macroeconomic frameworks is harder to find, but there are useful sections in Hirsch (1973), Armstrong and Taylor (1978) and Richardson (1978). On input–output analysis, see Miernyk (1965) and Richardson (1972); and for applications, Morrison (1973) and Pullen and Proops (1983).

4
Growth and Decline in the Urban Economy

In Chapter 3 we discussed the determinants of structure, both economic and spatial, in the urban economy and sought conditions under which equilibrium can be attained. However, we have recognised throughout that we are dealing with essentially dynamic forces which may not even lead to equilibrium. In this chapter we shall: introduce dynamics into the macroeconomic model of the city economy; consider the development of spatial structure within the city through time; and consider the dynamic links between the individual urban economy and the rest of the economy.

4.1 Dynamic Aspects of the City Economy

In this section we shall review the implications of a number of alternative models of economic growth for the city economy. We shall start with the neoclassical model and then go on to develop urban base approaches before considering non-equilibrating models of growth.

A Neoclassical View of Urban Growth

The neoclassical model suggests that there is a natural self-balancing correction mechanism at work to stabilise economies, not just internally in the sense of maintaining a balance between the various sectors of the economy, but also between economies. This starts with an aggregate production function for the city and hence is essentially a 'supply-based' model of the economy which views aggregate output as the simple summation of individual industry outputs. Since output in the economy depends on inputs of the various factors of production (principally labour, capital and land), it is clear that the possibilities of growth in the economy depend either on the growth of availability of those factors or improvements in the ways in which the factors can be used together. Basic to any such approach is the idea that there is a limit to the extent to which one input to the production process can be increased without increasing the others—this is the notion of diminishing marginal productivity. Since land is a key input to urban production and is much more fixed in supply in the sense that it cannot be imported from outside, this fixity would limit the extent to which scale economies can be achieved without causing rapidly rising costs (due to falling marginal productivity) to other factors.

There is a considerable amount of potential productivity improvement which can be gained even from a strictly fixed amount of land by increasing the density of its use, and from technical progress in the transport sector. The latter is not usually considered explicitly: in fact, many neoclassical views of a spatial economy manage to ignore space in any practical sense and just concentrate on the overall size of the city. It is clear, however, that historically the rapid growth of cities has typically been associated with major improvements in transport technology. Urban railways, the street tramway and the growth of private car ownership have all played their part either as cause or effect of changes in city size. As we saw in the context of locational decisions by firms in Chapter 3, the inclusion of this transport element as an input to the production function which can be traded off against other inputs is critical. It may be especially so in the case of aggregate city growth since it is clear that there are certain critical thresholds in city size which enable the introduction of new transport technologies to permit continued growth, the absence of which will impose a severe constraint on the city.

It is easy to show that urban rail or mass transit systems are more efficient users of land than the private car in terms of the land requirements per unit flow of traffic. This is partly because of the technical requirements of infrastructure and the associated control systems. Many passengers can be carried in a single train which occupies less space than the number of cars which would be required to carry the equivalent number of passengers; in addition, the ability to effect centralised control over the passage of trains along a given length of track permits a greater density of usage of the given infrastructure than would be possible in attempting to effect such control over many individually controlled private cars. Furthermore, such mass transit systems are much more efficient users of another scarce resource, energy. However, the investment in infrastructure required is much greater and hence high volumes are necessary to make it a practical proposition. This means that such transport systems are only suitable for major traffic corridors where large numbers of people effectively make the same journeys and hence demand and supply can be equated at a market clearing price for travel. This implies either linear cities, or cities which are large enough to enable the installation of an efficient mass transit system for certain key trunk haul routes in and out of the city with distribution at the outer ends being done by feeder systems of more flexible transport: bus or private cars. The time penalty imposed on such necessary changes of transport mode again means that only where total journey lengths are on average much greater can such a system be effective.

Table 4.1 illustrates the differing patterns of journey to work for cities of different sizes both by distance and by time. It can be seen from this that cities which are large enough to effect a more efficient transport system can expand in terms of distance without residents suffering a time penalty. It could also be noted in this context that equivalent access time can often be had from living at much greater distances from the city and being able to use long-distance rail services such as are available at the extreme edge of the urban transport system.

Much of the interest of the neoclassical model then centres on the possibilities of increasing the supply of the more conventional inputs of labour and capital. The interesting feature of the regional or urban economy within the national economy for this type of model is that supplies of factors can be increased by means other than natural increases in population or increases in savings since a key feature is the openness of the economy for factors as well as goods. Hence, migration of labour is a key element in determining the rate at which population will increase, and interregional capital

Table 4.1 Average Journey Length by Place of Work and City Size, 1978/79

	London		*Conurbations*		*Other Urban Areas*		*Rural Areas*	*Great Britain*
	Centre	*Outer*	*Centre*	*Outer*	*Centre*	*Outer*		
Distance (miles)	12.4	5.9	6.2	5.2	4.4	5.0	4.1	5.2
Journey time (mins)	43	31	31	25	20	21	16	22

Source: Department of Transport (1983) *National Travel Survey, 1978/79*, HMSO.

flows are correspondingly important in allowing for increases in regional capital stocks.

Migratory flows of labour and capital are determined in this system by the relative rewards to the factors in the various local economies, there being a net flow of a factor towards a region with a relatively higher wage rate or return on capital. If it is assumed that there is a perfect market in the factors, the wage rate or return on capital is then given by the appropriate marginal factor productivity which, as we have seen, is assumed to fall as factor supply increases, and hence we are back in the self-balancing situation.

In a regional model the logical outcome of this is to ensure that wages, for example, are equalised in all regions. Any empirical failure to identify this happening is mainly the result of the presence of imperfections in the various markets, especially in information. In an urban model there is a problem that the *raison d'être* for cities is the availability of scale economies etc. as discussed earlier, and we should expect therefore that an urban–rural wage differential would not only exist but would be maintained because of the maintenance of this scale economies 'gap' which itself becomes reflected in the differing industrial structures of these more localised economies. This has led those seeking to define some notion of optimality in city size to turn to broader definitions of factor remunerations including, for example, the non-pecuniary benefits of urban dwelling (access to a wider range of amenities) and the financial costs and external diseconomies of pollution etc. which need to be offset against these. In other words, the decision to live in a particular location depends on more than just job availability and wage.

The Neoclassical Growth Model

To summarise the basic form of the neoclassical view of an economy's growth we set down a simple formulation based on an aggregate production function of the form:

$$Y = f(K, L, T) \tag{4.1}$$

where Y is output and K, L, and T represent inputs of capital, labour and technology respectively. It is assumed that the per unit land requirements of capital are given at any moment in time so that we can ignore this as embodied in the state of technology and the level of capital inputs and similarly the current state of transport technology is included in the technology input. We can thus write the growth of the economy in terms of the growth of the various inputs and technical progress as:

$$y = ak + bl + t \tag{4.2}$$

where a and b represent the shares of capital and labour in total output since $a = (\Delta Y/\Delta K)(K/Y)$. If the rate of return on capital employed (r) is equal to the marginal productivity of capital, then $a = r.V$ where $V(=K/Y)$ is the capital-output ratio. In a perfect market r must be equal to the rate of interest which will equate savings and investment and hence the rate of growth of the capital stock, k, will be given by the savings ratio (S) and the required capital output ratio (V) as $k = S/V$. The labour force will grow at the natural rate of increase of the population, n, assuming that economic activity rates remain the same. If we open the economy up to inflows of capital and labour we can respecify k and l as follows, for economy i:

$$k_i = \frac{S}{V} + \sum_j k_{ji} \qquad \text{where } k_{ji} = f'(r_j - r_i) \tag{4.3}$$

$$l_i = n_i + \sum_j m_{ji} \qquad \text{where } m_{ji} = f''(w_j - w_i) \tag{4.4}$$

If we return to equation 4.2 and assume for the moment that there are constant returns to scale in the use of capital and labour such that $a + b = 1$, we can rewrite equation 4.2 as:

$$y - l = t + a(k - l) \tag{4.5}$$

This can be interpreted as showing that the rate of growth in labour productivity ($y - l$) is composed of the sum of two parts: the rate of technical progress and the rate of increase of capital per head (capital deepening). The absence of capital stock figures has typically rendered attempts to estimate the relative importance of different elements in equation 4.5 rather imperfect (Dixon and Thirlwall 1975b) although the recent estimation of capital stock figures at a regional level should enable some progress to be made here (Harris 1983). However, as Harris clearly demonstrates, it is necessary for production purposes to make a clear distinction between both gross and net capital stock and the utilisation of that stock. At a regional level some more prosperous regions, such as the East Midlands, have had a relatively low rate of growth of capital stock but a consistently high rate of utilisation, whilst other, less prosperous, regions such as the Northern region have had much higher rates of growth of capital, but typically lower and highly fluctuating rates of utilisation. Used in a CES production function, utilised capital suggests rather higher rates of substitution than pure capital stock measures.

One of the interesting elements of a local economy model is: what assumption is to be made about the variation in t between different economies? Here there has been a difference in stance between, on the one hand, that of the non-spatial regional economists (e.g. Dixon and Thirlwall 1975b) who have tended to assume that in a unified economy there should be no difference in the rate of introduction of new technologies in different areas and, on the other hand, the spatially explicit models of innovation diffusion favoured by geographers and regional scientists (Hägerstrand 1967; and see discussion in Vickerman 1980, Chapter 4). Our discussion of the composite nature of technical progress, above, noting that in an urban area it involves both capital-land intensities and a transport input, suggests that it would be wrong to assume technical progress is spatially invariable.

Export-Base Theories

In contrast to the preoccupation of the neoclassical model with supply side elements, later growth theories have attempted to stress rather more the role of demand side elements: sometimes this has been to the total exclusion of any consideration of production function elements which, we have seen, will be an important determinant of at least the competitiveness of an economy's output.

The simplest form of such a model is provided by the export-base theory which we have already encountered. This places the burden of growth on that part of demand which is exogenous to the city economy. Aggregate output consists of two parts—output for export (the base) and output for the local economy:

$$Y = Y_x + Y_l \qquad (4.6)$$

Y_x is given and exogenous to the model; Y_l is determined by the total level of output in the economy since it comprises services sold to the export base and services and goods sold to the residents of the city employed by either sector. Hence:

$$Y_l = a + bY + a + b(Y_l + Y_x) \tag{4.7}$$

and therefore

$$Y_l = \frac{a}{1 - b} + \frac{b}{1 - b} \cdot Y_x \tag{4.8}$$

and

$$Y = \frac{a}{1 - b} + \frac{1}{1 - b} \cdot Y_x \tag{4.9}$$

In terms of growth rates:

$$y_l = y_x \cdot \frac{bY_x}{a + bY_x} \tag{4.10}$$

and

$$y = y_x \cdot \frac{Y_x}{a + Y_x} \tag{4.11}$$

Thus, in this formulation overall output growth depends on exogenous export demand and its growth, and on the parameter *a* which is the autonomous element in local output: the larger this is, the lower will be overall growth. This model thus suggests that it is important to keep the size of the local sector within the constraint imposed by the rate of exogenous demand growth. Any attempt to boost total output growth by increasing Y_l independently through investment in local infrastructure or import substitution could be counter-productive.

Unbalanced Growth

Closely related to the philosophy of this type of model is that of Baumol (1967) which aimed to show the way in which unequal performance in different sectors of a local economy could lead to problems. Baumol thought in terms of a service sector highly dominated by municipal services, not serving the export market at all, in which the scope for productivity improvement was limited.

The base sector, on the other hand, has scope for continued productivity growth. Baumol aimed to show that there was no necessary mechanism of a neoclassical type which would restore balance between these sectors on the basis of their relative productivity growth but, in fact, the sector with the worst productivity record would tend to develop to the exclusion of the base sector.

Formally, the model assumes that the service sector, s, has constant productivity and the base sector, x, has productivity growing at a constant rate, r, per unit of time. If we ignore inputs other than labour, the outputs of the two sectors in time, t, can be written as:

$$Y_{st} = aL_{st} \tag{4.12}$$

$$Y_{xt} = bL_{xt}e^{rt} \tag{4.13}$$

If both sectors compete in the same labour market and wages are assumed to keep pace with productivity in the base sector, then wages will be determined for the entire economy as:

$$W_t = We^{rt} \tag{4.14}$$

Costs per unit output in the two sectors can therefore be written as:

$$C_s = \frac{We^{rt}L_{st}}{aL_{st}} = \frac{1}{a} \cdot We^{rt} \tag{4.15}$$

and

$$C_x = \frac{We^{rt}L_{xt}}{bL_{xt}e^{rt}} = \frac{1}{b} \cdot W \tag{4.16}$$

Here W is a constant representing wages at some arbitrary starting point in time and hence relative costs in the two sectors are:

$$\frac{C_s}{C_x} = \frac{be^{rt}}{a} \tag{4.17}$$

Thus costs in the service sector relative to the base sector increase at a constant rate through time.

Assuming prices proportional to costs and unitary elasticity of demand for output in both sectors, relative expenditure on the two sectors will be constant, since

$$\frac{C_s Y_s}{C_x Y_x} = \frac{We^{rt} L_{st}}{We^{rt} L_{xt}} = A \tag{4.18}$$

and hence relative output in the service sector would decline over time, since

$$\frac{Y_s}{Y_x} = A \cdot \frac{C_x}{C_s} = \frac{aA}{be^{rt}} \tag{4.19}$$

If, however, prices are not proportional to costs, e.g. because of subsidy, or if the demand elasticities are not unitary, then this is not the case, since from 4.19 we can write:

$$\frac{bY_s}{aY_x} = \frac{L_s}{L_x e^{rt}} = K \tag{4.20}$$

and if $L = L_s + L_x$

$$L_s = (L - L_s)Ke^{rt} \tag{4.21}$$

$$= \frac{LKe^{rt}}{1 + Ke^{rt}} \tag{4.22}$$

and

$$L_x = \frac{L}{1 + Ke^{rt}} \tag{4.23}$$

and hence through time L_s approaches L and L_x approaches zero, so employment in the base sector gets squeezed by the lagging service sector.

Baumol's model of the possible cumulative effects of a shift of urban economic activity towards sectors which have intrinsically lower rates of productivity growth could well be applicable to many large cities in which the simple fact of bigness tends to lead to the need for a greater service support sector. It will be noted, however, that there is no attempt to include any cumulative linking mechanism explicitly. In a later version of a model in the same basic vein Oates *et al.* (1971) have tried to identify an explicit linking between the level of output and a measure of urban deterioration. This is presented in a recursive manner with income in one period a function of deterioration in the previous period:

$$Y_{t+1} = r - sD_t \tag{4.24}$$

whilst deterioration is itself a linear function of the level of income in that period:

$$D_t = u - vY_t \tag{4.25}$$

In both these equations the key parameters s and v are assumed to be positive, so that the mere fact of size in urban income or output is assumed to lead to deterioration which reduces the level of income in the subsequent period to below what it would otherwise have been. From equations 4.24 and 4.25 we get

$$Y_{t+1} = r - su + svY_t \tag{4.26}$$

$$= b + aY_t \tag{4.27}$$

where $b = (r - su)$ and $a = sv$. For urban income to converge to an equilibrium level we need $Y_t = Y_{t+1}$ which will occur at:

$$Y_e = \frac{b}{1 - a} \tag{4.28}$$

The possibility of convergence to an equilibrium level of income thus depends on the value of $a(=sv)$. Since s and v are positive, so is a; if a is less than unity Y_t will converge on Y_e, and if a is greater than unity a cumulative divergence will take place from Y_e, though the model itself does not predict whether this will be growth or decline: that will depend on whether Y_e is greater or less than the current value of Y. What, then, determines the values of s and v and hence a? These are seen by Oates *et al.* to be determined by such variables as local tax rates and public expenditure levels reflecting partly the Baumol notion of the influence of slow productivity growth public service sectors, and partly the tradition of the Tiebout (1956) model of the optimal local public sector as being determined by the relative values of such variables through the ability of people to move towards combinations they prefer and away from those they do not.

For example, if income depends on the level of urban services provided, *inter alia*, and the latter depends on both the level of the tax base, B, and the level of education, E (which is assumed to reflect individuals' perceptions of the value of the services provided), we can specify the model of equations 4.24 and 4.25 more precisely as:

$$Y_{t+1} = \alpha + \beta S_t \tag{4.29}$$

$$S_t = \gamma + \delta B_t + \eta E_t \tag{4.30}$$

$$B_t = \theta + \kappa Y_t \tag{4.31}$$

$$E_t = \mu + \xi Y_{t-1} \tag{4.32}$$

From equations 4.29 to 4.32 we can derive an expression for Y_{t+1}

$$Y_{t+1} = b + a_1 y_t + a_2 Y_{t-1} \tag{4.33}$$

where $b = \alpha + \beta\gamma + \beta\delta\theta + \beta\eta\mu$, $a_1 = \beta\delta\kappa$, and $a_2 = \beta\eta\xi$ and for equilibrium

$$Y_e = \frac{b}{1 - a_1 - a_2} \tag{4.34}$$

Here again, the critical factor is the value of the parameter $a(= a_1 + a_2)$ which depends on the sensitivity of the various key variables on each other: urban income on urban public expenditure, the level of public spending on the tax base and on the population itself as measured by education levels, and the dependence of both of these on previous levels of income. The model is, of course, much oversimplified: it takes only a small selection of relevant public expenditures, it does not interlink these to the base sector of the economy, and it does not consider the way in which openness in the economy may impose a constraint on the process of growth or decline through either the balance of payments with other areas or the migration of factors. It does, nevertheless, suggest that there are problems inherent in cities which may be related to their urban natures, which require increasing levels of service or public expenditure on a basic urban infrastructure, and which may very easily produce cumulative effects.

Core–Periphery Models

The discussion so far has been aimed at showing that there may be circumstances in which a cumulative process may be set in motion in economies where a basic distinction can be drawn between two sectors: base and non-base, service or public sectors. This distinction concentrates on the premise that the demand for such non-base services is income-related whilst they display less scope for productivity improvements. But what of the case where cities run into problems with their base sectors? Are there cases in which the structure of the base sector can cause problems, or in which differential performance of base sector industries relative to those same sectors in other areas can lead to a cumulative process of growth or decline? We have already seen that both structure and differential performance can have effects on the economic performance of the local economy in terms of the analysis of shift-share evidence, but now we must set down the mechanism through which such a process actually works.

Models of so-called cumulative causation in economic growth aim to show why the process of growth is a self-sustaining one, rather than a counter-balancing process of convergence to an equilibrium level, and why the relative rates of growth of different economies can tend to diverge, rather than produce a system in which all economies converge to a common growth rate. The cumulative causation model is usually related to Gunnar Myrdal's (1957) attempt to define what are generally termed the 'spread and backwash' effects of growth between economies. Hence, the effects of increased economic activity in one area would tend to diffuse to other areas by the increased demand for imports from those areas occasioned by faster economic growth and because the faster growth in the 'centre' areas would imply increased production at lower costs. This in turn would provide export surpluses to be sold at cheaper cost to the other areas, raising the real standard of living in both. This is quite consistent with the neoclassical view of the spread of the growth process, but Myrdal also believed that, instead of this process coming to a natural balancing conclusion, there would be a backwash effect of this faster growth which would tend to move valuable factors of production away from the periphery areas and into the centre areas (particularly risk capital and qualified labour), thus reducing the potential of the peripheral areas to benefit. It is the backwash effect which leads to an increased impetus to the centre.

Attempts by writers such as Prebisch (1950), Perroux (1955) and Seers (1962) to develop such a model more formally in a variety of situations concentrated on the essentially structural factors associated with income elasticities of demand for exports as an explanation of relative growth. Kaldor (1970) suggested that there may also be price elasticity effects and hence that differential productivity growth could be important. To produce a cumulative effect required that there should be no self-correcting mechanism to slow productivity growth in a fast growing economy because of the limits of increasing returns. This requires introducing the so-called Verdoorn relationship which makes output growth itself a determinant of further productivity growth through both economies of scale and the embodiment of technical progress in the capital formation associated with growing output (Kaldor 1972).

The Kaldor Model

Before sounding a cautionary note and discussing some criticisms of the Kaldor approach let us outline a general development of the model. The simplest approach is the attempt by Dixon and Thirlwall (1975a) to formalise the basic features of Kaldor's (1970) model. It is assumed that the economy is open and that exports comprise the major component of autonomous demand, so that the growth rate of exports determines the growth rate of the economy; and export growth will depend on relative prices (and price elasticities of demand) and income growth (and income elasticities of demand) in the rest of the world. We have already suggested that a purely open-economy model may be limited by effective balance of payments constraints and so we need to allow for a constraint on export growth (Dixon and Thirlwall 1979).

A version of a more complete model is written in equations (4.35) to (4.40).

$$y_t = \gamma x_t \tag{4.35}$$

$$x_t = \eta(p_{dt} - p_{ft} - e_t) + \epsilon z_t \tag{4.36}$$

$$p_{dt} = w_t - r_t + s_t \tag{4.37}$$

$$r_t = \bar{r}_t + \lambda y_t \tag{4.38}$$

$$m_t = \psi(p_{ft} + e_t - p_{dt}) + \pi y_t \tag{4.39}$$

$$p_{dt} + x_t = p_{ft} + e_t + m_t \tag{4.40}$$

Equation 4.35 is the basic growth equation: the rate of growth of output, y, in period t depends on the rate of growth of exports, x. (All variables are written as growth rates.) Equations 4.36 and 4.39

are the export and import demand functions carried forward from Chapter 3; 4.40 is the balance of payments equilibrium constraint. Equation 4.37 is the domestic price determination relationship where w is the wage inflation rate, s is the mark-up inflation rate and r is the growth in productivity which is itself dependent on the rate of growth of output and an autonomous component (4.38). In the trade equations, z is the growth in income in other regions and e is the change in exchange rate. Of course, in an urban model there is no exchange rate as such, but it is useful to leave in this component so as to demonstrate the possible policy device of attempting to give an exchange rate advantage to a particular region within a unified economy by differential fiscal measures.

If we ignore initially the balance of payments constraint, we obtain the equilibrium growth rate in equation 4.41. The critical factors here are the values of ϵ and λ, since γ and η are assumed to be positive and negative respectively. If w and s are higher in the city than elsewhere, then the growth rate will be depressed unless ϵ and λ are sufficiently large to overcome the price elasticity effect. If we add the balance of payments constraint we obtain the alternative form of the growth rate given in equation 4.42. Now the γ coefficient is no longer relevant since it is the ability to expand the constraint of equation 4.40 which is the decisive factor in growth. The key parameters now are the relative sizes of ϵ and π, the former expanding growth and the latter retarding it. The sum of the price elasticities $\eta + \psi$ is now the critical factor in determining the relative retarding effect of a higher rate of inflation, but also in modifying the effect of the Verdoorn coefficient, λ. Note that if $|\eta + \psi| > 1$ this reduces the value of the numerator if domestic inflation is more rapid than elsewhere, but increases the importance of the Verdoorn effect in raising the growth rate.

$$y_t = \frac{\gamma[\eta(w_t - \bar{r}_t + s_t - p_{ft} - e_t) + \epsilon z_t]}{1 + \gamma\eta\lambda} \tag{4.41}$$

$$y_t^B = \frac{(1 + \eta + \psi)[w_t - \bar{r}_t + s_t - p_{ft} - e_t] + \epsilon z_t}{\pi + (1 + \eta + \psi)\lambda} \tag{4.42}$$

This model suggests a very delicate balance of growth rate behaviour, with the four elasticities ϵ, π, η and ψ assuming a critical role.

If we now allow for capital inflows or the payment of grants to compensate for a failure of exports to keep pace with imports, equation 4.40 will not bind as such, and a higher growth rate can be sustained. However, the real rate of such inflows will have to grow at a faster rate than the volume of exports in order to raise the growth rate and that implies ever-increasing commitments to such compensation. Thre is no long-term substitute for improving the real performance of the economy.

4.2 The Dynamics of Land Use Patterns

We have concentrated so far only on the overall growth problem—the determination of gross regional product (GRP)—of the city and have igmored the internal elements of structure and changes in these over a period of time which may be seen as both cause and effect of changes in GRP and which indeed may themselves have some cumulative effect on these. One of the reasons for this collapse of the spatial structure of the city when considering dynamics is the sheer complexity of treating both space and time simultaneously since this introduces the effective need to integrate over two dimensions simultaneously. We shall have to be satisfied here with simply stating the problems posed by this and briefly reviewing the attempts which have been made to resolve this difficulty.

The dynamic spatial problem is essentially the way in which land use becomes reallocated through time as the city economy changes in structure and the population grows or declines. In a growing city it is likely that the faster growing activities display rising profitability and hence bid-rent functions are likely to move outwards and allocate more land to the faster growing activities—a process which we noted in connection with the market nature of the basic model in Chapter 3. Similarly, if faster growing industries need to bid up wages in order to secure necessary supplies of labour, those employed in these industries will gain higher incomes and thus may change their optimal locations within the city creating a need for a reallocation of housing stock. If the city is also growing in total population terms, there will be a need for new housing stock. Changing size and structure of land use of the city implies a change in the transport system since journey lengths may change as may patterns of travel to and from work. If the demand for labour changes more rapidly than the population of the city, or if there is a constraint on the availability of land for housing purposes within the city, then in-commuting from the surrounding area may increase. This in-commuting may either be from potential new residents in advance of their moving in, or from old residents who either choose to, or have to, move out. The effects of these changes on the demand for transport are typically found in terms of the increased allocation of land for transport purposes in inner areas of cities and rising effective transport costs within the city as a whole. Both of these effects may increase costs of production through both land and labour costs.

Relocation of Employment

There has been relatively little study of the real spatial impact of growth in the productive sector of the urban economy. As we have seen in the discussion of industrial location models there has been considerable research into specific decisions to move the location of manufacturing industries, often in response to some of the effects of urban change. In the work of Keeble (1966) in London (summarised in Keeble 1976) and the work of Cameron (1969, 1973) in Glasgow, the process of searching for new sites is well documented, but the general finding of much of this research has been that actual moves of plants are relatively unimportant in the process of the movement of employment (cf. the work of Dennis 1978; Fothergill and Gudgin 1982; Danson *et al*. 1980). During the same period that manufacturing activity within cities was tending to move outwards, service industries were tending to absorb the land and to a lesser extent the labour left behind. This trend continued well into the 1970s, but showed signs of having peaked and begun to decline in importance towards the end of the decade as recession set in. Of course, service industries have demands for all factors of production very different from manufacturing industries, even though they may often be regarded as part of the economic base of the area since, especially for large metropolitan areas, the service sector is part of its regional or even national specialisation of function. Service industries do typically have much less extensive demands for land than manufacturing industry and higher densities of development are possible; but location and accessibility in general are much more critical. More recently, it may be possible to argue, the growth of modern electronic processing and communications systems has reduced this locational requirement, both from the point of view of contacts with potential customers and in terms of the reduction in the need for access to supplies of less qualified clerical staff.

In terms of the dynamic effects on the city economy as a whole the key relationship which needs to be analysed in this context is that between the location of employment opportunities and residential location. There is a clear presumption in most basic models of residential location that the key factor which individuals consider when deciding on the optimal residential location is that of the workplace—this can then be used as a proxy for accessibility in general. To the extent that the workplace is assumed typically to be in a central business district location where the bulk of other activity such as shopping, entertainment and culture is also likely to be located this may not pose a problem. However, the differential rates of decentralisation of different activities, the differential rates of decentralisation of different types of job for different skill levels, and the different degrees of access to different housing markets for different socio-economic or occupational groups render such simplistic approaches incomplete. The extent to which it is employment decentralisation or residential decentralisation which leads in this process has been questioned by Steinnes (1977, 1982). Aggregate evidence presents us with a rather ambiguous result from which it is not clear whether jobs move out due to the various locational pressures faced in more central locations and take with them individuals intent on optimising residential location, or whether the process of decentralisation of residents, motivated essentially by considerations of improving housing and environment, forces employers to follow.

In either case there is the possibility of the observed social imbalance in individual movement occurring because of constraints operating in both housing and employment markets. Recent work by the author (Vickerman 1984) attempting to interlink migration and commuting, using both aggregate and disaggregate data, suggests that there is very little direct connection between change of workplace and change of residence in the context of the London region, although there have been substantial changes in the pattern of commuting over a number of years (see also Mogridge 1979; Congdon 1983).

Housing Market Dynamics

More precise attempts have been made in the housing market to develop dynamic models. One approach which has been followed by a number of authors is to consider housing as a capital asset in the context of a vintage capital model (Evans 1975; Muth 1976). This has the advantage of enabling the temporal aspect of the model to be handled discretely as housing is only considered in terms of its vintage and not dated in terms of continuous time. The important features of such a model of the housing market are that they can be used to simulate the likely rate of depreciation of the housing stock, which is an important consideration in terms of the association between income and the degree of delapidation of housing through subdivision and undermaintenance in central areas. Whereas, however, fairly precise estimates can be made of the relationship between population growth and the growth and depreciation of the housing stock, it is much more difficult to assign particular vintages and particular rates of depreciation to specific locations within the city, except as part of a simulation exercise.

Pines (1976) and Anas (1976) have attempted to show something of the spatial impacts of such types of model over very broad subdivisions of a typical theoretical regular city. Two interesting features of these models and their results are associated with the assumed degree of reversibility of housing investment and the degree of myopia on the part of city residents taking housing investment and location decisions. The conclusions which seem to appear from these are that with irreversibility (i.e. the inability of a particular unit of housing stock to be costlessly converted to another use or to a different type of housing), considerable discontinuities may emerge in the rent structure of the city which are associated with a lack of smoothness in the density gradient and with irregular growth—features which are quite typical of the growth of many real-world cities. The myopia of individual decision makers in the housing market may also lead to discontinuities at the edge of the city where most of the new development takes place. Simulated over longer periods of time, such a model (Anas 1976) produces situations in which suburbanisation takes place because of the inability of the housing market to redevelop areas within the existing city sufficiently quickly. Again, it is clear from casual observation of the development process within cities that unnecessary suburbanisation does often take place, leaving undeveloped areas within the city which it would be more optimal, from an aggregate point of view, to have developed.

Market Interactions

Consideration of both the housing market and the process of workplace–residence choice and commuting patterns does raise the difficult question of the validity of assuming that optimising market clearing processes are at work in all the various markets when the speed with which adjustments can be made by individuals is quite slow and quite different between markets. In an earlier paper, the author outlined some possible approaches using sub-optimising procedures, and attempted to see whether the sort of patterns suggested by such approaches fitted the experiences of some British cities (Vickerman 1979). No clear-cut conclusions could be firmly supported, but the exercise certainly suggested that an approach based less on the general equilibrium clearing of a series of markets may be a more appropriate approach to the dynamics of urban development (see also Vickerman 1980 and 1984).

This is a difficult area, where there is only limited guidance from mainstream economic theory as to the likely ways of formulating and predicting results from a situation in which individuals are having to search for the best outcome in a series of markets simultaneously, or according to some preconceived notions of the most satisfactory ordering of searches. In such circumstances, the presumption that individuals will also seek to optimise on a period-by-period basis in each market does seem rather extreme. The difficulty posed in the context of attempting to assess the overall outcome of a series of separate decisions in an urban economy is that different markets involve different types of decision maker—individuals, public and private institutions—all with different time horizons for the outcome of their decisions. It seems unreasonable to suppose that all these decision makers are totally ignorant of the sort of feedback which they may encounter in their decision making; hence they may be inclined to make some allowance for their imperfections in both their own *and other agents'* knowledge. An approach to this problem through the use of sub-optimising decisions is given in Vickerman (1979).

Also critical in such a world is the distribution of economic power between the various agents in the economy, and the perceptions of that power by others. For example, if a local authority has both considerable economic power through its role in providing a large portion of economic activity and controlling others through its land-use policy and is perceived by both firms and households to be in control of the general level and nature of economic activity, then it can manupulate others' decisions to suit its own purposes. Its policy towards land release in peripheral areas, rezoning of inner areas for new activities and public transport investment and pricing should convey a total picture of the city it envisages. If it miscalculates because, for example, of its inability to foresee an energy crisis which both changes the outlook for the economic base of the city and renders inappropriate the spatial pattern of development planned, then it is often others who must bear the costs of this miscalculation: for example the individual living in a house in a new suburb who faces, first of all, the cost of travel to and from work which he cannot afford and, secondly, the loss of his job without accessibility to areas where there are potential jobs available.

Transport and Dynamics

We have touched on the issue of transport provision in a dynamic context: its role of linking together job and housing markets in many cities and the problem of coping with the spatial implications of major changes in transport prices because of exogenous shocks such as large rises in oil prices. We need to look a little more closely at the role of transport in the dynamics of the urban economy. Once again, this is a relatively little researched area, despite the considerable literature on transport itself, and once again this is due to the analytical complexity of dealing in several different dimensions.

A theoretical transport system is not too difficult to handle because it can work on the assumption that transport, like the houses of housing models, is a homogeneous entity. Transport in the typical urban model is thus a unimodal affair which has a precise land use requirement per unit of transport capacity provided and which is made available in response to the demand for commuting services. The main problem is that of congestion: the cost of providing the transport service from a given capacity increases as demand increases beyond a certain point. That increase in cost is perceived, albeit imperfectly, by the consumer who may adjust his bid-rent function for land at a particular location to reflect the increasing transport costs in accordance with the conventional trade-off model.This internal adjustment does have implications for the long run growth of the city since, in the absence of other factors, congestion costs will stunt the growth of the city. The response to this is either to provide additional capacity (which would typically require an increase in the allocation of land to transport and might thus not change the overall implications for land use very much but just affect the distribution or incidence of costs), or to innovate transport systems with greater capacity.

Real-world cities are not so simple. They almost always have several competing transport modes which have different land use requirements and different costs. The main factor, however, is that these different transport systems are not under a unified control; hence the signalling for an optimal allocation of transport between transport modes, as well as an optimal provision of transport capacity in aggregate, has to be done through a market system of prices and/or other controls. Futhermore, since there is no simple relationship of residential location to workplace, as assumed by the simple urban model with its central area employment and regular distribution of housing zones about it, we need to consider the way in which transport costs and prices may lead to a reallocation of journeys between workplaces, residences and other activity locations, as well as between transport modes. In this world it is not just a case of determining the optimal population of the city through the effects which transport costs have on rents, but of the distribution of activity through the city and between transport modes. Different internal distributions may give stable equilibria but result in differently sized cities which may grow or decline at different rates.

To demonstrate this last proposition Glaister (1976) considered a very simple city situation but allowed for different transport modes and different pricing policies adopted towards them. The result was what we should expect from the above discussion: rates of growth differed, final sizes of the cities differed and the overall welfare evaluation of the outcome of the different policies also showed great variation. We shall discuss this, together with a more detailed assessment of the policy options towards transport, public and private, in Chapter 6.

4.3 Dynamic Aspects of an Economy of Cities

We have tried so far to separate those factors from the dynamic process of economic change which relate to the individual city within the wider economy and to show how they lead to changes in both aggregate levels of economic activity and to its spatial organisation within the city. In this section we shall try very briefly to show two further aspects of the dynamics of the urban economy: the extent to which the processes of urban growth in individual cities lead to convergence or divergence in the relative performances of cities, and the way in which national economic growth is affected by the performance of individual cities and their interrelationships.

Rank Size Orders

We have already met the convergence–divergence problem on several occasions because it does lie at the heart of an understanding of both the static structure of the city and its growth processes. The neoclassical view of urban or regional growth is very much a relative growth theory since it relates local growth processes to relative productivity. Stemming from this is the notion of there being some form of stable ordering of city sizes within the economy. Obviously, the theory does not imply that all cities will finish up exactly the same size: initial advantage has led certain cities to achieve a pre-eminence within the economy as a whole and that pre-eminence in terms of agglomeration economies is maintainable. The convergence notion here is one of relative convergence such that beyond a certain point absolute inequalities will not increase, and a stable pattern of trading will ensure that although cities will differ in size, the *per capita* wellbeing of residents will converge to greater equality, with the greater benefits of the larger city being offset by the correspondingly greater costs. This relativity between cities must therefore mean that there is a fairly strict relationship between city sizes, since the potential benefits of agglomeration are likely to depend not just on absolute size, but on relative size. This arises because many of the agglomeration benefits are related to city function within both its regional and its national context.

The rank size rule for city size is an essentially empirical recognition of this belief. It has been shown that it is possible to fit a stable function of the form

$$RP = K = P_1 \tag{4.45}$$

where R is the rank order of the city, P is its population and P_1 is the population of the largest city in the system. This form, due to Christaller (1966), is a special case, where $q = 1$, of a more general form

$$R = KP^{-q} \tag{4.46}$$

in which the value of q tells us something about variations in the 'shape' of the rank ordering. If $q < 1$, the system has a relatively larger number of large secondary cities, and if $q > 1$, the big cities are highly dominant. Like many relationships in the so-called social physics approach to regional science (e.g. Zipf 1949), the rank size rule is essentially arbitrary and with no underlying theory (although, as with the related gravity model, many have attempted to develop one). The rule is very close, however, to two distributions which have found a place in economic reasoning concerning the measurement of the distribution of other economic variables such as income, the log normal function and the Pareto distribution—see Richardson (1973b) for a detailed review.

Divergence in Growth Rates

Despite the stability of the rank-size ordering of cities within an economy, there is also evidence that the sort of *per capita* convergence in income levels or wellbeing which this might imply does not actually occur. Implicit in the unbalanced growth or cumulative causation models is the notion that growth rates may diverge, and by diverging may lead to cumulative inequalities in the welfare of the residents of different cities beyond those which, in terms of the neoclassical view, are simply the result of market imperfections preventing the free movement of resources.

If we think of the model in equation 4.41 as a two-region model, it gives us a relationship between growth rates which demonstrates how it is the key elasticities that determine whether these are likely to converge onto common equilibrium paths. Of course, growth at the same rate does not imply absolute convergence to the same level of *per capita* incomes in the two economies.

We have, therefore, every reason to expect that city growth rates, and hence *per capita* incomes, will diverge through time and that encouragement to mobility of factors will not correct this imbalance but may actually worsen it, posing policy issues of a type which we shall need to take up in the following chapter.

Interregional Approaches

We also need to think about the dynamic interrelationships between city economies and the national economy which they together comprise. Quite obviously there is a limit to the extent to which we can simply translate international economic theories to an inter-city level within a single national economic policy framework. We need to find an appropriate level of compromise between traditional theories of self-balance and new theories of divergence.

One way in which an element of self-balance enters the system is the fact that 'imports' to city economies consist of both 'imports' from other cities in the country and 'real' imports from cities and regions in other countries. The latter enter into the national balance of payments and hence form part of a much more real balance of payments constraint which will affect income growth in all cities of the country and hence the potential 'export' demand from within the country for any one city's goods. If the largest cities within the country have an exceptionally high propensity to import from other countries and the country's economy as a whole faces a balance of payments constraint on its international account, this could result in a depressing effect on the economies of the potentially faster growing small cities. Suppose also that those cities for which there is a potentially favourable overseas export demand (in terms of the income elasticity of demand for existing products) face potentially faster rising costs than their overseas competitors: this would reduce their rates of growth below what could be obtained and have a cumulative impact as a result of the national economic constraint. Why should this be likely?

We have seen that the key factors which may influence local costs are land rents and transport costs within the city, both directly on firms and indirectly through their influence on labour costs. If these are rising faster than costs in other cities, at home or abroad, then this may counteract the potentially favourable income elasticity effect. Potentially richer cities could be penalised by national economic policy measures, such as grants given by national government to local government, which may favour lagging regions for perfectly genuine reasons (the desire for equalisation) or may discriminate against local authorities who attempt to maintain lower transport costs. Lower transport costs may not just have a direct effect through industrial transport costs, or the transport costs determination of land rents, but also through the transport cost element in the determination of wage rates, or even the desire to work in a city. If two countries have very different attitudes to the public subsidies given to urban public transport there may be a major long run effect not just on the prosperity of individual cities but also on national economic performance as a whole.

This dimension of urban economic analysis and policy making is not one which has yet received much attention. We must not forget that not only is it dangerous to consider one urban economy in isolation from others in the same country, but it is equally dangerous to consider an inter-urban economy within a country independently of the international situation. To this end current attempts to develop inter-regional economic models which cut across national boundaries (and which therefore provide a basis for this much wider linking of economic activity directly rather than through a sequential or hierarchical structure of towns, regions, and nations) are a major step in the right direction (see Issaev *et al.* 1982).

Further Reading

There is a vast literature on economic growth models which underlies the discussion here. The classic statement of the neoclassical model is in Borts and Stein (1964); Myrdal (1957) has much to say about the basic core–periphery models; good summaries of the state of the art in regional growth at that time are contained in Richardson (1973a) and Holland (1976). The Kaldor model appears in Kaldor (1970), refined in Dixon and Thirlwall (1975a, 1975b, 1979). Specifically urban models start with

Baumol (1967) and see Mills and de Ferranti (1971) and Eversley (1972). There are good summaries in Richardson (1973b) and Cameron and Wingo (1973). Dynamic spatial models appear in the collection edited by Papageorgiou (1976), and they have been discussed by Vickerman (1980) and in more detail by Paelinck (1982).

The issue of structural change has become an important theme in economics generally: at the local level, Fothergill and Gudgin (1982) and Bartels and van Duijn (1982) contain useful discussions.

For some contrasting views to those presented here, see Broadbent (1977) and the collections edited by Harloe (1977) and Dear and Scott (1981).

PART TWO

Urban Problems and Policies

5
Welfare and Control

In Part I we concentrated on the more abstract aspects of the urban economy: its reason for existence, its structure and the factors influencing its growth and decline. This we illustrated by the features of real cities and their economies, but we did not turn our attention to the real questions of analysing and attempting to solve the problems which beset so many cities today.

In this second part of the book we shall take up key issues identified by our overall view of the city and attempt to look not just at their causes and likely outcomes, but also at the possibility of using government policy measures at national or local level to alleviate their effects or removing them altogether. However, before we can assess policy in detail towards transport, or housing, or levels of public expenditure and taxation, we need to stand back from the individual issues and ask some questions about what our aim should be. In a way, this is the provision of what could be termed a *normative* framework to stand alongside the essentially *positive* economic framework of Part I. At several points during our positive analysis it became clear that there was an argument about not just income levels, but also about the distribution of income both within a single urban economy and between urban economies (and indeed non-urban economies) within the overall national economy. How are we to decide on the correct weighting of these? Similarly, we pointed out that there is a close connection between national economic performance and the economic performance of at least the largest urban areas within that economy. How much are we to transfer resources in order to subsidise the populations of the large cities so that they can compete more effectively internationally, and hence raise the potential level of national output and income?

In this chapter we need to establish this other framework, the framework for policy analysis, so that any recommendations emerging from detailed analyses of particular problems of sectors can be assessed for their normative as well as their positive implications. In doing this we must also be aware of the fact that government itself is not a costless exercise. It is to be hoped that at most levels the administrative cost of government is insignificant compared with the benefits generated, but increasingly the question is asked whether particular levels of government do fulfil this basic criterion. This is especially the case where we are requiring government to discriminate between different areas of a country with due regard to their specific needs.

We shall divide the discussion into five basic areas. First, we need to assess what the criterion for success in policy is to be: objectives of policy at both national and local levels and the inconsistencies between these. Secondly, we shall take up the issue of externalities and environment in the urban economy. Thirdly, we shall look at the range of activities which local government authorities may be involved in. Fourthly, we shall discuss the issue of the appropriate scale of such involvement, the size of the local public sector. Finally, we shall consider problems of collective choice and the implementation of policy.

5.1 Problems of Places and People

We have seen that in most economies, not only do local variations in income *per capita* emerge, but there is both theoretical and empirical evidence to suggest that such divergences can bę both lasting and cumulative. We have also seen that this shifting of the economic base of a national economy in space is a likely result of the changing economic structure. New industries are unlikely to have similar locational requirements to older industries. The problem which this poses is that the residents of declining areas become disadvantaged relative to those of the newer, growing areas. Hence the basis of most economic policy towards regions has been to compensate their residents for the loss of the region's economic base. This has, in most countries, involved not simply a financial compensation, but an attempt either to halt the trend of decline, or to divert the new industries from their more favoured locations to locations where redundant resources exist. Where such a policy is successful, it obviates the need for continuing compensation being paid to that region's residents. However, to be successful it may involve the continuing payment of subsidies to firms which are encouraged to locate there, such that the total costs are not dissimilar.

This is a familiar story in the history of regional policy (see Armstrong and Taylor 1978 for a fuller account) but it raises a difficult question: the relative success of some aspects of regional policy in limiting new growth in parts of the economy may have contributed to the new economic problems of inner city areas in formerly successful regions—for example, the decline of London and Birmingham in the case of the United Kingdom. This resurrects an old debate which has appeared in various guises over the years and which centres on whether it is more appropriate to move jobs to workers, or workers to jobs and hence whether it is more appropriate to create prosperity for given geographical areas or for people, regardless of their location. Although this is a serious policy issue, it gets confused with the argument about the usefulness of government intervention at all, since a policy aimed just at promoting the welfare of people—what may be termed a people-prosperity objective—can be allied with a free-market stance of no government intervention. This is a pity because there does remain a serious issue about the correct objectives of policy for an interventionist stance: people- or place-prosperity.

The economics of the debate are quite simple to outline. If the relevant geographical area for decisions to be made is at the national level, then the objective of policy is presumably to secure the maximum degree of output or income at that level consistent with an acceptable distribution of that income over the population. In a free market situation, where profit maximisation is the basic criterion, firms would choose the best location consistent with that maximum being achieved. In such a situation governments would have two basic roles: one would be to ensure that harmful externalities did not arise (there might be a need to control the degree of agglomeration where the market failed to account correctly for its social costs), and the other would be to compensate those individuals who fell outside the acceptable bounds of the distribution *and* who were unable to relocate because of the actual or incorrectly perceived cost of that relocation. If firms have to be induced to move to different locations, then it is presumed that these are less favourable from the point of view of the national, as well as the firm's, output. The relevant consideration is whether the cost of this interference in location is greater than the compensation required under a free location system. The basic question which then emerges is: who should have the greater rights—the firm, to locate where *it* wants, or the individual, to locate where *he* wants? One cannot expect the market to provide an answer to this question.

Measurement Problems

Whilst it is not too difficult to outline this issue in an abstract case, there are a number of practical problems which can arise which make it much more complex. First of all, there is the obvious point that the world is not one of free markets so that it is no more likely that firms make the correct decision in their location policy than do individual households in deciding not to move from the area in which they have spent their whole life just because the local economy is in decline. Perhaps more serious for the potential policy maker, however, is the measurement problem of the possible objective indicators. As far as personal income is concerned there is less of a problem, but if it is decided that transfers should be made between areas according to some average income criterion, then the definition of the area becomes critical. This is because areas defined by local government boundaries, or indeed by any other criterion, are rarely if ever homogeneous in terms of the characteristics of their population. Transferring income from a generally high income area to a generally low income area thus only makes sense if it is coupled with a general policy to ensure that there is redistribution between high and low income families. The danger is that what is actually achieved is a redistribution of income from the less well-off in the high income area to the better-off in the low income area. This could happen if jobs were diverted from a low unemployment area where marginal workers have gained employment to a high unemployment area where local businessmen receive the benefit.

The crudeness of regional policy, operating at best over very large sub-regions, also presents problems here since the areal transfer could be from a high unemployment/low income inner city area in a prosperous region to a low unemployment/high income small town in a development area. It may, of course, be true that analysts can assess the extent to which changes in the mean value of a variable for an area are misleading by looking at what is happening to the variance or to percentiles, but policy is rarely sensitive enough to discriminate in such a way as to make these other measures of a distribution realistic policy indicators.

We have already suggested that there are problems of variation within regions which may affect the efficacy of regional policy. It is also true that there are variations within urban areas which may work in a similar way. For example, the attempt to provide a measure of relief to inner city depressed areas by lifting a large number of restrictions on development in so-called Enterprise Zones creates artificial boundaries within a city. Whilst such measures may or may not generate new economic dynamism (and we shall discuss this in more detail in Chapter 7), the concentration of the production activity in such areas does not necessarily mean that the income of residents of that area is increased: the workers in new factories can commute from wealthier areas of the conurbation; and the profits may be creamed off into other parts of the region (just as the profits from regional development areas have often accrued to firms setting up branch plants in the region in the form of enclave economy investments).

We have used this argument as a criticism of area-based policies which broadly aim at improving the productive potential of areas which score badly on a certain indicator. It could also be used to criticise the compensation policies which would be necessary under a freer market attitude to location since typically such compensation would be paid in the form of a grant to the local authority; and it would normally be very difficult to assess the extent to which an individual in a particular region should benefit. Such grants might help to alleviate the rate burden on residents in declining areas where, as we have seen, there may be increasing burdens of local infrastructure to be maintained. Such benefits typically have greater impact on those with the greatest liability to such taxation, and not typically on the poorest sections of the community. It is true that the non-pecuniary aspects of wellbeing (as embodied in various social services and the public transport infrastructure) ought to be included as well as the purely financial aspects, but of course access to most of these is not means-tested. Hence cheap transport benefits those in work more than those not in work, whilst on the other hand special prices of services available to the unemployed may discriminate against those in work but in exceptionally low-paid work, where net income is lower than it would be from the full array of income support benefits.

In short, therefore, we face an almost insurmountable problem in defining both the appropriate indicator and the appropriate spatial unit for its measurement. We must be careful in interpreting any policy just in terms of the numbers of jobs created, the effect on average incomes or levels of unemployment, and the cost per job created. All of these are highly relevant indicators, but neither any one alone nor any combination of them tells the full story.

5.2 Externalities and the Urban Environment

We have cited on a number of occasions the fact that externalities exist within an urban economy as a reason for government intervention in order to ensure that any optimum size of city or structure of economy that is achieved can be interpreted unambiguously as a social optimum. Such a society must be defined so as to include those outside the city as well as those inside it, otherwise very different answers may be obtained. Richardson (1973b) suggests a range of possible values which would satisfy the notion of optimal city size, using both average and marginal, private and social, cost and benefit notions (see Figure 5.1). Using rather arbitrary but commonsense notions about cost and benefits derived from urban living, it can be seen that very different city sizes will satisfy different groups. Existing city residents, for example, would prefer to be at *E*, where the difference between average costs and benefits is maximised, than at *O*, where marginal social costs and benefits are equated. On the other hand, assuming that the net benefits of city life, over and above the benefits of non-city life, are included in these cost and benefit definitions, new entrants will be encouraged into the city up to *M*, where net benefit falls to zero. In a period of decline the failure of individuals to take into account the social costs of their actions may lead to the reverse happening: the

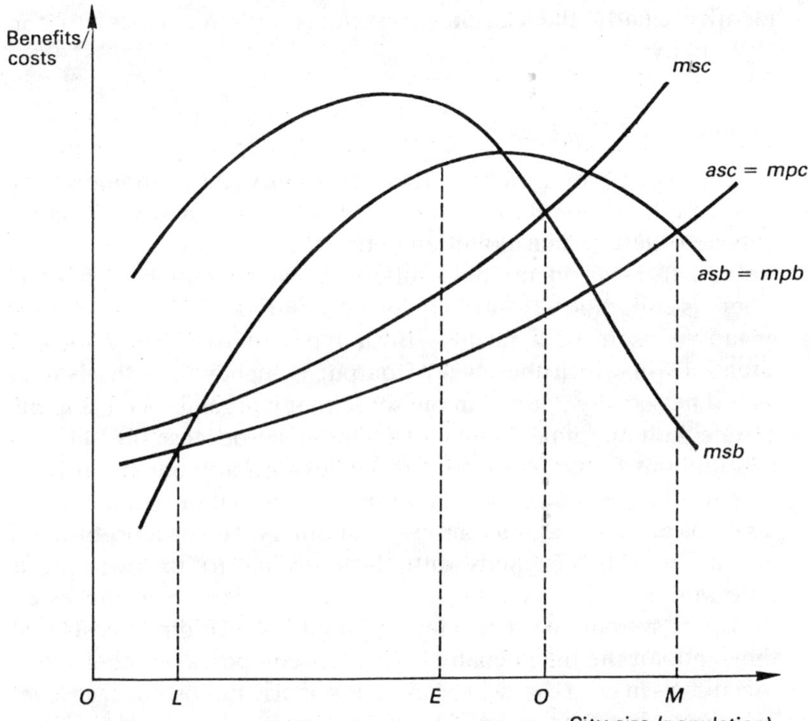

Figure 5.1

city would decline to a size below its socially optimum size. This obvious importance of externalities means that we do need to look at the nature of these in a little more detail than hitherto.

Many of the externalities which we have referred to as both agglomeration economies and economics of urbanisation need not concern us here because they are fully taken into account by individual decision makers when choosing an urban location. The external effects are internalised because they have a market value, and this implies that they can be traded. The externalities which do not possess this property are potentially the most serious, however, since they are more likely to involve not the typical producer/producer external effects of the above type but producer/consumer or consumer/consumer effects. A market does not normally arise to enable the effective internalisation of such externalities because they involve either unequal economic power or the inability to identify clearly the causer (or sufferer in some cases) of the externality.

Pollution and Congestion

The most common forms of urban externality can be thought of as either pollution or congestion externalities. The basic distinction between these is that pollution externalities involve a transfer of welfare from an identifiable sufferer to an identifiable polluter, whereas congestion typically involves a shared loss of welfare by a group of users of a facility. Both types of externality involve situations in which the level of output is higher than that which would be socially optimal in the sense that marginal social benefits equate with marginal social costs. This arises because the decision taken about output or usage only takes into account the private costs to the decision maker and not the external or social costs of dirt, noise, time-loss, etc. imposed on others. Hence a profit-maximising industry expands output according to its own profit criterion, ignoring pollution costs. A traveller on a congested transport system only takes into account his own direct costs and time and not the time penalty his presence imposes on others. The social costs in each case will be in excess of private costs at each level of output where the externality exists. Hence, assuming downward sloping demand curves representing the benefits, optimal output will be less than actual output.

The optimising solution in each of these cases is a tax-subsidy measure to ensure that output occurs where social costs and benefits are equated. Hence, polluters or motorists causing congestion can be taxed to make sure that they perceive the full social costs of their actions; equally, polluters can be subsidised to introduce pollution control equipment and public transport can be subsidised to induce traffic away from congested roads—a policy which we shall consider in more detail in Chapter 6.

There may be a spatial problem with such a solution, however, since benefits and costs may not arise within a single community. If the industry is a base industry, much of the benefit from its output accrues to consumers outside the city, whilst the costs are incurred internally. Any attempt to reduce pollution may lead to a loss of competitiveness and ultimately to a loss of employment for city residents. Local firms may thus have considerable bargaining power to continue to impose external costs. Similarly, the redistributive effects of congestion taxes may have undesirable consequences when translated into a question of who pays and who gains.

Cumulative Degradation

A further type of externality which has been of considerable importance in urban areas is the way in which property values may depend not only on the quality of the immediate property, but also on the quality of surrounding properties and the environment. This can lead to an incentive to undermaintain properties since the return on maintenance expenditure will be reduced by surrounding, less well maintained properties. On the other hand, if other properties are better maintained, there is a potential net gain in return. As long as an area is fairly homogeneous the externality can be effectively internalised, as individuals with similar preferences can assess the preference patterns of neighbours and act accordingly. Once individuals stop taking into account others' preferences, for example when different types of individuals move into an area, areas can deteriorate rapidly.

5.3 Scope of an Urban Public Sector

In this section we shall turn our attention to the sort of activity which may be provided by the public sector at an urban level, how this may take effect, and how the public sector may control the private sector in order to achieve the same ends. We shall leave until the following section the question of the extent of that activity, either in total or in part. We have seen that the rationale for the public sector intervening is essentially that of market failure in one guise or another, i.e. the public sector has an essentially allocative role, correcting for mistakes in the private sector. However, the local public sector has typically been denied access to an adequate source of revenue to support such involvement.

Why should there be a need for a local public sector at all if there is a national public sector with better financing prospects? The traditional reasons given for the existence of public authorities at different spatial levels are twofold. First, there is the need to reflect spatial variations in need or demand for public services which is best met by local control. The needs for certain services in urban and rural communities certainly differ, although it may be arguable as to whether these are best met by having separate authorities rather than just variations in national provisions. As we shall see, the assumption of more and more financial responsibility by central government has been associated with increasing sophistication in the devising of need indicators on which grant settlements are based. This effectively removes the greater part of local discretion over the level of provision. Secondly, there is the supply side argument that economies of scale are exhausted at different spatial or population size levels (Hirsch 1973) in the provision of public sector services. Hence there is the need to assess the most appropriate units for the provision of such services in order to minimise the unit cost of provision. This, however, raises a number of issues. There is no reason why optimal units for the provision of different services should coincide at particular sizes of authority. There may be some evidence for the grouping of ranges of services at different levels of provision (Hirsch 1973; Richardson 1973b) which would imply a rationale for a multi-tier system of government provision. But there is no obvious reason why this should require separate local authorities, rather than just a differing spatial organisation of the direct providing agencies of a central government body, especially as the latter may involve certain broader economies of an administrative or financial nature.

Historically, a very wide range of services has been provided by local authorities: indeed, in Britain as in many countries, the local authority sector was the origin of direct public provision of services. The growth of municipal power in the late nineteenth century coincided with the period of consolidating urbanisation and the growth of new public utility services, which for various reasons were thought to be better placed under municipal control: gas, water, electricity, telephones, the street tramway, were all examples of this. Nineteenth-century benevolent attitudes led to municipal development of public baths and parks and the start of public education, especially in higher education. In the twentieth century, the growth of road traffic led to increasing concern with the provision of highways within urban areas and, later, the desire to provide public housing and personal social services led to local government agencies being seen as the natural focus of new types of state intervention.

Many of these ventures were overtaken by technological change. The need to provide constant standards of service over wide areas, as well as to plan new developments systematically, led to it being less appropriate for local authorities to control the traditional public utilities. These passed into State ownership with the early nationalisation of gas and electricity, with the nationalisation of the telephone (achieved at a very early date) and with the later nationalisation or reorganisation on a national basis of the water undertakings. Education, too, was affected by a desire for national consistency following the 1944 Education Act. Subsequent attempts to secure varying degrees of national conformity led to local authorities being used as little more than agencies of central government, with little power to design a service to meet precise local needs or demands as evidenced by local votes. Similarly, personal social services and housing are often provided on little more than an agency basis by local authorities, since many of the services are controlled by national standards which limit effective freedom of action. National standards in playing field provision and similar standards coupled with the administration of many specific central government grants to local authorities (through national agencies which can insist on conformity to a national standard for the award of a grant—for example, the Sports Council in the case of sports centres, or the Arts Council in the case of many cultural activities) also reduce the extent to which genuine local initiative or control can be exercised. Table 5.1 summarises some of the main shifts in the nature of public expenditure at a local level over the long period derived from the important work of Foster, Jackman and Perlman (1980).

The one sector where substantial local control and initiative has been available has been in the key sector of urban transport. Although highways have become less important as a subject of expenditure over the years (partly because of the rise of other activities and partly because of the transferring of responsibility for a national network to central government) local government has very largely retained control of urban public transport. Indeed, there have been some advances in the degree of local control in recent years: first, through the provision for Passenger Transport Authorities in Metropolitan Counties to assume financial responsibility for local rail services and for local bus services (not only those directly provided); and secondly, through the general responsibility

Table 5.1 Changing Distribution of Local Government Expenditure, 1900–75 (%)

	1900	*1950*	*1960*	*1970*	*1975*
Current Expenditure					
Education	11.6	30.3	37.3	35.1	35.9
Poor relief & welfare	11.1	2.9	3.1	3.0	6.1
Housing	0.1	9.5	15.0	14.7	16.6
Highways	12.0	7.4	6.0	4.7	3.6
Hospitals & health care	1.3	3.8	3.7	3.1	–
Sewerage & refuse disposal	4.6	4.5	4.1	4.2	1.9
Parks	0.8	1.6	1.5	1.2	1.3
Fire	0.5	1.6	1.5	1.2	1.3
Police	6.7	5.7	5.8	5.6	5.4
Public utilities	8.9	4.6	3.4	2.9	–
Transport	3.6	8.9	6.5	3.4	0.8
Capital Expenditure					
Education	8.4	8.5	5.1	12.9	10.2
Poor relief & welfare	4.8	0.9	0.9	1.2	1.8
Housing	3.2	70.6	56.9	48.4	65.9
Highways	12.9	1.5	4.6	9.7	7.5
Hospitals & health care	1.3	3.8	3.7	3.1	–
Sewerage & refuse disposal	8.0	3.1	6.4	7.4	0.5
Parks	2.0	0.4	0.5	0.7	1.8
Fire	–	0.1	0.4	0.3	0.2
Police	–	0.7	0.6	1.0	0.9
Public utilities	32.1	4.8	4.9	4.1	–
Transport	12.0	3.7	1.7	1.3	0.4

Source: Foster *et al.* (1980), Table 1.4.5

of local authorities to make provision for the maintenance of unremunerative services which fulfil a social need. This degree of local autonomy has, of course, had financial implications which have affected central government and, as we shall see in more detail in Chapters 6 and 8, has led to renewed powers being sought by central government to curtail this freedom, at least insofar as its financial implications are concerned.

Thus far, we have concentrated on the direct provision role of the public sector where it may be argued that municipal provision has been essentially a phase determined by particular technical conditions of supply and which has now largely outlived its usefulness in many areas (partly because of the financial implications). Local authorities do have other functions, however, which may have an important impact on the local economy. The most obvious of these is the local planning function of providing and implementing land-use policies for the city. Apart from certain strategic planning functions of a more regional kind which in Britain have largely been left at county level, this is an area where local control has been maintained or even strengthened (although the planning legislation allows for appeal procedures to higher authority and also provides national guidelines on the treatment of, for example, historic buildings or issues which may have wider regional or national implications). Structure Plans and District or City Plans serve as a legally binding framework within which specific planning decisions are taken. Such a procedure is necessary both to ensure consistency in planning decisions (the adoption of the plan itself involves long periods of public consultation) and to provide as much information as possible to individuals planning to undertake future developments within the area. Planning controls through the framework of the local plan thus have elements of both carrot and stick in that they can encourage certain types of development in certain areas as well as provide legally-based controls on indiscriminate development in the public interest. The sort of cumulative uncertainty found in decaying areas can thus to some extent be minimised in order to avoid what has sometimes been termed 'planning blight'.

The ability of a local authority to use its planning powers towards economic development is, of course, limited. Ultimately, it can only use such powers in a passive or responsive way when dealing with individual planning applications submitted to it.

Whilst there has been little direct economic initiative by local authorities of a traditional fiscal kind, a number of the larger authorities have seen that there is a role to be played in entrepreneurship for the sake of economic development. Thus larger metropolitan authorities in particular have introduced schemes for industrial restructuring within their areas or for taking a financial stake in the operations of certain key firms as a venture into risk capital, acting typically in the role of a local enterprise board. To a large extent this new role has often been a defensive one to counter the uneven impact of central government policy in the recent recession and to fulfil a task which could equally be, but has not been fulfilled by central government.

We have, therefore, again identified a rather confused picture of what the urban public sector is likely to be involved in. Specifically, it does appear that there is no stable range of activities for which a clear rationale for provision at the urban level exists. The precise range provided at any time is a reflection of both demand and supply characteristics of the individual services. Increasingly, we have also seen, it has become a question of the acceptability of local public sector involvement to central governments which are even more worried about the growth of the public sector in total and the growth of the local public sector in particular to compensate for curbs on central government expenditure. This brings us to the question of the aggregate size of the public sector.

5.4 Size of an Urban Public Sector

Since the public sector typically emerges to compensate for some market failure, it has long been a question of interest to public sector economists whether there is any way of defining an optimal size for the public sector in the absence of the market test. This is an aggregation of the problem of determining the optimal supply of a public good. Samuelson (1954) argued that essentially there is no test of whether a particular level of provision is optimal: partly because of the basic definition of public goods preventing any of the usual principles of exclusion and competitiveness in consumption from being applied, and partly because there might be every incentive for individuals to misrepresent their own demands or evaluations of particular levels of supply.

On the basic question it was suggested by Tiebout (1956) that although pure public goods at a national level would pose the problem identified by Samuelson, the provision of such goods at a local level did not pose quite the same degree of difficulty: it was possible to conceive of the existence of a market in the goods if different local authorities provided differing levels of service at different rates of taxation. In such a situation, individuals could choose to vote with their feet and move towards preferred combinations of goods and tax rates and away from less preferred combinations. Although the Tiebout hypothesis is an attractive one, it would depend for its operation on the existence of some very restrictive assumptions: individuals would have to be perfectly free to move only in response to packages of public goods provision; they would need perfect knowledge of the range of services and tax rates available; the costs of provision of a unit of service would need to be the same in different areas, and so on. As we have already seen in the course of this chapter, the scope for local variation in provision is severely restricted. Nevertheless, there have been some attempts to verify whether a version of the Tiebout hypothesis does hold. Oates (1969) looked at educational expenditure, tax rates and property values in a selection of local areas in the United States. The hypothesis was that area preference would be reflected in property values and that if the package of public goods (in this case education as measured by expenditure) was a significant factor in area choice, then a positive relationship would be expected; at the same time, preferences for lower rates of taxation to finance any given level of expenditure would lead to a negative relationship between the local tax rate and property values. The Oates tests suggested that there was some evidence of a Tiebout effect, but we must be careful not to base too much on this evidence as it does depend on taking a rather restrictive set of assumptions about the determinants of property values and the measure of output is, as we have seen above, an unsatisfactory one (see, for example, Edel and Sclar 1974).

Other attempts have been made to assess whether it would be possible to use not revealed but stated preferences of individuals to determine optimal levels of provision. The usual objection to this is whether individuals tell the truth, especially in a situation where their ability to interpret the outcome of their statement may vary. Hence a person with a low tax liability may be happy to overstate his actual preferences for public services, whilst one with a high tax liability but no altruism would understate his to reduce his expected tax bill. This would particularly be the case in which it was thought that whatever response was given to the question the same right of access to the service would be accorded. This is the classic free-rider problem of the public good: where individuals do not have to pay for a service directly, they will consume it without paying, or consume at a higher level then they need.

One way round this problem in conceptual terms is to think of the provision of the public good being undertaken by a club (Buchanan 1965). Assume, for simplicity, that all individuals have the same preferences. As more and more people are allowed to become members of the club the average cost of provision falls and hence so does the marginal benefit from adding each new member to the club (marginal benefit is the reduced cost of the service). Each new member may impose a marginal cost on existing members. If this cost is zero, the club will expand infinitely so long as marginal benefit remains positive and there is a pure public good problem which remains unresolved since there is no competitiveness in the use of the service. However, for a wide range of goods of a public nature there is likely to be a range of output over which the marginal costs of additional consumption are perceived by consumers to be positive, and when these exceed the marginal benefit of increasing output the optimum size of the club is obtained. Later analysis (e.g. Pauly 1967, 1970) has again shown the limitations of such a method of preference revelation in large-scale situations or where preferences vary between individuals and questions of distribution become relevant. However, there may be scope for use of the club analysis for the determination of certain types of locally-provided public service. It has also been suggested (Evans 1972) that the club analysis can be extended to the determination of city size as a whole in the way that was demonstrated in Section 5.2 with variations in the benefits to existing and new residents.

Interest has recently been reawakened in the idea of the optimal production of local public goods as part of the determination of the optimal size of the city itself. Individuals' preferences for public goods form part of their decision whether or not to reside in a particular area. Both the public good and the private goods which are also demanded by residents require inputs of labour. The size of the city affects the level of demand for private goods and hence the viability of local industries. Through the process discussed in Chapter 3, these various demands for land within the city produce a rent gradient for the use of land at various points. This rent gradient expresses the premium over the opportunity cost of land in a non-urban use, payable at a specific location. The rent is, therefore, a pure economic rent to the land owner. It is not difficult to demonstrate that the total rent in the city will be just sufficient to pay for the provision of the public good. It represents the surplus out of production which can go into the provision of urban facilities (Stiglitz 1977; Arnott and Stiglitz 1979). This economic rent provides the tax base for the city.

A further issue is posed, however: can the city reach an optimal situation only if it contains individuals with identical preferences? Such a situation would imply that individuals would have an incentive to live exclusively in cities with others sharing similar preferences and to exclude non-conforming individuals, as in the club concept. It can be argued, however, that as long as the production function for at least the private goods requires labour of different types, the collective benefits from a diverse city outweigh the losses attributable to having to support what to the individual is a non-optimal level of public goods provision (Stiglitz 1983).

If the city is not an island, but instead is part of a unified economy, this also raises the problem of inter-governmental grants as compensation for any loss of welfare to local residents which arises either from an effective export of benefits to other areas inadequately compensated by the market (for example, where there is local pollution) or from an inability of individuals to adjust location quickly enough in response to changing economic conditions.

It can be seen, therefore, that we need to consider in more detail the way in which such preferences can be revealed and the balance between local and national preferences taken into account.

5.5 The Possibility of Urban Economic Policy

In this chapter we have presented some of the reasons why a simple positive application of economic policy may run into problems in an urban context. We must now reconcile the positive needs of securing efficient and balanced economic growth within both the nation and its individual urban areas with the need to secure an equitable distribution of the benefits of that growth and any costs associated with it over the population as a whole. This requires us to introduce two new dimensions to our theory: a theory of conflict resolution between interest groups and a theory of bureaucracy.

The essence of government from an economic standpoint is that it is necessary to resolve conflicts which the market cannot handle (or handles unsatisfactorily). To a large extent, however, this simply translates the direct economic conflict into a conflict between groups for votes or for power. As we have already suggested at various points, and as has been vividly expressed by Parry Lewis (1979), the conflicts in an urban area are not necessarily just between clearly identifiable groups of individuals because individuals play a number of roles: as consumer, producer, employee, etc. Even spatial loyalties are not clear-cut: an individual may live and work within a single town, but he depends on other areas of the country for much of his consumption and, typically, for his employment as well if the firm is based outside the area (or a large proportion of its share capital is controlled from outside). Conflicts thus occur within individuals as well as between individuals. If government is to exist, and especially if government is to exist at different levels to service different spatial needs—national, regional, local—then there is conflict, too, within the government organisation. If we add to this the interrelatedness of the various dimensions of government interference in general economic policy, in industrial policy, in policy towards land use and housing and transport and the environment etc., we clearly need to know something of the way in which organisations work and hence to understand bureaucracy. In the final analysis there is little point in identifying the need for a policy (which should be implemented by a given series of measures that would be likely to have certain predictable effects) if there is no organisation capable of introducing, administering and monitoring that policy.

Conflict Resolution and Democracy

The basic attempt to provide an economic theory of conflict resolution derives from a long-standing interest by economists in the aggregation of individual preferences into community preferences. A considerable literature about social or public choice has developed (Mueller 1979; Sugden 1981) which in general shows the difficulty of devising a system for the unambiguous revelation of a community's preferences. This tends to suggest that there is little scope for basing any form of economic policy on the objective assessments of the preferences of the individuals affected in accordance with an acceptable overall presumption of social wellbeing. If the policy maker is prepared to impose the distribution of social wellbeing on the community, then it will be possible to devise coherent policies which work towards this. If the policy maker has to seek acceptance of the distribution as well as of the policy itself there are more problems since the method of revealing the acceptance also becomes critical—i.e. the voting system must be both neutral and acceptable. The essential problem faced by a democracy is that it quickly becomes impossible for individuals to vote separately on all issues which affect them (and even if it were possible they would also need to vote to assess the relative importance of the issues to the extent that they would be likely to conflict, at least in the use of resources) and once the options available become more than binary most voting systems fail to give unambiguously transitive results.

Most theories of voting and economic behaviour tend to assume the simple case in which there is a clear relationship between the voter, the decision maker and the policy. A politician puts forward the combination of policies which he stands for and the individual chooses whether or not to support that package (Downs 1957). The individual loses welfare to the extent that the package does not reflect his own preference rankings for the decisions on each issue and for the weighting of one issue relative to another and his only choice is a blanket acceptance or rejection of the package. If there were enough candidates it would, in theory, be possible to find a candidate whose package satisfied the individual's own choice. The danger to the individual, as the number of candidates increases, is that he may be more likely to allow a definitely unpreferred candidate to get into office while choosing between the more preferred candidates in a first-past-the-post system. Other voting systems allow for the proliferation of subtle variations between candidates, but a first-past-the-post system tends to lead to the concentration of alternative packages into a small number of likely winners. The system itself thus forces the individual to compromise his preferences.

Consider now the situation in which there is not one authority but several tiers of authority, each of which provides certain clearly definable services. This may be a preferable situation to the extent that the individual can then vote on a narrower range of issues. If, for example, separate authorities controlled health, education, transport, housing etc. and each of these had elected members, the individual could vote for his personal preferences in each field, as well as for his overall national government choice which would enable him to vote for the allocation of resources between the separate sectors. If the sectoral authorities were also formed at a more local level, it would be possible to vote for a geographical as well as a sectoral split. However, note that in this situation the individual has to be able to assess the feasibility and consistency of his various preferences in order to be able to vote in such a way as to be satisfied by the final outcome. The apparent failure of politicians to carry out their 'promises' is often the inability of those voting for them to recognise the inconsistencies in their own preferences.

Here we have the classic dilemma of the local government authority which is elected to carry out certain sets of policies that are predominantly allocational in the various fields of land use, housing, transport, etc. These policies are, however, severely constrained in terms of the overall availability of resources from a separate level of government which has been elected to carry out an inherently different set of national policies concerning the level of economic activity, public sector spending, etc. What is missing is any opportunity for individuals to express their preferences about the spatial distribution of that national level of activity since the constraints on the local authorities tend to operate differentially in different areas—no one is typically asked to vote for a redistribution of resources away from the residents of large cities or towards the residents of certain other areas. As we shall see in more detail in Chapter 8, the key constraint on the local politician's ability to deliver the goods is not the local electoral reality of failing to keep promises or having to raise taxes or curtail expenditure by more than expected as a purely local decision, but coping with an externally imposed constraint on spending or tax rates (either by grant limitation or by failure to underwrite borrowing) so that the local authority effectively goes bankrupt.

So far we have considered the public sector simply as a tool of collective preference. There are problems in determining the means of revealing that preference and its consistency, but the individual is assumed to be voting for a particular package of taxes and expenditures which the politicians put together. The politician's behaviour is largely one of deciding on a package which is thought to be capable of winning the most votes (or the number of votes needed under a particular electoral system). Whilst the individual is attempting to maximise his own utility, so is the politician in terms of a utility function which includes his own probability of winning (Downs 1957). A government may, however, behave in a rather different way since it, too, is a coalition of interests: the leading politicians in a party need to be able to maintain the support of the other elected members as much as the elected members need to maintain the support of the electorate: but the government may also be able to appeal to the electorate over the head of the individual elected member. As Breton (1974) has suggested, governments can behave like monopolists: they can control the flow of output of certain key services and use their monopoly power to 'buy' the votes they need to carry through other measures, especially measures which may not have popular support. Hence a government which promises tax cuts convincingly enough may be able to acquire the votes of those less concerned about some of the expenditure implications of reducing government revenue.

Bureaucracy and Control

The mechanism of turning preferences for particular combinations of outputs into actual outputs raises the basic issue of the control of a bureaucratic organisation by its political masters, and ultimately by the electorate—the individual whose preferences are to be satisfied. Tullock (1965) and Downs (1967) tried to extend the basic model of democratic government to cover this issue which was more fully developed by Niskanen (1971) (and see Jackson 1982 for a more recent review).

There are two essential features to note: first, there is the nature of the output of most government agencies; secondly, there is the question of the decision model of the bureaucrat in implementing the policy of the politician. The rationale for most government interference is likely to be market failure, and in many cases that means the non-existence of a market because of the nature of the good in question. The basic features of public (or near-public) goods is that they do not possess the two key features of a private good: excludability and competitiveness. Typically, in purchasing a unit of output of a private good, an individual is competing with other potential users for a limited amount of supply and can be excluded from consuming by the operation of the market (usually by the price being raised to a level where he does not find it worthwhile to buy). To some degree these elements are missing from the public good case: use of a unit of road space does not use up that unit to prevent anyone else from consuming it (even if there is severe competition for road space under congested conditions). If a municipal sewage system operates, then, even if the individual who refuses to pay does not have his house connected to the system, it is typically not feasible to exclude that individual from the general community benefits of having a system to which most people belong.

If output is difficult to measure in this way—how much road space is used up, how much education is produced, how much social service is produced, what the units of all these are—then we have difficulties in relating the output measure to inputs and hence determining the productivity in the production of the goods. Typically with many of these types of goods the usual response is to relate output directly to the inputs used: education depends on the number of teachers and other resources put into it; the welfare of old people is determined by the staffing and resource inputs of old people's homes; the output of the transport system depends on the capacity of the system. It may be possible to determine a sort of intermediate output in many cases: educational output can be related to examination successes, social service outputs to the number of clients, transport output to the passenger or freight kilometres generated; but all these are unsatisfactory. Simply coping with more old people, or travelling more, does not mean that any more welfare is created or that people are exercising a true preference. In the case of transport it is easiest to demonstrate the absurdity of the situation: the closure of a direct link between two points five kilometres apart, between which 200 people travel every day, and its replacement by a more circuitous link requiring a journey of eight kilometres, will increase output of passenger–kilometres as long as at least 125 people still travel. It is difficult to argue that the output of welfare has unambiguously increased—although it may of course increase if any cost savings can be used to compensate the apparent losers. The real problem for bureaucracy is that, in the absence of direct measures of productivity, output is measured by inputs and hence any output-maximising criterion is achieved by maximising inputs—typically by maximising the budget of the providing agency.

The concept of the budget-maximising bureaucrat lies at the heart of Niskanen's theory of bureaucracy and is closely related to similar behavioural theories of the firm in a 'managerial capitalism' context. The essential assumption in such a model is that the individual bureaucrat is primarily motivated by his own personal utility which is related to such factors as job security, personal advancement and status. Status within an organisation is typically thought of as being reflected in the number of subordinates for whom the individual is responsible, or the size of the total budget administered. Promotion to higher office is often conditioned by accumulated experience in controlling other personnel and budgets and hence the system is self-perpetuating. Within a large organisation such as a local authority, therefore, an order of priority of departments becomes established according to their size. Large, and large-spending, departments such as housing and social services tend to take priority simply because the senior administrators in these departments are the most experienced (because of the progressions referred to above). The real problem with this is that it becomes exceedingly difficult for the organisation to respond to changing priorities across traditional departmental boundaries even though considerable sophistication is employed concerning the precise allocation of expenditures within departments. The general conclusion is that this process lies at the heart of the growth of public sector expenditure in recent years.

There is the further question of the way in which large organisations set performance targets at the operational end. A department of a local authority may have certain priorities established centrally, but it must translate these into instructions which can be followed by individual administrators: housing managers, transport managers, leisure centre managers, etc. Since there is a general presumption against market-pricing and profit-maximising behaviour an alternative target indicator has to be set. Typical social service indicators, which have on the whole been best analysed by economists, tend to get adopted for a wide range of activities in which it is essentially the level of service which is maximised subject to a budget constraint. Hence, leisure centre managers may attempt to maximise use of their facilities subject to some general directives about the distribution of users between certain target groups (the young, the unemployed, etc.). Transport managers may be asked to maximise the passenger miles carried subject either to an overall budget constraint or, since revenue is derived from such operations, subject to a constraint of subsidy per passenger mile implied. Similar examples can be found elsewhere. In other areas of activity, such as the public housing sector, all reference to the market may be omitted and allocation made on a purely administrative basis according to essentially social priorities—though the effect of this is typically to devise a surrogate market in terms of levels of deprivation, with points for unemployment, numbers of children, single parents, etc.

How would we expect the manager of a facility to respond in a situation where he is left free to provide a range of services subject to an overall constraint of the grant budget? This presents an interesting extension to the typical supplier's model of behaviour since the supplier in these conditions is interested both in the direct public demand for the service (from which part of his revenue derives) and also in the indirect demand for the service in general (which derives from the grant aid support given by the government authority as a result of it being one of the elements in the package of public provisions on which it is elected). If the manager ignores direct demand and relies entirely on his grant aiding in the current period, then he may suffer in the future since the authority may determine that the absence of direct demand either means that the facility is not worthwhile or that the manager is incompetent. On the other hand, too great a success in raising direct revenue may mean the removal of grant which could prove a serious future constraint on development of the facility. In many cases also it may be taken as a failure on the part of the manager to provide a genuine social element in the service since, if it can be made to pay, the rationale for government interference may also disappear. Examples of this could be a theatre manager failing to provide enough minority interest productions; a leisure centre manager making profits from high-income squash and badminton players to the exclusion of low-income group interests; or a transport manager who caters only for profitable peak traffic and removes evening and weekend light-traffic services. Thus, rather as in the shareholder control model of firm behaviour where an element of satisficing enters (achieving a level of operation which can be sustained but which falls short of the best possible short-run position), we can find a likely situation in which the manager's main concern is his future level of grant aid (see Austen-Smith 1982 for a complete model of such behaviour).

Intergovernmental Relations

In this section we have tried to provide a sketchy outline of a very large literature concerning the ways in which government may work, at both a political and an administrative or bureaucratic level, as a means of explaining, in Mueller's (1979) words, the 'slippage between the lips of the voter and the flow of outputs from the government's cup'. It is also not just a question of the potential distortions between collective preference and actual provision in an allocational sense: we have noted again the fact that government activity may tend to grow in size through time for cumulative reasons. This adds to the rather more abstract notion of the effect of intergovernmental activity in a dynamic model noted in Chapter 4 which suggested that grant aid to compensate for so-called 'balance of payments' deficiencies on the part of a local economy would also be cumulative. Against this background it can be seen that the real title of this section should perhaps have been 'the impossibility of a coherent urban economic policy'. We have noted that there are potential conflicts between organisations and within organisations and extreme difficulties in passing coherent targets down from one organisational level to another, both between and within levels of government. The themes sketched here will recur throughout this second part of the book, especially within sections on pricing and investment and on the public finance aspects of intergovernmental relationships. This indeed seems to lie at the heart of the whole future of assigning local economic policy or public control of facilities to a local level of political organisation where the scope of such activity might be too large for a central government to be able to ignore it if it wished.

Further Reading

The people-versus-place issue is usefully discussed by Whitman (1972). Richardson (1973b) gives a compendious account of the work on city size; and see the valuable papers in Cameron and Wingo (1973). More recently, attention has swung towards city growth problems and urbanisation in the context of less developed countries: see Richardson (1981) and Renaud (1981).

A guide to the wider issues of environmental economics is Pearce (1976). The specific problem of congestion derives from a classic paper by Walters (1961), but see also Beesley and Walters (1970) and Gwilliam and Nash (1972).

A basic introduction to theories of public choice is given by Sugden (1981); Mueller (1979) provides a much more comprehensive review.

Theories of bureaucracy are well developed by Niskanen (1971) and Jackson (1982). For specific discussions of British local government in a political context see McKay and Cox (1979), Dunleavy (1980) and Saunders (1979), and the chapter by Stewart in Cameron (1980a). For a factual account of the growth and development of local government finances in Britain, see Foster *et al.* (1980).

The Tiebout model (Tiebout 1956) is central to much of the discussion on local public provision. There have been many theoretical reassessments and attempts at empirical tests, but see particularly Oates (1969), Buchanan and Goetz (1972), Edel and Sclar (1974), Stiglitz (1977, 1983), Arnott and Stiglitz (1979) and, for an admirable review, Pestieau (1983).

6
Pricing and Investment in Urban Infrastructure

6.1 Urban Infrastructure: An Introduction

We have recognised the importance of infrastructure to the urban economy at a number of points. It is a critical input to the urban agglomeration economies which provide the rationale for the city's existence. Large parts of infrastructure take up valuable land which cannot be used for productive purposes and the quality and efficiency of the infrastructure will affect both willingness to live in the city and the costs of living there. For these reasons, it is in the provision of infrastructure that the public sector has principally exercised its ability to interfere in the working of the local economy. Such interference comes both through controls over the price mechanism (because of some notion of market failure to produce the right price) and through the provision of subsidy to ensure that the supply price of urban infrastructure is kept lower, and the volume of supply higher, than would otherwise be the case. The two principal concerns of this chapter will be the determination of a correct price and the assessment of the right level of public subsidy.

We shall concentrate on two aspects of the urban infrastructure: transport and housing. As we have seen in our more abstract models of the city economy, these are likely to be the key elements. However, there exists a wide range of public utilities (water, gas, electricity, sewage disposal), cultural and leisure and educational facilities (libraries, schools, colleges, etc.) health care and personal social services, all of which together make up the infrastructure of the city in which individuals live and work. They form part of any study of the public sector (not just at a local level) but whilst they do have important spatial elements, they play a rather less important role in the model of the local economy developed here than do transport and housing which enter into all of the basic decisions about location of both individuals and firms.

We shall look at the specific policy problems posed by each of these sectors in turn in later sections of this chapter. First, though, in Section 6.2, we shall establish some general principles to guide the later discussion—principles which aim to relate solutions for any individual sector to the urban economy as a whole. Let us begin by making general observations about supply and demand conditions in urban infrastructure sectors which serve to highlight the important similarities that exist between all of these.

A key feature is the incompatibility between the units and the nature of the demand for, and supply of, infrastructure. Supply decisions generally relate to the provision of a *stock* of physical infrastructure: houses, road space, rail capacity, etc. There is a concern, therefore, with the long-run decision about optimal levels of investment and their finance; and in the short run, with decisions about the allocation of available capacity which it is difficult to change rapidly. Demand decisions typically relate to a *flow* of housing or transport *services* provided by the given stock of infrastructure, purchased out of current income. Furthermore, these demands are typically derived demands in that people seldom want transport for its own sake, but rather for getting them from one place to another in accordance with a set of primary demands which have a spatial dimension. The same is true to some extent of housing services in that the basic requirement for housing is the provision of space in which a number of activities can take place—such as eating, sleeping, etc.—which involve the maintenance of human capital. This basic distinction is then confused by the possibility of individual consumers owning elements of the infrastructure which are used to supply these services.

On the supply side there is also a further problem, especially pronounced in the case of transport, that the actual supply of the service involves a further type of capital, the vehicle, running on the basic infrastructure. This provides additional flexibility in the capacity of the infrastructure. It is in this area that the confusion in ownership can become most pronounced, with the transport service being provided both by commercial transport operators and by owner-drivers who compete for use of the available infrastructure. Adequate planning and pricing thus has to take into account both the infrastructure capacity and the provision of transport service capacity, and the market conditions applying in both output and input markets. In housing markets there is a related problem in that individuals may either own the house in which they live, or may rent it from either a public or a private landlord. The added complication here (which, as we shall see, affects the degree of subsidy to some extent) is that the owner may either be the outright owner of the equity in the asset or, by having a mortgage, may only be the owner of some part of the equity. This then adds the fact that, where ownership of an asset is involved, the demand for the product can no longer simply be related to current activities and income, but requires consideration of longer-run aspects of both consumption patterns and wealth.

The significance of the contrast between the owner-provider of a service and the use of a market-provided service is that in both these sectors market provision is likely to imply some form of aggregation of demands to make supply an economic proposition. For the owner-provider the compromises which this implies are likely to be on a much smaller scale. Supply will be tailored much more closely to the precise demand for either movement or housing. The public transport user is constrained to board and alight at recognised points which present compromises, is constrained to travel at specific times which are also compromises, and may also have to compromise on the choice of destination. The private transport user can gain access to and egress from a network with greater ease, travel at the most suitable time, and to the best possible destination. In the housing market, the renter is again constrained in terms of the types and range of housing services on offer, since the landlord must compromise in terms of the precise way in which housing attributes are bundled together in order to gain access to as wide a market as possible. The owner-occupier may also be dictated to by house builders and developers as to the types of houses available in specific locations, but will generally have greater freedom both in choosing a precise location and in modifying the basic house to suit his own particular demands for housing services.

A final general point which needs to be borne in mind throughout our discussion of infrastructure is that demands for any element in the urban infrastructure are not independent of other elements. We know, from the model developed previously, that transport and housing interact with one another, and with all the other urban infrastructural services, in the utility functions of individuals. Hence, any consideration of the pricing mechanism for one of them needs to take into account the effect on any other so that they are not contradictory. There is little point, for example, in providing cheap subsidised housing in a peripheral location if it is also decided to charge a full economic cost for transport to and from that location. Similarly, schemes to charge low fares for public transport imply that there is a market which is price-sensitive. With this in mind, we now turn to examine the general economic issues involved in pricing and investment decisions in urban infrastructure.

6.2 Optimal Pricing and the Optimal City

We have identified the essential problem as one of determining both an appropriate price and an appropriate level of subsidy for urban infrastructure—in the longer term this also implies determining an optimal level of capacity and hence investment. We shall take up the specific factors affecting the two main sectors with which we are concerned in the following two sections, but we can make certain broad assumptions about the general nature of demand and supply conditions for transport and housing here to establish the broad analytical framework. The overall income and price elasticities of demand for the use of infrastructure in general are fairly low, but the own-price and cross-price elasticities for the outputs of individual suppliers may be more substantial. This reflects the fact that there is, typically, a multi-level demand decision to be made concerning both the quantitative and qualitative (mode of transport, tenure of housing) dimensions. On the supply side, response is likely to be relatively slow and lumpy, especially where a change in capacity is required. Also, whereas the demand side is characterised by large numbers of relatively small users, the supply side consists of two parts: the supply of infrastructure which is largely in the hands of monopoly suppliers (although there may be some oligopolistic competition between, for example, rail and road) and the supply of individual services where there is much more competition (although there may also be evidence of regulation in some markets).

The determination of optimal pricing policy in the context of the urban economy as a whole does not just involve the equation of demand and supply, however. We also need to introduce the objective function, which will typically involve considerations beyond the clearing of individual markets. There are two basic considerations which enter into these calculations. One is the merit good aspect of the good: it is considered socially desirable that consumption levels should be higher than those which would obtain if there were no interference. The other is the externality effect (especially on the economic performance of the city economy itself) which arises through subsidising transport and housing. Lower living costs within the city should be reflected in lower labour costs related to both lower money wages than would otherwise obtain and higher productivity through better quality of life. This involves a transfer between the community and the individual of some of the costs of urban living in return for the creation of greater economic welfare. In effect, the determination of optimal pricing for an urban infrastructure sector involves the assessment of both social benefits and full social costs. The optimal price for transport services is that which ensures the correct level of usage of the right amount of infrastructure for a city which is of the right size. Rightness in size is, as we have already seen, a rather elusive concept but will be related to a maximisation of the net social benefit of residents. If the average price of transport is too high, the city will fail to grow sufficiently to take advantage of all the benefits of greater size. If, however, too great a level of transport subsidy is given, and the price is allowed to fall too low, the city may become over-large and the subsidy burden may impose too great a cost on the residents. The same factors also apply to housing and to any of the other urban services mentioned. The overall solution must involve some compromise since, as we saw in Chapter 5, the optimal size of the city may vary considerably with respect to each of the elements of the urban infrastructure—hence the need to solve them simultaneously and not independently. The value in terms of net social benefit would need to be the same per pound of subsidy in each sector. This concept could also be used in an interurban context to assess which subsidy distribution between cities was the most effective.

This basic notion of value for money in determining the total size of a particular sector goes hand in hand with a view on the optimal distribution of the burden of paying for that capacity between users and city residents in general (through taxation) and between residents of the city and non-residents, who pay for part of the provision through any equalising grants. These latter groups can also be assumed to gain benefits through the various spillovers which the city economy confers on the national economy as a whole.

In practice, it may be that rather simpler rules of thumb are adopted which tend not to produce such balanced results. In transport, it is often simpler to adopt an objective of maximising traffic flows or passenger-miles carried subject to some overall external financing constraint. In housing, certain norms or standards may be adopted relating housing entitlement to individuals' abilities to score points against certain characteristics—typically, indices of deprivation. The adoption of such rules may lead to a tendency to encourage openendedness in the provision of subsidy, since greater subsidy confers greater benefit in terms of the crude indicator of benefit adopted. The danger is that increasing subsidy is also associated with increasing real costs of provision of the service, so that the basic rule of maximising benefit relative to the subsidy is lost. In many areas the response to this has been to place the blame on the subsidy itself and attempt to remove the subsidy altogether. We shall need to be very careful in the assessment presented here to preserve the various dimensions of the original balance in order to produce answers which relate to genuine optimal levels of subsidy in the context of the city as a whole.

Pricing Rules

Let us now consider a rather more precise model of the pricing problem. The conventional approach is to argue that the efficiency rules of allocation require that prices equal marginal cost, so that the individual consumer's willingness to pay at the margin equals the market valuation of the resources used up in production. In a situation where we can, for the moment, assume that marginal costs are constant, social considerations will lead to a higher output of the service (at a lower price and with at best only a break-even situation) than any policy aimed at creating some profit for the enterprise. This basic result is shown in Figure 6.1 and can be seen

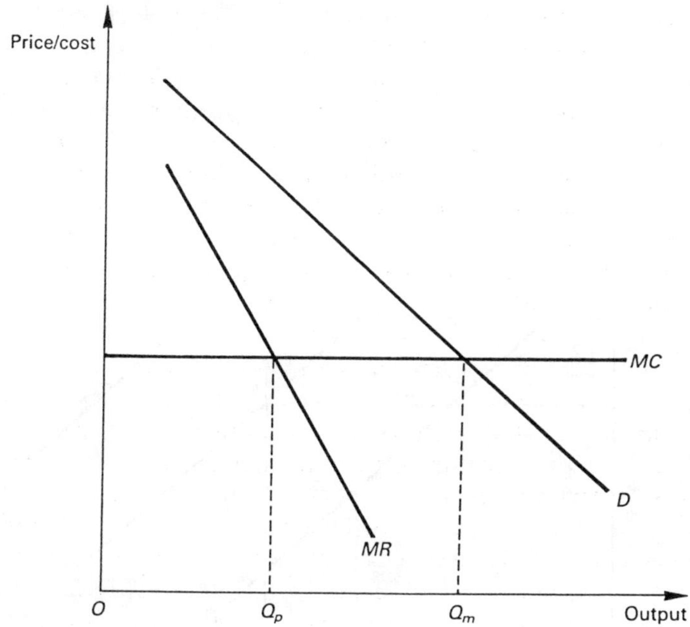

Figure 6.1

to derive from the concern of a marginal cost price with the actual demand curve, whereas a profit-motivated supplier will be more interested in the marginal revenue. It is therefore essential that this demand curve accurately reflects any social valuations of the output of the form discussed above.

This is a purely short-run situation, however: even with constant short-run marginal costs, it is unlikely that long-run marginal costs will be equal to the former since extra capacity means more capital expenditure. Thus the situation in Figure 6.2 has to be considered which suggests that the relevant consideration will be to decide whether demand is at D_1D_1' or at D_2D_2'. At the former level of demand, capacity is sufficient and short-run marginal cost pricing is adequate simply to ensure the optimal allocation of that capacity. At a level of demand given by D_2D_2' a higher price is necessary to allocate the effective congestion arising in the use of capacity. Note, however, that unless demand were to rise to a higher level, say D_3D_3', there might not be a case for expanding capacity, since at a price of OP_2 it is not possible to cover the long-run marginal costs

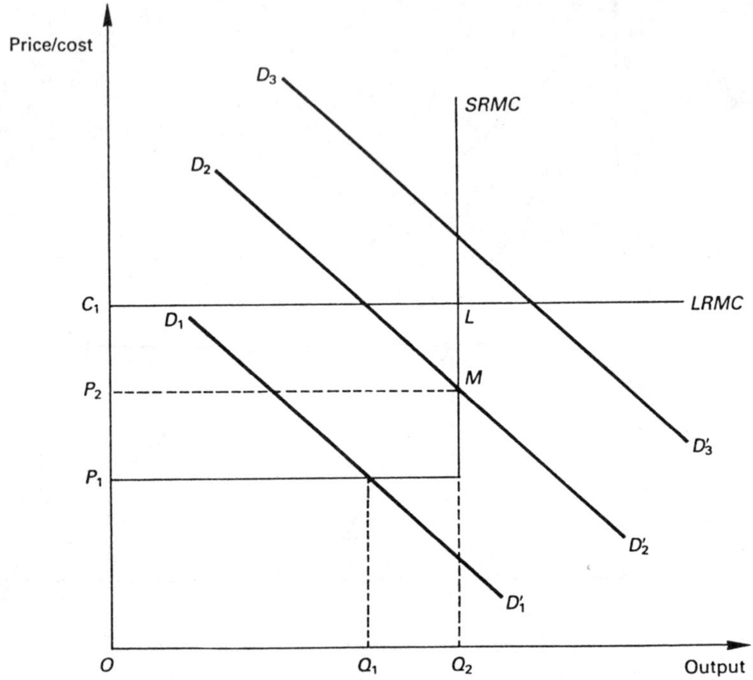

Figure 6.2

of OC_1. Decisions about appropriate levels of capacity will then depend on whether the gain from additional consumers' surplus generated from the new capacity outweighs the additional resource outlay.

The analysis of Figure 6.2 gives us some basic rules for deciding on optimal outputs and prices for particular urban services, and we can assess from this the financial implications for the provider. At a level of demand of $D_2D'_2$ the service will lose an amount equivalent to C_1LMP_2 and this will need to be made up in some other way. Suppose that this is a bus service and that there is an alternative means of travelling between the two points for which the demand curve shown in Figure 6.2 represents demand. Let us represent the total traffic available by OT in Figure 6.3 and the marginal private costs of travel by the alternative mode of transport by SS'. Now the issue becomes one of the prices charged on both modes of transport. Of course, prices as such may not be charged if

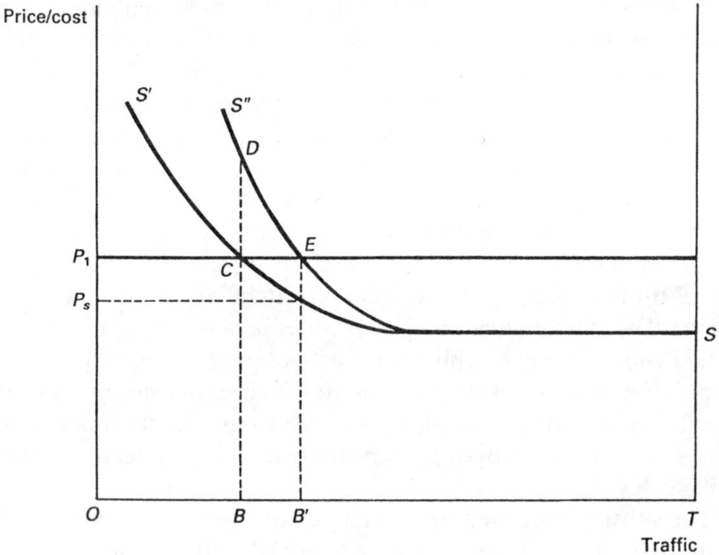

Figure 6.3

the alternative is the private car where SS' is the perceived private cost of travel, the rising part of the curve reflecting increasing congestion (Walters 1961). We assume that the traveller always uses the mode with the cheapest private cost to himself and that the public transport operator always charges a fare based on short-run marginal costs including any congestion surcharge. Under these circumstances, the distribution of traffic between the two modes is that OB goes by bus and BT uses the car. This leads to a welfare loss of CDE due to the unaccounted for social costs of car traffic, given by SS''. In such a case, we can either tax the car users to equalise the social costs of resources used up, or we can achieve the same distribution of traffic by lowering the price of bus travel through an effective subsidy of P_1P_s on each traveller.

This solves the transport sector's problem of internal allocation, but what about other considerations? These are not so easy to demonstrate by means of a simple diagram because we cannot continue to assume a given volume of identical traffic on a single route. Suppose the logic of the result of Figure 6.3 is adopted city-wide: there is considerable road traffic congestion and hence a policy of subsidy to each public transport passenger is adopted.

Some travellers are induced by such a policy to switch modes and a social benefit accrues because of this. What of the travellers who do not switch? The existing bus travellers receive a subsidy bonus; the remaining car travellers benefit from a reduction in costs and may still not be paying the full social costs of their travelling. The switchers may be a particular group of people who are able to switch because of their location relative to the transport network. Remaining car users may be prepared to change modes but unable to find a suitable bus service. In these cases, there is a spatial distribution of the benefits which may affect land values and house prices. The changes in house prices occasion a windfall gain (or loss) to existing residents, whilst altering potential rates of growth of population in different areas of the city. These considerations would also be important in a similar approach to the question of housing prices and allocation between tenures with differing decisions about subsidy levels.

The subsidy proposed in the analysis of Figure 6.3 is open-ended and implies that there is no effect on social welfare from the means of collecting the tax revenue used to provide the subsidy. A more typical situation is one where there is a strict limit to the total level of subsidy available and the transport or housing authority has to decide how best to allocate this. In such circumstances it is optimal to deviate from a strict adherence to marginal cost pricing. Following the analysis of Baumol and Bradford (1970), it can be shown that the correct proportionate deviation from marginal cost in each market is given by the inverse of the own price elasticity of demand. Hence it is optimal to load any excess charge more heavily on the market with the least price-elastic demand; for instance, charges for public transport at peak times should be raised more than those at off-peak times.

This solution assumes that cross-price elasticities between either time periods or modes of transport are very low. Let us use the example of Figure 6.3 again, but now relax the assumption that total traffic is fixed. In our initial analysis, the implicit mechanism at work was that the allocation of traffic varied according to the relative cost elasticities of the two modes. Now we need to consider the case where it is desired to secure an optimal allocation of traffic but where the price of one of the modes, car travel, cannot be controlled. A similar situation would also occur for a housing authority unable to control the price of owner-occupied houses. In such circumstances it will again be optimal to deviate from marginal cost pricing for the service for which price can be fixed. The optimal discount on marginal social costs of the publicly provided service depends on the excess of marginal social costs of the private service over private costs (i.e. the uncharged social premium), the relative levels of demand for the private and public services respectively, and the relative sizes of the cross elasticities of private sector demand with respect to public sector prices and public sector demand with respect to private sector costs (see, for example, Glaister 1974; Glaister and Lewis 1978).

Thus we can see a conflict between the prices *desirable* for optimal allocation of resources and the prices *necessary* to meet the financial constraint on the public sector's operations. This makes it desirable to consider another point: the value of the subsidy itself in terms of changes in social surplus generated by a change in the level of subsidy at the margin, assuming that prices are fixed as optimally as possible within the public sector's operations. The change in surplus consequent on the change in subsidy level comes about from the switching between private and public sectors and the possible change in operating costs in the latter. We shall look at this issue again in the context of the specific problems of the two sectors.

6.3 Transport Problems and Policies

Demand and Supply of Transport

Demand for transport services consists of the simultaneous recognition of preferences for both a quantitative and a more discrete qualitative dimension. The quantity is quite easy to deal with. An individual wishes to travel from one place to another: this involves a certain number of potential passenger-kilometres. A firm wishes to transfer goods: this involves a quantity of ton-kilometres. The qualitative dimensions tell us about the manner in which that quantity is purchased. For the transport journey there are decisions about timing, about route and, most importantly, about the mode of transport to be used. Both these types of decision—quantity and quality—will be determined by a similar range of factors of which household income and the relative prices of the alternatives will be the main features.

The traditional way of handling these decisions is through a sequential procedure. The individual is assumed to decide, first, to make a journey for a given purpose; then, where and when to go; and finally, how to go in terms of mode and route. The problem with assuming such a strict sequence is that although it simplifies the structure of the decision (often into a series of choices which can be relatively easily handled in empirical studies), it typically does not allow for feedback between the later stages of the decision and the earlier. Hence, the characteristics of individual transport modes cannot affect the decision about whether to make the journey at all or where to go. Since such a situation is obviously not realistic, attempts have been made with more sophisticated models of choice (Domencich and McFadden 1975; Hensher and Dalvi 1978) to include either recursive or fully simultaneous decisions. Hence the range, variety and characteristics of transport modes available at a particular location, together with the individual's preferences for one mode rather than another (which can be used to weight each of these), are all part of the 'price' of access to particular destinations. The prices of these various destinations may affect the decision of how much travel to undertake (Vickerman 1980, Chapter 3).

For the individual traveller we can write down demand in a probabilistic way where the probability that a given alternative is selected depends on the characteristics of both the individual and the alternative. Many of the characteristics of the alternative will typically be generic to all feasible alternatives (meaning that the choice of one alternative does not affect the value of those characteristics). For example, for journeys to city centres, most modes of transport provide a service which only differs in terms of speed, comfort, cost and ease of access. Many other dimensions of the choice are constant across all modes. For peripheral journeys, however, this is less true and destination and mode choice become more closely related. Hence the characteristics of destinations and preferences may play a role in the selection of the mode of transport used; this characteristic is no longer generic.

So far we have only considered individual demands in a probabilistic way. What we actually observe is their aggregation into a flow of traffic. Let us now turn to look at this in more detail. Four aspects are particularly relevant: the purpose for which a journey is made; the mode of transport used; total and average

Table 6.1 Trends in the Purposes for which Journeys are Made (%)

	1972/73	*1975/76*	*1978/79*
To/from work	22.0	22.1	18.8
In course of work	3.2	3.5	4.1
Education	10.3	9.9	9.5
Shopping	20.7	19.1	21.8
Personal business	7.7	9.3	10.6
Eating and drinking	3.7	3.1	2.5
Escorting and others	5.7	5.4	4.7
Sport	1.7	2.2	2.4
Entertainment	4.5	3.5	2.6
Social	14.3	15.4	18.0
Holidays, pleasure	6.2	6.5	5.1
Total	100.0	100.0	100.0

Source: Department of Transport (1983) *National Travel Survey, 1978/79.*

distances travelled; and the timing of travel in the day. They are summarised in Tables 6.1 to 6.4. These tables convey that over time the journey to work has become less important as a proportion of total daily travel (which has itself been generally increasing) and, although the use of public transport has generally declined, it has maintained a better share of journeys to work, especially in the larger urban areas. Total distances travelled and average length of journeys have also increased, reflecting the decentralisation process in many cities. It is clear that this is also related both to the change in the mode of transport used and in changing socio-economic factors which in turn have affected levels of car ownership. Finally, it is clear that despite attempts to spread working hours, traffic in urban areas is still heavily peaked in morning and evening rush-hour periods.

The switch from public to private transport, despite changes in patterns of journey purpose, journey lengths and journey timing, is the source of many of the most serious problems which we shall need to consider further. A given volume of people wishing to travel

Table 6.2 Trends in the Mode of Transport Used for Journeys (%)

	1965	*1972/73*	*1975/76*	*1978/79*
British Rail	2.3	1.8	1.7	1.6
London Transport				
Underground	1.5	1.1	0.8	1.0
Total rail	3.8	2.9	2.5	2.5
Local bus	30.9	20.7	16.5	16.9
Long distance bus	0.5	0.5	0.5	0.6
Works or school bus	1.5	1.5	1.7	1.2
Other public transport	0.8	0.7	0.6	0.8
Total public transport	37.5	26.3	21.9	22.1
Car, van, lorry	40.1	57.3	59.4	58.7
Motor cycle	2.6	1.3	1.2	1.4
Bicycle	7.6	3.8	4.3	3.6
Walking (over 1 mile)	12.1	11.1	13.0	13.7
Other private transport	0.2	0.2	0.2	0.5
Total private transport	62.5	73.7	78.1	77.9
Total	100.0	100.0	100.0	100.0

Source: Department of Transport (1983) *National Travel Survey 1978/79*.

by private transport requires more road space than the equivalent flow catered for by public transport. Hence there is a demand for expanding transport infrastructural capacity, and also a need to cope with congestion problems. The critical parameters are therefore the relevant price and income elasticities (including cross elasticities) of demand for each of the various modes, for which we shall provide some evidence later.

We need to look first at the question of supply. We have already noted the distinction between the supply of infrastructure and the supply of transport services. A critical feature of all transport infrastructure is that it is costly but involves considerable economies

Table 6.3 Trends in the Length of Journeys to Work (%)

	1975/76	*1978/79*
Distances		
Under 1 mile	17	14
1 and less than 2 miles	19	17
2 and less than 3 miles	13	14
3 and less than 5 miles	18	20
5 and less than 10 miles	19	21
10 and less than 15 miles	7	7
15 miles and over	7	7
Total	100	100
Average length of journey (miles)	4.9	5.2
Average weekly mileage (miles)	44.5	43.5
Travel times		
Under 15 mins	37	28
15 and less than 30 mins	37	33
30 and less than 45 mins	16	16
45 and less than 60 mins	5	6
60 and less than 90 mins	4	4
90 mins and over	1	1
Total	100	100
Average duration of journey (minutes)	21	22
Average weekly time travelling (minutes)	202	190

Source: Department of Transport (1979, 1983) *National Travel Surveys 1975/76 and 1978/79.*

of scale. A four-track railway has capital costs per track-kilometre roughly one-third less than those of a two-track railway (Foster and Joy 1967; Thomson 1974). Savings of nearly thirty per cent are possible per lane-kilometre in building a twin four-lane road as opposed to a twin two-lane road (Thomson 1974). The implication of this is that the cheapest way to provide a given infrastructure in a

Table 6.4 Distribution of Journeys by Journey Start Time (%)

	All journeys		*Bus journeys*	
	1975/76	*1978/79*	*1975/76*	*1978/79*
0000–0559	0.9	1.0	0.7	0.5
0600–0659	1.0	1.0	2.1	1.9
0700–0759	3.8	4.5	7.0	6.8
0800–0859	8.7	9.6	11.3	12.8
0900–0959	5.5	5.3	4.4	5.3
1000–1059	6.7	6.4	6.4	6.0
1100–1159	7.0	6.4	6.1	5.8
1200–1259	8.0	7.9	6.3	6.4
1300–1359	6.9	6.6	6.3	6.3
1400–1459	6.4	6.2	6.1	6.0
1500–1559	9.5	8.8	9.8	9.2
1600–1659	8.7	9.0	10.8	11.8
1700–1759	7.2	7.5	7.9	8.1
1800–1859	4.8	4.8	4.0	3.7
1900–1959	4.7	4.5	3.1	3.0
2000–2059	3.4	3.3	2.0	1.8
2100–2159	2.7	2.8	1.7	1.9
2200–2359	4.1	4.3	2.7	2.6

Source: Department of Transport (1979, 1983) *National Travel Surveys 1975/76 and 1978/79*.

city is to ensure that a small number of large-capacity links are built, rather than spreading capacity around the city. Such a policy has important implications for the shape and size of the city. If we also introduce the comparison between different modes of transport, it is clear that given infrastructure costs can produce very different capacities for moving people: rail is generally superior for moving large numbers of people over links with few access points; roads are better for diversified traffic flows.

Turning to vehicle-related costs, there are a number of elements involved: capital costs of the vehicle, running costs and administrative costs. Of course, it is also true that railways typically have to cost and provide their own means of controlling traffic on the infrastructure—signalling, for example, which is typically included in capital costs—whereas this is not provided by the operator for road transport, although a tax is usually paid for the use of the infrastructure. This tax is, however, usually assessed on a licence fee basis, so that the payment is related to vehicle size and assumed costs imposed on the infrastructure through deterioration and other factors like accident costs, but not to the actual level of road usage made (see Department of the Environment 1976 and Department of Transport 1979 for further discussion of this point).

To the operator, however, there are some clear scale economies in vehicle size in both passenger and freight transport up to a certain size. These derive both from the capital costs of the vehicle and from haulage costs so that the cost per unit capacity falls. Since labour costs are predominant in all forms of transport, accounting for over 40 per cent of road hauliers' costs and up to 70 per cent or more of bus operators' costs, these too can be shared between capacity units better in larger vehicles. There are fuel economies as well from larger vehicles. However, that a larger vehicle is cheaper to run per unit of capacity provided does not mean that it is necessarily the most economic proposition since the operator has to balance the likelihood of filling that capacity and the resultant 'load factor' at different times. Simply costing capacity units may not be a sufficient means of costing the provision of a service, although it does suggest again that there is a strong incentive to concentrate traffic as much as possible.

There do not appear to be significant scale economies in the size of fleet operated. A number of studies of both freight and passenger fleets (e.g. Edwards and Bayliss 1971; Lee and Steedman 1970; Wabe and Coles 1975; Walters 1982) have suggested no economies of scale, and either constant or even slightly decreasing returns—results which are confirmed by studies in other countries. Consequently, there seems to be no particular advantage in having services controlled by large monopolistic operators. Whilst conditions differ so much between cities, and particularly between cities of different size (concerning factors outside an operator's control, such as traffic congestion), it does seem that small operators in small cities generally have higher productivity in needing fewer staff and getting a higher mileage out of their vehicles (see Monopolies and Mergers Commission 1982 for some recent evidence).

Actual costs of individual services provided do, of course, involve rather more complex calculations relating not just to capital and other fixed charges against direct running costs, but also to the attribution of fixed costs to peak and non-peak operations (Nash 1982, Chapter 3). The broad conclusion we can draw, however, is that there will be a strong incentive to concentrate the service provided as much as possible into high density traffic corridors. Allowing for lumpiness in the provision of additional capacity, and for the discrepancies between peak and off-peak costs, it seems likely that marginal costs of transport operation will not be very different from constant, and possibly not very different between cities. The level of average costs may also not differ systematically with city size since larger cities can accommodate transport systems with higher initial capital costs but with greater scale economies.

Service Quality in Transport

We have concentrated thus far on the quantitative aspects of demand and supply. We must now turn to the important question of the quality of service required and provided in terms of speed, frequency, comfort, and so forth. Much of this quality aspect of transport can be assessed through the use of time as an additional dimension by which services are priced. This has the advantage that it is convertible into money terms for the evaluation of social surplus by the use of appropriate time values. Here we would need to assess not just the time spent in travelling in a vehicle (which reflects speed and hence congestion levels), but also the 'excess' times of waiting and of gaining access to a vehicle (e.g. walking to a bus stop or a car park) which reflect the density of service on a route and the density of routes and stops in an area.

An operator is thus faced with an almost bewildering array of possible policy variables which he can control: he can alter fare levels, he can alter the peak versus the off-peak differential, or he can alter any of a series of service levels. Each of these constitutes some weighted element of the generalised cost of travel by that mode, and has its own associated elasticities of demand of both 'own price' and 'cross price' types. Each also has a cost of implementation and hence a price in terms of additional resources or requirements for subsidy.

Whilst it is possible to calculate and evaluate these various elasticities and costs, they are rather unwieldy instruments for the planning of individual transport services, especially as they tend to be estimated from city-wide evidence rather than from the specific situation of individual routes. What is needed is a rule of thumb which reflects the concerns of the theoretical measures whilst being much simpler to understand and operate at the managerial level. For example, London Transport has for some years used the notion of maximising passenger miles carried subject to the constraint of the overall level of subsidy available. Here passenger miles serves as a proxy for social benefit (Glaister and Collings 1978; Nash 1978). The authority sets a passmark for the number of passenger miles per £ of subsidy required to justify a service being run. The passmark is determined rather like the notion of the value of the subsidy in terms of marginal social surplus (met above) but with a different maximand, on the basis of the optimum fares and service levels for existing services. It can thus be used at a relatively junior managerial level, since all that is required is the expected marginal revenue and marginal cost of any proposed change in the system: the net cost at the margin should be equal to the inverse of the passmark. It should be stressed that the results are not the same as for a social surplus maximisation, but they do show that quite sophisticated concepts can be turned into relatively easily applied rules of thumb. Glaister and Collings (1978) have shown how weighting systems can be used to create an equivalence. These weights approximate to the adjustments necessary in the social surplus maximisation to allow for different own price elasticities on different routes (or between peak and off-peak) and for cross-price effects between modes arising through congestion.

Urban Public Transport Policies

The policy role of governments at all levels in the transport sector has largely been determined by the existence of externalities and the need to control any monopolistic power conveyed by these (Mohring 1972). The analysis of these has, however, been set against an essentially static background. The pressing problems of transport which have most typically triggered policy action have developed rather more as a response to the dynamics of city growth and decline, or technical change in the transport sector itself.

During the 1960s and 1970s, despite the decline in the rate of growth of many cities (becoming negative in some), mobility was still increasing. This was associated with the rising real incomes of city dwellers and the growth of car ownership, coupled with declining real prices of fuel. The problem emerged, therefore, as one of inadequate road space as a large switch from public to private transport took place (see Table 6.2). Since the early 1970s, the decline in the economic fortunes of many cities has, as we have seen, accelerated, and this has shifted the major emphasis of the problem from being a purely allocational one to being one aspect of the financial problems besetting local government. This financial problem arises because of the increasing need to provide revenue support to urban public passenger transport now faced not only with a continuing shift of demand to private transport, but also with a reduction in the total demand for transport because of the economic decline.

The emphasis in transport planning has accordingly changed from one of highway planning based on detailed analysis of traffic modelling to a much broader concept of total transport planning. The need is now to ensure a more balanced provision of transport infrastructure to meet current and future needs, although little real attention has yet been given to the role which such planning plays in the overall economic planning of urban areas. As we have seen, the variables which are available for policy formulation are the prices charged, the allocation of investment to infrastructure, and decisions about the total size of any subsidy available to transport (whether a financial subsidy to public transport or an implicit subsidy to private transport). However, these are not independent factors, although, since they carry varying political weights, the temptation has often been to treat them as such. Furthermore, design of an optimal policy on the basis of a theoretically optimal allocation of resources may also pose problems for day-to-day decisions about levels of service.

There have clearly been problems which have arisen from the diversity of responsibility for different modes of transport: not only different responsible authorities, but different levels of responsibility and freedom of action. Road and rail have typically been conceived in national terms, with central government having both strategic and financial control (indirectly in the case of rail). At the local level, local authorities have powers over secondary roads, but only agency roles over primary routes so that, whilst they can prepare cases for road investment, the final decision on priorities is taken centrally. Local authorities do have some degree of control over public road passenger transport. This, too, varies: at one extreme, Metropolitan Counties have until recently been able to exercise complete control over service and fare levels as both operator and strategic planning authority (including powers to control and provide revenue support to other operators including British Rail). At the other extreme, some local authorities can only exercise control through their ability to offer subsidies to National Bus Company or independent bus operators to maintain unprofitable services on the basis of social need. This latter provision has largely been made for rural needs and so is of little relevance here.

We cannot hope to review all these dimensions fully, but the case of the Metropolitan Counties and of London is the most interesting because it helps to illustrate both the divergences which have occurred at the local level in the philosophy of public transport support, and the friction which has developed between national and local views of what constitutes an appropriate level of support.

As we have seen, the size of operations is not a source of great economies. There is some mild evidence of diseconomies in large transport undertakings, but these are essentially management-related and can be overcome by decentralisation. Such factors tend not to affect fare and aggregate subsidy levels, though they may affect the latter to some extent through the efficiency of local service planning. Historically, transport in major cities was, with one or two exceptions, a municipal responsibility, but very largely sold on a self-financing trading basis. Investment was the subject of the greatest interference by the authority since this would typically require loan sanction. The 1968 Transport Act, as amended by provisions in the reorganisation of local government in 1974, set up Passenger Transport Authorities in the conurbation areas which, together with Passenger Transport Executives, were to plan and operate (respectively) local public transport. Since, after reorganisation, the PTA for an area was the Metropolitan County, public transport planning was under the aegis of the same authority which also had responsibility for other strategic planning matters, including roads.

Up to 1974, subsidies to operational revenue were relatively unimportant, but since that date they have become increasingly important, both as a source of total grants to public transport (Table 6.5) and of the financial expenditure of local authorities on transport (Table 6.6). However, there are substantial variations in the contributions made through subsidies to public transport

Table 6.5 Public Expenditure on Transport 1971–81 (in £ million)

	1971	*1972*	*1973*	*1974*	*1975*	*1976*	*1977*	*1978*	*1979*	*1980*	*1981*
British Rail grants from central government	75	141	189	391	502	481	491	561	677	711	867
British Rail grants from Passenger Transport Executive	–	8	9	15	19	25	33	39	45	57	61
London Transport grants from Government & GLC	9	27	30	31	63	63	42	45	63	76	83
Fuel duty rebates	21	21	20	32	38	45	57	59	60	78	93
New bus grant	10	18	21	23	31	39	43	52	62	80	56
Concessionary fares	7	12	20	37	79	95	109	124	137	162	190
Infrastructure grants	1	1	1	2	2	2	1	1	1	1	1
Local authority revenue subsidies	6	10	14	76	185	191	166	165	185	250	400
GLC depreciation & capital grants	1	2	6	7	8	17	13	14	25	29	41

Source: Department of Transport (1982) *Transport Statistics, Great Britain, 1971–81*.

Table 6.6 Local Authority Expenditure on Transport, 1975/76–1981/82 (in £ thousands)

	1975/76	*1976/77*	*1977/78*	*1978/79*	*1979/80*	*1980/81*	*1981/82*
Current expenditure							
Bus and underground services:							
Revenue support	177,314 (Revenue support and Other combined)	183,022 (Revenue support and Other combined)	158,531	169,154	188,591	278,226	365,220
Other			5,586	8,514	26,835	38,990	50,991
Rail and other services	24,811	24,407	28,748	32,290	36,608	45,245	34,234
Concessionary fares	69,267	79,205	94,041	112,948	130,589	136,616	155,859
Total	972,407	1,061,916	1,100,016	1,245,164	1,450,445	1,644,541	1,858,815
Capital expenditure	422,996	399,759	352,973	368,846	459,415	564,510	542,624

Source: Department of the Environment, *Local Government Financial Statistics*, published annually.

operations, both between cities in Britain and in comparison with other cities in other countries (Table 6.7). What is noticeable in the domestic situation is the way in which, since the early 1970s, current revenue subsidies have increased in importance at the expense of capital grants. To some extent this followed strong criticism of the effects of grants such as new bus grants and those for the provision of elaborate bus–rail interchanges made by Foster and others in evidence to the House of Commons Expenditure Committee (1972). However, the total level of subsidy to public transport has not shown any tendency to increase in recent years, a reflection of the fact that service reductions have borne the brunt of more recent financial pressures on operators. It remains an open question whether the generally higher levels of subsidy and lower real fares in other European countries, often coupled with very substantial investment in the infrastructure of new underground railways and light rail transit systems, has had a significant impact on the economic welfare of urban dwellers in those countries when the full cost has been assessed.

Although, in Table 6.7, we can see some important differences in philosophy between different areas—for example the low fares/high subsidy policy followed by South Yorkshire—this has never reflected total freedom since central government has laid down very strict controls on the capacity of local authorities to pursue such policies. Until 1974 such finance, other than central responsibility for various classes of road and capital grants such as New Bus Grant (aimed at securing national agreement on a rapid transition to higher productivity one-man operated buses), came out of the authorities rate revenue plus rate support grant (RSG) and borrowing. Since 1974 an additional system of Transport Supplementary Grants (TSG) has operated, designed partly to compensate authorities with a very high expenditure on transport which would not be reflected in their needs elements or definitions of grant related expenditure (see Chapter 8 on these), and partly to exercise a general control on transport expenditure. In the settlement for 1983/84, over 70 per cent of TSG was allocated to London and the six Metropolitan Counties (Table 6.8).

The TSG system essentially involves counties making bids under various headings for their estimated transport expenditures, current and capital, in a given year. Expenditure in excess of a given threshold, which is determined principally by those elements of

Table 6.7 Levels of Subsidy and Costs of Public Transport Support

	Fares as % of Total Expenditure		*Grants per head in*
	1975	*1979*	*1979 (£)*
Britain			
London	61	75	25
Manchester	78	75	13
Merseyside	72	59	18
South Yorkshire	60	35	29
Tyne and Wear	91	68	15
West Midlands	62	76	10
West Yorkshire	78	75	7
Glasgow	85	76	8
West Germany			
Frankfurt-am-Main	45	50	30
Hamburg	75	67	19
Munich	77	52	30
Stuttgart	61	50	28
France			
Lyon	76	59	22
Paris	45	44	68
Belgium & Netherlands			
Brussels	28	30	66
Rotterdam	31	28	47
Scandinavia			
Helsinki	42	49	77
Stockholm	45	43	79
North America			
New York	33	28	n.a.
Philadelphia	53	49	20
Toronto	81	75	26

Source: Allen, J.E. (1982) 'Public Transport—Who Pays?', cited in Bus and Coach Council, *The Future of the Bus*.
Note: n.a. = not available

Table 6.8 Transport Supplementary Grant 1977/78 to 1983/84

	Public transport revenue support (%) Bus	*Rail*	*Highway mainten-ance (%)*	*Other current (%)*	*Capital expenditure (%)*	*Total allowable expenditure (=100%) (£ thousands)*	*Grant (£ thousands)*	*Grant as % of allowable expenditure*	*% of total grant*
1977/78	15.7	3.1	47.1		34.1	722,900	204,945	28.3	
1978/79	15.7	3.2	49.0		32.1	774,300	219,193	28.3	
1979/80	15.0	3.4	48.2		33.4	917,200	257,111	28.0	
1980/81	16.0	3.3	49.9	0.7	30.1	959,000	273,326	28.5	
1981/82	15.3	3.2	46.5	0.9	34.1	1,112,900	315,000	28.3	
1982/83	16.0	3.3	48.2	0.7	31.8	1,631,800	456,900	28.0	
1983/84	17.4	2.9	45.3	0.7	33.7	1,831,693	450,000	24.6	
Distribution of 1983/84 grants by type of authority									
Greater London	24.6	–	24.8	1.3	49.3	461,818	200,722	43.5	44.6
Greater Manchester	23.9	18.4	38.7	0.4	18.5	100,476	23,426	23.3	5.2
Merseyside	26.6	17.5	32.1	0.6	23.1	82,766	30,688	37.1	6.8
South Yorkshire	26.3	7.3	48.2	0.4	17.9	47,887	9,993	20.9	2.2
Tyne and Wear	27.1	3.1	41.3	0.1	28.4	47,960	12,825	26.7	2.8
West Midlands	20.5	6.3	5.1	0.3	27.7	94,891	18,585	19.6	4.1
West Yorkshire	28.5	10.2	40.9	1.0	19.4	87,902	24,611	28.0	5.5
All Metropolitan Counties	25.1	11.5	40.5	0.5	22.4	461,882	120,128	26.0	26.7
Non-Metropolitan Counties	9.8	0.04	58.1	0.5	31.6	912,493	129,150	14.2	28.7

Source: *Transport Statistics Great Britain, 1971–81: Rate Support Grant Report, England*, HC 1982–83, 149.

expenditure which can be met from allocations under RSG, is then eligible for grant at a given rate (currently about 70 per cent). Hence authorities typically receive between 20 and 40 per cent of the expenditure agreed and accepted by central government. This system has two principal advantages: it involves all types of expenditure on all modes of transport (except for central government subsidies to British Rail for services outside the Metropolitan Counties and such things as airports, canals, etc.) and it requires authorities to submit the current year's bid for TSG in the context of a longer term proposal for the Transport Policies and Programmes (TPP).

However, the existence of the TPP means that an authority has, in effect, to declare publicly its compliance with, or deviation from, the central government's policy towards transport: hence the government is able to declare the proposed expenditure programme unacceptable and get it reduced by a reduction in the effective rate of grant. There are substantial differences between the individual counties' bids and their accepted expenditures. As Mackie and Garton (1979) have shown for 1976/77 TSGs for London and the Metropolitan Counties, accepted expenditure on revenue support was only 47 per cent of total bids under this heading. However, the actual expenditure achieved was rather different since nearly 70 per cent of the original bids were actually spent, and in four of the six Metropolitan Counties expenditure exceeded the original bid. This level of overspending was typically met by underspending on capital programmes, though how far this was due to accidental reasons through uncertainties in capital spending and how far due to deliberate attempts to maintain politically important elements in the bid is not always clear.

This failure to control an individual authority's expenditure level because of its ultimate ability both to switch expenditure between heads and to raise own revenue through rates has become one element in central government's resolve to reform both the expenditure and the revenue raising powers of local government.

Following a legal battle fought over the GLC's attempt to raise subsidy levels in London, the central government decided to clear up the confusion, and to act in a way which sharpened its ability to control transport expenditure. The essence of the argument was set out in a White Paper in November 1982 (Dept. of Transport 1982) which subsequently became the Transport Act 1983. The main requirement of this new Act was that PTEs, the GLC and the Metropolitan Counties had to set out annually proposals for fares, service levels and subsidy on a common basis. In addition it required three-year plans of financial prospects, capital provision and the most effective options for balancing services and fares in relation to costs, revenues and travel needs in accordance with annual guidance from the Secretary of State. This plan, effectively requiring a detailed breakdown of revenue support options within the TSG bid, was to be used in conjunction with the TPP submission to determine TSG. The White Paper noted that the target set in this plan had also to be consistent with the total expenditure target for the authority set in its RSG allocation overall—the authority had to decide for itself whether it could afford its target. Whilst on paper this raises sensible questions about transport, in a wider context of levels of control, accountability and responsibility it raises serious questions about who should run or determine levels of expenditure on key local services—an issue which we shall take up again in Chapter 8.

Whilst this political activity can be viewed as a straight battle about authority, can we form any judgment about the economic merits of the proposed changes, or indeed about the policies of the several authorities which prompted the action? Recent controversies over transport, including attempts by the central Government to remove responsibility for public transport in London and the Metropolitan Counties from local political control and by the GLC to exercise stricter control over lorry traffic in Central London, have centred on the conflict between the financial implications for operators and the responsible government authority and the much less easily quantifiable external factors and cross-price effects on road traffic, congestion, pollution and accident rates. Following the work of Glaister and Lewis (1978), Beesley *et al.* (1983) have developed elasticity values for all modes of passenger transport in London which incorporate both price and service quality effects resulting from changes in congestion levels on the various modes (Table 6.9). These values can then be used as a basic input to estimates of the total social welfare gains or losses associated with various policies towards both fares and service levels.

The results in Table 6.9 suggest that bus demand has been rather more sensitive to own price effects than has the demand for other modes, although comparison with estimates for 1971 suggests that

Table 6.9 Transport Elasticities for London, 1981

	Elasticity of passenger miles by mode with respect to given price change					
	Car	*Tube*	*British Rail*	*Taxi*	*Bus*	*Walking*
Bus fares	+0.019	+0.103	+0.069	+0.127	−0.397	+0.234
Tube fares	+0.011	−0.335	+0.031	+0.270	+0.145	+0.042
Petrol prices	−0.121	+0.020	+0.025	+0.005	+0.033	+0.027

Source: Beesley *et al*. (1983)

there has been a decline in this sensitivity. The cross effects on car usage are much lower than on other public transport modes—a confirmation of earlier findings by Baum (1973) that public transport fare levels would need to be very low indeed to effect a major reduction in road traffic. However, it is noticeable that the effects of changing prices for car usage (both own and cross-price effects) are rather stronger than in the reverse direction. It would be a mistake, therefore, to assume that cross-price effects are symmetrical.

Beesley *et al*. (1983) have used this basic data to experiment with a series of policy measures, increasing and decreasing both fares and service levels (passenger miles) by 10 per cent globally. They have also experimented with specific service alterations on individual routes in order to assess the overall effects on, *inter alia*, social net benefit, subsidy levels and value per £ of subsidy at the margin. The general conclusion from this exercise has been that higher subsidies do on the whole generate higher social benefits, but that the incidence of these subsidies—on lower fares or varied service levels of different modes—is very different. There is some evidence of declining net returns to subsidy, but the model discussed suggests that a 1979/80 level of subsidy some 2.8 times the actual level of subsidy in 1979 could be justified. This would imply fare reductions of 65 per cent for buses, 69 per cent for the underground, a 2 per cent reduction in bus service levels and a 12 per cent increase in tube service levels. Perhaps more significant, however, was the evidence that considerable variation in net benefit could be achieved from a given global level of subsidy. For example, for each £ of subsidy a 10 per cent decrease in bus fares is estimated to yield an increase of 6.73 passenger miles travelled and £0.53 of net surplus benefit, whilst a 10 per cent increase in service level would produce slightly less increase in travel (5.76 passenger miles) but a *decrease* in net benefit of £0.31. This arises because the increase in service levels has an immediate effect on other modes through congestion.

In a more recent reworking of a similar model Glaister (1984) has attempted to provide both some comparative data for other metropolitan areas and to assess alternative rules for the allocation of subsidy.

The general conclusion is that, ignoring the opportunity costs of the subsidy in other public sector activities, restricted transport subsidy levels have deprived the community of some available net benefits. Furthermore, within the existing levels of subsidy, redistribution between authorities and within authorities between alternative policies could also produce greater benefits. In general, authorities tend to overprovide public transport service at too high a fare.

If we were able to extend the analysis to take in a wider range of external benefits (both directly transport-related, such as accident and environmental costs, and indirectly related, such as employment growth *vis-à-vis* the attractiveness of city centre locations with low access costs), it is likely that net benefits to subsidy would at least stay the same, and most likely increase substantially. We shall take up some of these issues relating to the labour market, residential location and commuting in Chapter 7.

We have so far concentrated on the public transport fare-subsidy issue since it dominates much current debate on urban transport. There are other dimensions to transport policy, however. Clearly related to the subsidy issues is that of the role of competition. Local public transport in Britain is subject to licensing by Traffic Commissioners who have traditionally granted operators monopoly rights over individual routes and areas of operation. In the last few years, the Conservative government has tried to break down the protection that this provides to the large municipal and state-owned bus operators despite evidence from both the Monopolies and Mergers Commission (1982) and the Commons Committee on Transport (1982) that such a move might not be in the best interests of the public. So far, those schemes which have been tried experimentally do not appear to have been a great success and often have reintroduced some of the worst aspects of the pre-1930 situation when the licensing scheme was first introduced.

Further issues concern the correct level of road taxation for private users, especially the distribution of the burden between different users, the environmental issues surrounding lorry size (Department of Transport 1980), and the question of the control of competition through the various licensing schemes involved in freight transport (Department of Transport 1979).

6.4 Housing Problems and Policies

Demand and Supply of Housing

The demand for housing services can be considered in much the same way as that for transport since, again, there are both quantitative (size of house) and qualitative (style, design and, most importantly, tenure) aspects. Once again we also face a potential problem in determining the correct sequence of decisions about these various aspects. Many attempts to understand housing demand have started with the assumption that individuals decide tenure first, independently of other aspects of demand, and then settle other issues within tenure. More studies of the quantitative demand have been carried out in the owner–occupier sector simply because the degree of administrative interference in the public rental sector makes it much more difficult to assess genuine consumer demand. Recently, however, attempts have been made to treat tenure choice and the quantitative demand for housing as simultaneous decisions (King 1980). Preferences over, and access to, different housing tenures thus condition household demand for a house with given characteristics (see Maclennan 1982, Chapters 2 and 3 for a comprehensive review of the housing demand).

Quantity is, of course, a rather difficult thing to assess in the case of housing. Individuals often express their preferences for different houses in terms of these being 'larger', 'smaller', 'too small' and so forth. In a recent survey (Gordon *et al.* 1983) 25 per cent of those who had moved house in the previous eighteen months stated that house size was the major factor in causing the move. To measure these preferences objectively one must combine various attributes and assess the implicit valuation of these across a wide range of housing types. This assessment of the implicit prices attached to bedrooms, kitchens, living rooms, gardens, etc. is very different from the cost of building such features and is usually referred to as the measurement of a hedonic price for such features. Generally, however, it has been assumed that markets are capable of resolving these issues in terms of a single price for the house which can then be used as a weighted generalised measure of quantity and quality.

There has been considerable debate in the housing literature over the years about the value of the income elasticity of demand for housing. Most studies have suggested that the short-run income elasticity of demand for housing based on current income of households was typically rather less than unity. However, such a low value would not explain the growth in housing demand which has occurred. Recognising the asset value of housing as a further dimension suggested that more of a permanent income long run elasticity should be used, and studies which have measured this do indeed suggest a higher value of around unity. Attempts to apply similar techniques to the demand for rental property obtain rather lower values of income elasticity, suggesting that much of the income determinant of housing consumption is actually related more to the investment value of the house than to its housing value. Price elasticity of demand is also rather low for housing, suggesting that there is very little variation in housing consumption which can be induced by marginal price changes.

Table 6.10 summarises the pattern of tenure and housing demand in the major urban areas in Britain. It will be seen that there are considerable variations in the size of the council housing sector between cities. Over the long run, the expansion of owner occupation and the growth of council housing have largely removed the private rental sector from all but small sections of the housing market (typically, the very poor and the very rich). In this, Britain has had rather different experiences from most other countries, especially those in Europe, in which private rental markets have remained an important part of the total housing sector and in which a much higher proportion of people live in various forms of multiple occupation of buildings. This different approach to housing has made a major difference to densities and hence to city size, shape, structure, costs and efficiency.

The housing supply process is rather different from that for transport. In the transport sector, supply cannot be stored: it has to be produced as it is consumed. In one sense this is true of housing, too, since housing services are consumed continuously through periods of time. However, the flow of services is typically not controlled by a supplier but rather built into the infrastructure of the house. The relevant decisions are then those of the builders of houses: where, and what sort of house, to build. This also relates to the tenure into which houses are built since, at least until recently, tenure of property rarely changed between public and private sectors. The basic nature of this decision is similar to any development decision of the type discussed in Chapter 3. It relates expectations of the type of resident of a given location to considerations of the cost of the land and other factor inputs to the building. There have been a few attempts to incorporate the developer's supply decision into the access-space trade-off model of Chapter 3, the most notable of these being the path-breaking work

Table 6.10 Patterns of Tenure, 1981 (% Distribution of Households)

	Owner occupation	*Public rental*	*Private rental*
Great Britain	55.7	31.2	13.2
Greater London	48.6	30.7	20.7
Inner London	27.3	42.8	29.9
Outer London	61.9	23.2	15.0
Outer Metropolitan Area	63.8	25.2	11.0
Rest of South-east	63.8	21.6	14.6
Greater Manchester	57.0	33.0	10.0
Manchester	36.0	47.1	16.9
Merseyside	52.0	33.0	15.0
Liverpool	40.6	39.6	19.8
Rest of North-west	67.7	23.3	9.0
South Yorkshire	46.9	42.7	10.3
Sheffield	44.5	45.0	10.5
West Yorkshire	59.0	30.5	10.5
Leeds	53.5	35.3	11.3
Rest of Yorkshire & Humberside	60.6	25.7	13.7
Tyne and Wear	38.7	49.0	12.4
Newcastle	38.9	45.7	15.4
Rest of North	52.3	35.6	12.1
West Midlands	53.7	36.7	9.6
Birmingham	52.6	34.6	12.7
Rest of West Midlands	61.3	27.6	11.1
East Midlands	59.9	28.6	11.5
East Anglia	58.9	26.8	14.3
South-west	63.7	22.1	14.2
Wales	60.8	29.3	9.9
Central Clydeside conurbation	29.3	63.0	7.7
Rest of Scotland	37.5	50.4	12.1
Great Britain, 1971	48.0	30.4	21.6

Source: Census (1981)

of Muth (1969); see also Bradbury *et al.* (1977) and MacDonald (1979). The essence of these models is to use the city's factor supplies in a housing production function which provides the housing services input into the individual's utility function of the form of equation (3.9). However, as well as there being the production function of housing services, there is a developer with a profit function. The effect of the profit motive is to lead to variations from the supply side (as well as from the demand side) in the density of development and hence the nature of the housing supply process also affects the overall city structure.

One of the problems of housing supply is that, since houses are required to produce housing services, to vary the supply of housing typically requires infrastructural investment, which takes time. This is certainly true of new housing which only forms a fraction of the existing stock (perhaps no more than two per cent in a year) and part of this is replacement. Of course, it is possible to vary housing output by reconstruction or by rapid depreciation of existing housing stock, which is a more difficult decision to incorporate. However, it is clear that a considerable amount of variation in housing demand is met through a filtering process in which houses are modified to vary the output of housing services. Whilst the precise location of new housing developments may reflect local pressures, it is also clear that the overall level of activity in the housing construction industry is a reflection of national macroeconomic factors. The speculative nature of much new housing, typically by small builders, means that loan finance is critical both to finance construction and to ensure the existence of finance for final purchasers. Table 6.11 gives some indication of the aggregate levels of activity in recent years.

The Price of Housing

Optimal pricing issues in the housing sector are a little different from the transport sector, but this is mainly because of historical differences in responsibilities and rather different objectives. The main concern in housing has been one of securing adequate supplies at an acceptable price to meet assumed housing needs. Needs have tended to dominate revealed demand because of the merit good characteristic of housing. The allocational rule which would need to be followed if the government controlled the supply of all housing

Table 6.11 Trends in the Value of Housing Output, 1971–82 (1975 = 100)

	Public sector	*Private sector*	*Total*	*Public sector as % of total output*
1971	107.6	135.3	121.7	43.3
1972	96.1	147.6	122.3	38.5
1973	93.6	153.9	124.4	36.8
1974	90.8	110.9	101.0	44.0
1975	100.0	100.0	100.0	49.0
1976	110.7	106.6	108.6	49.9
1977	100.6	100.9	100.8	48.9
1978	94.6	114.3	104.6	44.3
1979	78.5	105.4	92.3	41.7
1980	64.4	83.7	74.2	42.5
1981	40.7	73.4	57.4	34.7
1982	34.5	85.7	60.6	27.9

Source: Department of the Environment, *Housing and Construction Statistics*, published annually and quarterly.
Note: Figures for 1980–2 are provisional.

would be that price could be set below marginal cost, supposing that there were distortions in the pricing of non-housing goods or that the government wished to alter individuals' revealed marginal rates of substitution between housing and non-housing goods.

The problem arises because the government does not control all housing supply, nor is the supply controlled by a homogeneous set of private sector suppliers. Hence, unlike the transport case where in the private sector there is reasonable homogeneity of supply, the presence of both a private rental sector and an owner-occupier sector confuses the issue. Of particular concern is the private rental sector since any subsidy may be enjoyed by either the tenant or the landlord—note that a similar problem would arise in transport if roads were privately owned. This distributional issue arises because of the distinction between asset ownership and consumption. Although it does not occur as a distributional issue between individuals, there is still the same problem with owner occupation since subsidies may fall more heavily on the purchase of the asset than on the price of housing consumed.

The usual mechanisms for influencing housing prices are rent control and tax reliefs in the private sector and rent control and direct subsidy in the public sector. Added to this are various effective personal subsidies in the form of rent and rate reliefs for low income families, which apply across tenure groups. If the objective is to secure the desired amount of housing, the policy must aim to treat the tenures neutrally—unless there are differences in the marginal social costs of building or maintenance between tenures.

The typical analysis of intervention in the housing sector is depicted in Figure 6.4. For an individual consumer, given the free market prices of housing and non-housing goods, the budget constraint is BB', and OH_1 housing is consumed. If the government intervenes to reduce the price of housing to, say, an equivalent of

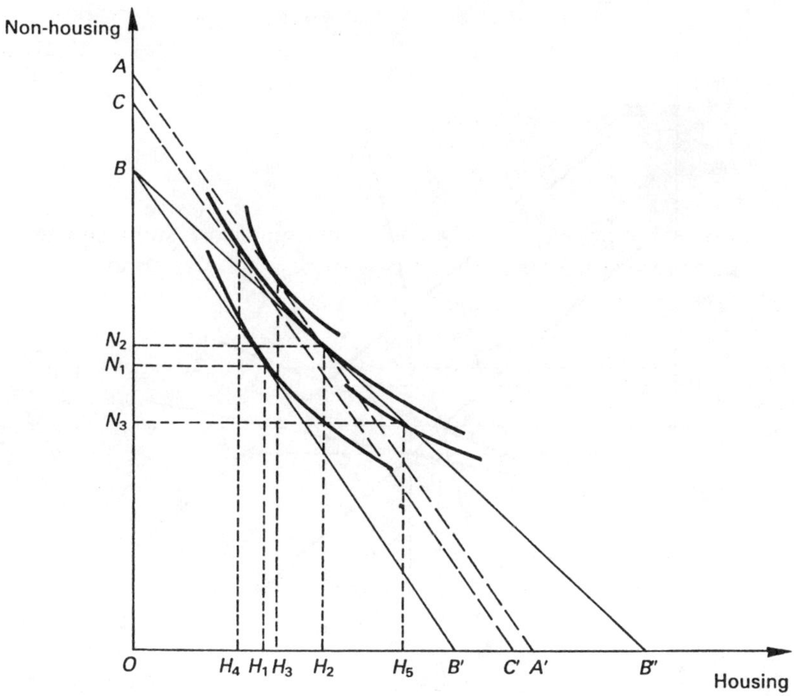

Figure 6.4

budget line BB'', then housing consumption will be increased to OH_2. The individual is better off since he is on a higher indifference curve and can consume more non-housing goods as well. However, for the same cost the government could provide an income subsidy to the individual raising his budget line to AA', which would lead to an even higher level of welfare, though to a smaller rise in housing demand of H_1H_3. There are two arguments against the income subsidy: first, that it is less effective in raising housing consumption (those who benefit are seen as squandering the subsidy on non-housing goods because of their failure to include the external benefits of better housing in their own preferences); secondly, that a failure to control prices may mean that the increase in demand raises prices of housing as shown in Figure 6.5, because of the inelastic nature of housing supply. Hence, instead of an increase to OH_3, a lesser increase to, say, OH_6 occurs, implying a lower level of welfare. A policy of income subsidy may thus require a parallel policy of rent controls.

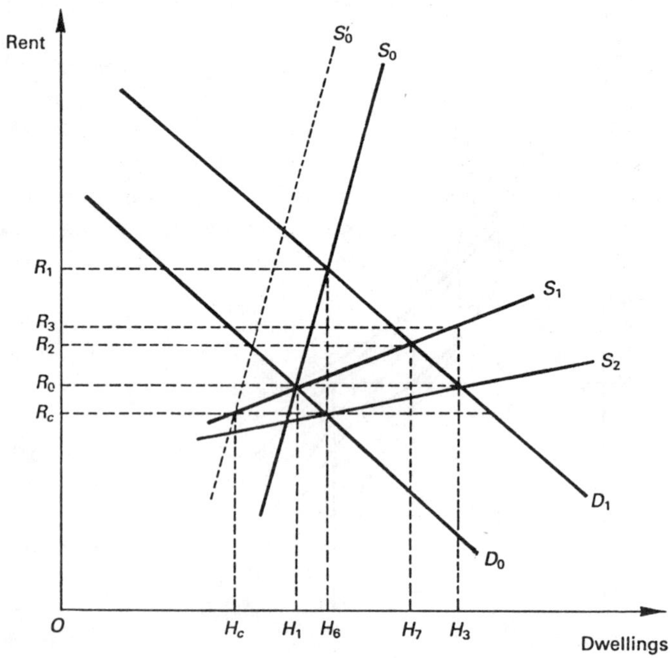

Figure 6.5

An alternative objective could be to achieve a given level of welfare through income subsidy rather than price subsidy, leading to lower cost and raising the budget line to CC' and housing consumption to OH_4. This would still leave the supply problem of Figure 6.5, however.

Many public housing schemes involve both price and quantity intervention since council houses carry subsidised rents and only provide housing in pre-determined quantities. Assuming the price subsidy is the same as in the first example with a budget line BB'', the authority now imposes on the individual a quantity of housing, OH_5, which necessitates a reduction in his non-housing consumption to ON_3 and a lower level of welfare.

Let us now return to the supply problem in Figure 6.5, where S_O represents the short-run supply of rented accommodation in the private sector. This is assumed not to be entirely fixed, but to be relatively inelastic in the short run. The effect of a rent control at OR_O is to produce excess demand for rental accommodation of H_1H_3. To secure any long-run increase in supply to match this demand requires an increase in rent received by landlords to at least OR_2 if the long-run supply curve is S_1, but this would still leave H_7H_3 unsatisfied demand. The only way of securing the full OH_3 supply of rented accommodation is to subsidise landlords to the extent of R_OR_3 so that the supply curve becomes the equivalent of S_2 in Figure 6.5. The provision of subsidies to suppliers exercising monopoly power in a market is usually regarded as inappropriate.

The situation could be even more worrying than we have so far suggested. Rent controls are often an attempt to reduce rents below the current market price rather than just to prevent them rising to meet new demand. Figure 6.5 shows that if the controlled level is at OR_c, below OR_O, the long-run supply of housing is reduced from OH_1 to OH_c. This depends on knowing the long-run equilibrium rent for rented accommodation which will be determined by the rate of return on equivalent assets, or the capitalised value of the asset which could be obtained by selling the house into owner occupation. It requires the existence of security of tenure provisions for tenants to be able to avoid this course of action although, as Frankena (1975) and others have pointed out, such provisions may just lead to landlords increasing the rate at which they depreciate the asset, since market controls may set price and quantity, but not always quality.

One attempt made in recent years was to divorce the economic price of rental housing received by the owner from the subsidised price paid by the consumer, much as happens in agricultural markets. This resulted in the notion of 'Fair Rents', introduced in 1965. The fair rent was to be set on the basis of the characteristics of the property (rather than of the tenant) but on the assumption that there was no shortage in the market, i.e. rents could not include any element of scarcity value. The outcome thus neither satisfied market requirements, nor tenant subsidy requirements, although the latter could be dealt with under rent rebate and, more recently, housing subsidy schemes.

The basic difference between local authority and private sector tenants is the provision that can be made for the former in preserving quantity and quality, although typically at the cost of a loss of perceived welfare. What of the comparison between local authority tenants and owner-occupiers? Owner-occupiers do not receive a direct price subsidy on their consumption of housing, but they do receive favourable tax treatment because they live rent-free in a house whilst not being taxed on the implicit rental income received from ownership of the asset. They often do not own the full asset since, typically, they have a mortgage on which they must pay interest, but they also receive tax relief on this. The degree of subsidy is thus often related to an individual's tax liability rather than to his housing needs. King and Atkinson (1980) have attempted to derive a comparison of the total subsidy received by residents in each of the two tenures. Such a calculation requires assumptions about the value of the house, the size of the mortgage, expectations of house price changes, the mortgage interest rate and the individual's marginal tax rate since these all affect the capital cost of housing to the individual, and the target rate of return for the local authority. For the individual owner-occupier to face higher annual net capital costs than the local authority for an equivalent house, King and Atkinson show that he must either pay tax at below the basic rate, or have a very large mortgage (above the £25,000 tax relief ceiling which applied until 1983) and have an opportunity cost of the capital of at least 12 per cent. They therefore conclude that the cost of housing is less to the owner-occupier than the equivalent cost to the council tenant.

Policy Issues in Housing

Whilst housing is a key policy issue in the urban economy, it is also the case that much of the discussion of housing policy has taken place in the national context as part of the general framework of social welfare. We have seen that to some extent transport has also increasingly moved in that direction in recent years as intervention in that sector has become more costly and more concerned with revenue subsidies. Local government has acted rather more as the agent of central government in just one sector of housing—the supply of public housing—since it has no power to control the degree of price control or subsidy to private rental or owner-occupier housing in the absence of locally-determined income taxes. The only effective control which local authorities can apply is in their role of planning authority and major land owner: they can control the rate at which land is released for private, as opposed to public, housing developments. Local authorities do have some influence in the public housing sector, since they are responsible for building, maintaining and fixing rents for council houses in their own areas.

Rents are typically fixed on an average cost price basis for a defined unit of housing services (Robinson 1979, pp. 120–4) which depends on the difference between the authority's total costs and subsidies coming from the government and its own rate fund (Table 6.12). Total costs depend very largely (more than 70 per cent, typically) on loan charges and variations between local authorities reflect both the age distribution of the housing stock (i.e. the historic cost of existing houses) and differences in the cost of new building. Central government subsidies to the Housing Revenue Account (H.R.A.) of each authority are partly calculated to reflect specific factors influencing these costs. The authority is notionally free to contribute to the H.R.A. from its rate fund in order to keep down its level of rents (Table 6.13). The financing of a major area of policy is, then, another source of potential conflict between central and local government.

There are two issues at stake here. The first issue is internal to the local authority sector: the averaging of rental prices per unit of housing service fails to distinguish between ages of dwellings and hence leads to cross-subsidies between tenants of old properties and

Table 6.12 Local Authority Housing Revenue Accounts, 1971/72 to 1981/82 (%)

	1971/72	*1972/73*	*1973/74*	*1974/75*	*1975/76*	*1976/77*	*1977/78*	*1978/79*	*1979/80*	*1980/81*	*1981/82*
Expenditure											
Supervision and maintenance	9.5	10.9	10.3	11.5	12.8	12.7	13.1	13.2	13.2	13.7	14.8
Repairs	14.7	18.7	16.9	16.4	17.1	16.6	18.0	19.2	19.6	20.1	19.9
Debt charges	69.3	66.5	68.5	68.2	66.2	66.3	62.6	63.3	65.8	63.2	59.7
Revenue contributions to capital outlay	0.5	0.7	0.7	0.9	0.7	0.9	1.2	1.2	} 3.1	} 3.2	} 3.4
Other	5.7	3.4	3.7	3.1	2.6	2.5	2.4	2.6			
Residual	0.2	−0.2	−0.2	−0.1	0.6	1.0	2.7	0.5	−1.7	−0.3	2.1
Total (£million)=100%	858	976	1,205	1,620	1,986	2,380	2,658	3,064	3,723	4,550	
Income											
Rents on dwellings	66.7	65.1	55.4	44.8	43.1	41.2	42.4	40.6	37.1	37.5	53.3
Rents on other properties	3.1	2.8	2.4	2.2	1.8	1.7	1.7	1.6	1.6	1.4	1.5
Exchequer subsidies	21.8	18.9	19.5	30.0	31.8	35.1	33.6	34.4	35.8	32.8	25.7
Rent rebates	–	–	11.0	9.4	8.3	8.9	9.3	8.7	8.1	8.3	–
Rate fund contributions	4.7	9.6	7.3	10.9	11.7	9.5	9.1	10.0	12.0	12.9	9.7
Other income	3.8	3.7	4.3	2.7	3.2	3.6	3.8	4.7	5.4	7.1	9.8
Total (£million)=100%	858	976	1,205	1,670	1,986	2,380	2,658	3,064	3,723	4,550	4,841

Source: Department of the Environment, *Local Government Financial Statistics*, published annually.

Table 6.13 Local Authority Contribution to Housing Subsidies, 1981/82

	Percentage of total housing costs				
	Gross rents	*Government subsidy*	*Rate fund contribution*		*Rate fund subsidy per dwelling*
			Mandatory	*Discretionary*	*£*
Greater London Council	33.8	27.8	0.6	29.1	726.06
Inner London Boroughs	37.2	38.6	0.6	22.3	435.39
Outer London Boroughs	56.2	30.8	0.8	11.0	141.73
Metropolitan Districts	71.8	23.3	1.2	9.3	82.41
Non-Metropolitan Districts	75.4	22.0	1.3	2.4	21.22

Sources: Department of the Environment, *Local Government Financial Statistics; Local Government Comparative Statistics* (CIPFA), published annually.

those of newer properties, whilst failing to keep prices commensurate with replacement costs. This means that the rate of return on investment in housing is depressed and that the ability to invest is reduced (Nicholson and Topham 1971). King and Atkinson (1980) estimate the real net rate of return on local authority dwellings to have been of the order of 2.8 per cent in the early 1970s, falling to around 2 per cent in the late 1970s, far lower than comparable investments. The extent to which this differential in rates of return exists is an estimate of total effective subsidy, and King and Atkinson suggest that raising the target rate of return to 3 per cent would imply an average increase in rents of 38 per cent, or a rise in housing costs from around 7 per cent of gross average earnings to around 10 per cent.

The second issue is the relationship between the local authority and the private (especially the owner-occupier) sector, where the effective subsidy on the latter is controlled by central government decisions and that on the former (albeit marginally) by local decisions. In any case, as we saw above, capital costs to the owner-occupier are typically well below the average rate of return in the local authority sector and, by implication, the notional total subsidy is much larger. Moreover, the relative cost of owner occupation tends to decline with increases in both income (or more exactly the marginal tax rate) and the rate of inflation. This could have important redistributive effects between population groups, and hence between cities, since it is related both to the average income of inhabitants and the level of home ownership.

A further dimension of policy which has led to substantial variations in practice between local authorities and, again, to friction between central and local government, is that of the sale of council houses. The argument on this issue has been largely dominated by political ideology and not by an overall assessment of the housing needs of a particular area and how best to achieve them. Even at a national level the economic and, more particularly, the financial effects of sales have been largely speculative (Maclennan 1982, pp.271–8), although recent evidence is that, despite running at lower levels than expected at the time of the 1980 Housing Act, councils have actually benefitted enormously from the windfall gains in their capital accounts amounting to nearly six hundred million pounds in 1982/83, according to some estimates (The Times, 1 November 1982). What appears to be the result of sales is that they reduce the demand for new owner-occupier housing in an area, whilst also freeing councils from the need either to provide new housing stock or to improve the existing stock for those most likely to buy (who are also those most likely to demand improved quality). The windfall in capital receipts is not matched by an increase in capital expenditure to replace the old stock. The longer-term financial prospects may be less rosy, however. The implication seems to be that the public housing sector will be squeezed, rather like the private rental sector, to become a smaller sector of low-quality housing for lower-income groups. Such a result may, of course, make it easier to effect a unified housing policy since each rental sector will become much more homogeneous so that rent controls and subsidies may have fewer undesirable consequences. Then there will be a need for reform on the effective subsidy provided by the tax treatment of owner-occupiers. At such a point, however, housing policy will be completely out of the control of local authorities.

Housing Policy and the City

What of the more general effects of housing policy on the urban economy? The existence of price controls in the rented sector and of subsidies to the owner-occupier sector seems to have the net effect of increasing the total consumption of housing to a level above that which would obtain without such intervention, and above that necessary for merit good reasons. However, there is a distortion within the market: in order to maintain levels of consumption in the rented sector, excess consumption is encouraged in the owner-occupier sector. A number of commentators have suggested a more unified treatment of housing taxation and subsidy to correct this (King and Atkinson 1980; Hughes 1979). If housing consumption in the aggregate is above its desirable level, the investment in housing must have been transferred from other investment opportunities because of the distortion in relative rates of return. Cities may therefore have tended to over-capitalise the housing sector with two possible effects. One is the diversion of capital from productive industry with potential consequences for the economic bases of the city. The other is that increased housing capital will often mean larger houses and, since housing finance does not usually distinguish between building and site values, this implies larger plots. This would lead to the city being larger than it might otherwise be, with consequent implications for other infrastructure, such as transport. This again highlights the way in which housing and transport subsidies interrelate and need to be considered together to avoid some of the conflicts which have often emerged.

At the present time, local authorities are having their housing budgets cut by central government by a planned average of about 15 per cent a year in real terms from 1979/80 to 1983/84. The early stages of this are apparent in Table 6.12. The discussion above suggests that there may be some basis for the need to reduce the total level of involvement: government housing policies have in many ways created as many problems as they have solved. However, it is also clear that it is much more the distribution of subsidy and its allocational impact which should be corrected, and there is little indication that the global cuts planned will achieve this vital objective. One important advance in recent years has been to try to separate the individual need for housing subsidy (on income grounds) from the market price of housing through a system of Housing Benefits. This, too, has fallen foul of the global constraint on public expenditure which itself is introducing many serious distortions into the allocation of subsidies, both between and within sectors.

Further Reading

A useful starting point is any text on public expenditure decisions, such as Rees (1976). On transport, there are some useful introductory texts which include much institutional background, such as Button (1982) and, specifically on public transport, Nash (1982). An excellent guide to the more technical aspects, which shows how to turn theory into practical evaluations, is that of Glaister (1981). A useful introduction to the whole issue of subsidies is given by Beesley (1972, 1974), and see also Frankena (1983), Pucher *et al.* (1983), Beesley *et al.* (1983), and Glaister (1984).

General policy towards transport is contained in a series of consultative Green Papers and White Papers of which the most relevant are *Transport Policy: A Consultation Document* (1976), *Public Transport Subsidy in Cities* (Cmnd. 8735, 1982) and, on the particular question of London and the South-east, *Public Transport in London* (Cmnd. 9004, 1983). At a more general level, the book by Collins and Pharoah (1974) gives very useful background, as does Thomson (1978). Official monitoring of the working aspects of transport policy has been undertaken by the Monopolies and Mergers Commission (1982) and the House of Commons Transport Committee (1982).

On housing, the literature is vast: particularly recommended for their economics-based approaches consistent with the discussion here are Robinson (1979) on the policy issues and Maclennan (1982) on the more general aspects of housing economics. The last fully comprehensive review of housing policy is that of *Housing Policy: A Consultative Document* (1977) parts of which, though much amended, became the Housing Act of 1980. For a valuable summary of housing policy, see Donnison and Ungerson (1982).

7
Labour and Capital in the Urban Economy

Much of the basic analysis of the working of the urban economy in Part I concentrated on the base sector of the economy and noted the importance of efficiency, productivity and competitiveness in the performance of urban industry. It was also noted that many of the problems faced by urban economies today are highlighted by the growth of unemployment, the out-migration of skilled labour, the decline of urban enterprise, and its replacement by new industries in new areas which are typically less urban. Our discussion of policy so far has rather suggested that the main policy area for urban government is in the provision of both physical and social infrastructure. This is, to a large extent, the way in which the situation has been perceived. It is a reflection of the view that urban areas constitute the core of the economy in general and that urban public sector intervention is largely a case of controlling the worst excesses of negative external effects of urban industry whilst promoting the more beneficial ones. Such variations in industrial performance as did occur through space were attributed essentially to regional variations in either structure or the pressure of demand. Hence, a large array of regional measures to assist industry through both investment incentives and labour subsidies in lagging regions, and through restrictions on developments in more prosperous regions, have been established (Armstrong and Taylor 1978).

These measures have typically not been able to distinguish between sub-regional variations, except in so far as distinctions have been drawn between the different levels of aid available in Special Development Areas, Development Areas and Intermediate Areas, and these distinctions have been made just on the basis of variations in main indicators such as unemployment rates in Employment Office areas. Certainly there has been no attempt to devise policy measures which discriminate between the analytically different problems faced in old urban, suburban or rural areas, despite the attempts made by the EEC to distinguish between such problems in European regional policy. In this chapter we shall try to provide a framework for the analysis of such problems and to discuss some aspects of policy which have arisen in recent years.

7.1 Urban Factor Markets

The key indicator which is used to identify the need for policy intervention has typically been the level of unemployment, and we shall devote a large part of this chapter to the discussion of both the determinants of unemployment and changes in labour market areas. However, it must not be forgotten that ultimately any policy intervention is constrained by the implicit production function for urban industries and that policies towards labour which fail to recognise the importance of securing capital investment will rarely succeed in establishing any continuing growth in the local economy. In this first section of the chapter we shall, therefore, spend some time establishing more clearly just what these relationships are in practice.

This is not a novel approach: indeed, regional policy in Britain and many other countries, although typically triggered by labour market indicators, has normally resorted to intervention in the capital market as the main instrument of policy. Hence, in Britain, investment grants and incentives have been the main tools of regional policy and, as we shall see in Section 7.4, new urban policy is largely geared to this end. It is based on the view that the financial investment is the *sine qua non* of any new development and that finance capital is typically more mobile than labour, and thus more easily attracted into regions (or possibly, more correctly, attracted back after being more easily attracted out of the region by lack of opportunity or return in the first place).

The only period in which a concentrated policy of specifically labour-based policies has operated was during the period of the Regional Employment Premium in Britain from 1967–77. This policy measure was essentially Kaldorian in its philosophy in that it attempted to effect a competitive advantage on a receiving region, operating rather like a currency devaluation would on an economy with its own currency. More recently, labour market policies connected with training and education or job opportunities for the long-term unemployed have been increasingly widespread nationally, but they have largely been directed at specific groups in the population, such as youth employment schemes, rather than at specific areas. Some attempts to focus these policies rather more at a spatial level have been made in the last few years, with priority being given to the worst-affected inner city areas, as we shall see in Section 7.2.

The basic criticism which is directed at policies of investment subsidy is twofold. The first argument is that if these policies are to succeed, in the sense of producing investment in an area which would not otherwise have attracted any, they must either divert investment from an area where it would be more productive, or create investment which is highly marginal. In both cases there is a diversion of investment funds towards less productive ventures, and in both cases there is the risk that in a downswing of general economic activity the project will fail, hence making assisted areas more vulnerable to cyclical swings than other areas—a subject which has attracted considerable attention. Where the investment would have been undertaken anyway, there would be just a simple transfer of resources to the investor or entrepreneur. What this emphasises is the need to consider investments not just as one-off independent events but to ensure that a series of linked and interdependent projects is undertaken.

The second argument is that concentration on investment incentives maximises the advantage secured by projects which are large users of capital, since it distorts the relative prices of the factors—hence capital-intensive investment will take place in regions which are characterised by shortages of financial capital but abundant supplies of labour. Whilst it is true that a capital subsidy will lead to projects which are more capital-intensive than they would otherwise have been (because of a substitution effect caused by price changes), this does not necessarily mean that less labour will be used in aggregate than in the absence of the incentive, since there will also be an output or income effect which raises the level of activity (see the discussion in Whiting 1976).

There is, perhaps, a more fundamental problem with the basic analytical assumptions underlying the use of such policy measures, one of which is particularly pronounced at the urban level. The analysis is principally based on essentially aspatial foundations: similar measures are used as aids to industry at both national and regional levels, and this is even more true of recent labour market policies. The analysis typically lacks a careful definition and assessment of the appropriate market within which the policy is to operate. We have already met and discussed the way in which attempts have been made to define labour market areas on the basis of commuting patterns or daily urban systems, using existing commuting patterns to define the limits to workplace and residential search. This raises a number of difficulties, principal among which is the impossibility of talking about a single urban labour market when in fact different occupations will have very different spatial labour markets in which they operate, and the rather different ways in which the dynamics of a local labour market can operate through both daily commuting and longer-term migration (Vickerman 1984). Hence, just as we saw the growth of cities as depending on the coincidence of acting as a market centre to a series of different-sized market areas for goods, so the overall picture of a local labour market depends on the overlaying of a series of spatially-defined occupational labour markets.

Labour markets only tend to become spatially defined because of the immobility of labour and the limits to search and to commuting which space imposes. Financial capital markets do not suffer from this restrictiveness and hence the tendency is to regard them as being aspatial. Capital markets are at least national, and probably international. Nevertheless, this probably does not stop very strong local market forces from operating. One such is the accident of entrepreneurship—the local demand for risk capital is not spatially independent. It is clear from international studies within Europe that very considerable differences in innovative ability have led to differences in performance (Jones 1981) and there has been considerable interest in examining the adoption and diffusion of innovation as a part of the examination of regional variations within countries (e.g. Ewers and Wettmann 1980; Thwaites 1982). Another is the perceived risks associated with investment in specific areas, whether through variations in local labour militancy or the risk of loss through vandalism, or the suggestion that banks and other financial institutions have been less willing to invest in certain inner city areas because of implicit racial discrimination. This would suggest that probably there do exist considerable spatial variations in both the demand for, and supply of, financial capital which do lead to distinct problems for some urban areas, as opposed to others.

It has been assumed generally that urban labour markets are rather easier to define by the use of commuting data but, as we shall see in Section 7.3, there are many problems with such an approach when we allow for the possibility of moving either or both workplace and residence. We shall look rather more closely at explanations of unemployment in the following section, but let us try first to draw some conclusions about the way we should expect the labour market, within some clearly defined boundaries, to behave.

First, we have already noted that we should not expect there to be a single unified labour market within an area. Skill differences, industrial differences, and age and sex differences will provide more or less clear divisions between sectors of the labour market. These distinctions are not rigid or permanent, however. Despite attempts to identify dual labour markets with primary and secondary workers, occupational mobility does occur, perhaps more between industries than between specific jobs; nevertheless, there is very little rigidity. Secondly, the intra-urban location of jobs may be important: cities are not like the cities of the theoretical model of Chapter 3 with all their employment in the central areas; particular types of industry will tend to concentrate in certain areas of the city and hence so will the demand for particular types of labour. This means that the relative location of housing of particular types will be important since occupation has a significant influence on housing demand, both through tenure and the quantity and quality of housing demanded.

A complete model of a local labour market must therefore take into account both demand and supply sides, both of which are interrelated and spatially dependent. As we shall see, a continuing problem with models of local labour markets is their tendency to ignore this simple fact (see Cheshire 1979 for a critique in a similar vein). Demand depends on the aggregation of different types of firms' labour requirements as given by a spatial production function. As we have seen, a spatial production function implies that there is an element of choice in the firm's location, in which potential labour supply in a given location is one element. To some extent firms will be attracted to central or highly accessible locations because that increases the size of the potential labour market. The labour supply in an area also depends on the potential employment prospects. That potential, since its value depends on access to jobs, will depend on such factors as transport availability and preferences. Labour supply in an area will also depend on housing availability since housing demand and job choice are clearly closely connected.

7.2 Urban Unemployment

Unemployment has come to be the major concern in urban economies. In so doing, it has replaced traditional concerns with transport and housing. This is partly a reflection of the growth of unemployment generally, but also of the way in which the greatest rises in unemployment have been concentrated in urban areas, particularly those in regions which traditionally have had relatively low unemployment rates (Table 7.1). Building on the analysis of markets referred to in the preceding section, it has come to be recognised that the analysis of the specifically urban dimension in unemployment requires the adoption of an increasingly sophisticated approach. There is a great danger that the use of over-simplified explanations of unemployment leads to the adoption of policies diametrically opposed to those actually needed. This arises because there is a difference between *describing* the *pattern* of unemployment and *explaining* the *causes* of that pattern.

Attempts at explaining these causes in local economies have followed rather different paths through time. Original interest centred on structural explanations, just as it had with more general explanations of regional variations in economic perormance. In the late 1960s, interest moved towards a demand-determined explanation: regions with higher, more volatile, rates of unemployment were those where the cyclical pattern of aggregate demand was more pronounced. This approach classified local unemployment as being principally of a Keynesian or demand–deficiency origin. Such approaches were examined mainly at the wider regional level, but as interest focussed more on the local urban level, it also became

Table 7.1 Unemployment in the Conurbations, 1971 and 1981 (Percentage of the economically active out of employment)

	1971		*1981*	
	Male	*Female*	*Male*	*Female*
Greater London	4.4	2.8	9.3	4.6
Inner London	6.0	3.5	12.8	6.3
Outer London	3.2	2.3	7.3	3.6
Greater Manchester	5.7	3.0	12.6	5.9
Manchester	9.8	6.2	18.1	7.5
Merseyside	8.4	3.8	17.8	7.2
Liverpool	11.5	7.6	21.6	8.9
South Yorkshire	5.4	2.2	12.0	4.9
Sheffield	5.2	3.9	12.6	4.5
Tyne and Wear	8.6	3.0	16.5	5.8
Newcastle	9.8	5.5	16.2	5.6
West Midlands	5.0	2.7	15.7	6.3
Birmingham	6.5	5.3	16.7	6.9
West Yorkshire	5.3	2.4	11.3	4.9
Leeds	6.2	4.1	11.2	4.9
Central Clydeside	11.1	6.7	17.3	7.7
Great Britain	5.0	2.6	10.5	4.7

Sources: Census (1971) and Census (1981)

clear that the characteristics of those unemployed showed considerable variation between areas and might also be a principal cause of that variation. Recently, attempts have been made to assess the spatial elements in the labour market more directly, revealing the important linkages between labour markets, housing markets, transport markets, and so on, on both demand and supply sides. Let us look at these approaches in more detail.

We have already seen that the crude relationship between a local economy's structure and its economic performance is a poor predictor of the latter at a more general level. Since one of the main indicators of performance has typically been employment growth, since also we would not expect natural growth rates of the labour force to vary substantially enough between local economies to explain the observed differences, we should expect employment growth and unemployment to be inversely related. This relationship may be affected by variations in activity rates or migration. If we assume initially that both of these depend on individual decisions which are based on rational economic judgments, we should expect individuals to respond positively to job opportunities. Hence, variations in both activity rates and migration will not tend to make unemployment variations differ systematically from employment growth variations, except that they may dampen slightly the interregional variations.

Assuming that major changes in factor proportions are not taking place, employment growth in an economy is a reasonably good indicator of demand pressure. The next stage, therefore, is to separate that part of local unemployment which is due to the pressure of demand in the local economy from the part due to the local economy's structure. It will be remembered from our discussions in Chapter 3 that the relevant demand is that which is exogenous to the local economy: demand for its exports. What we therefore need to assess is the extent to which demand for labour in the local economy is due to that economy's competitiveness (so that the demand for its products from outside is greater or smaller than in other regions), and also to that economy's structure which means that, regardless of its competitiveness, it concentrates on producing goods for which 'world' demand is growing faster or slower than demand in general.

Following the initial studies of Brechling (1967) and Thirlwall (1966, 1969) which attempted to identify the cyclical elements in regional unemployment rates, a standard approach developed. This aimed to separate unemployment into two parts—that matched quantitatively by vacancies (implying structural or frictional unemployment) and that for which there was a deficiency of vacancies. A qualitative matching by job type of the unemployed with vacancies would indicate structural unemployment within the non-demand deficient total (Cheshire 1973; Thirlwall 1974). At the regional level, demand-deficient unemployment has clearly dominated, but certain regions have experienced more pronounced structural influences at certain times.

At the local level there is a major problem in determining the appropriate labour market for measuring and matching unemployment and vacancies. At any level there is the problem of regarding the labour market as closed, ignoring the way in which migration or commuting may affect labour supply (Gordon 1977) and ignoring the more personal characteristics of individuals which may influence labour supply. The pure demand side approach also treats structure as given and ignores the way in which the pressure of demand affects different industries differentially, leading to structural change.

Most attention subsequently has been focussed on the analysis of the characteristics of the unemployed, both in inter-urban comparisons (Vipond 1974; Metcalf 1975) and in intra-urban studies (Metcalf and Richardson 1976; Evans 1980). The general conclusion of these studies—that high unemployment is typically associated with such factors as lack of skill, older workers, single workers—clearly has implications for areas such as older industrial cities and, in particular, inner areas of cities. However, there is the problem in such studies of sorting out cause and effect, demand and supply side factors. It is dangerous, for example, to conclude that, because lack of skill and high unemployment are related, a major policy response should be one of retraining. More skilled workers appear not to have fared particularly better within inner city areas: what they have been able to do is to escape and avoid the excessive spatial concentration (Richardson 1980; Evans and Richardson 1981).

This raises the spatial aspects of the labour market again. There are two questions: the actual size of the labour market and the inter-connectedness of labour markets. A number of writers—Cheshire (1973), Vipond (1974), Hoch (1977)—raised the question of whether, and why, the size of the labour market should have an effect on unemployment. The results were less strong in Britain than in the United States, but generally it was found that larger cities had lower unemployment, *ceteris paribus*, suggesting a lower search costs effect with more job opportunities available in a larger city. However, Evans and Richardson (1981) found some evidence in favour of an opposing thesis: that larger labour markets induce higher quit rates and higher expectations (reservation wages) which would prolong search, on average, and raise observed unemployment rates.

Strong evidence for this hypothesis comes from a study across the larger Metropolitan Economic Labour Areas (MELA), which are based more firmly on the economic, rather than administrative, boundaries used in most earlier studies (Burridge and Gordon 1981). This suggests that unemployment in a MELA is positively related to differentials between that MELA and a distance-weighted sum of both density and size of surrounding MELAs. The density variable aims to capture likely costs of search, the size variable the likely level of opportunities. Burridge and Gordon also estimated the effect of location and openness (lack of self-sufficiency as measured by commuting) of the labour market on the growth in employment necessary to compensate for an additional one per cent growth in local labour supply. In very open labour markets leakage through in-migration leads to the need for a 15 per cent or more growth in employment, whilst in a relatively closed labour market less than 2 per cent growth is needed. This approach has been repeated in an inter-borough study of the London region (Gordon and Lamont 1982) with similar results, except that the net effect of employment growth on unemployment was rather stronger. Nevertheless, in a local labour market which is 75 per cent open to commuting flows, job creation would have virtually no effect on local unemployment and on average job creation would need to be about 2.5 times the desired reduction in unemployment.

One of the major problems in interpreting and using these results is that there is a tendency for a cumulative effect over time. High unemployment in an area tends to produce high levels of unskilled workers remaining in the area which is associated with high levels of unemployment in a subsequent period. In practice, there is little evidence that particular skill or social groups in the population suffer differentially in different areas—an unskilled person is just as likely to be unemployed in a suburb or a small town as in an inner city. This leads to the observation made by most studies that the spatial pattern of unemployment is remarkably stable through time.

There is a fair measure of agreement that job creation policies alone are unlikely to solve unemployment problems in specific areas, particularly policies which are aimed at changing skill levels. This is partly so for the reasons already noted: that increasing skill levels will tend to increase the chance of those individuals who are able to move away, whilst the creation of new jobs in an area may just lead to increased movement into that area on either a temporary (commuting) or a permanent (migration) basis. Evans and Richardson (1981) suggest that such policies ultimately lead to the problem moving to another part of the city and that it cannot be solved at the local level.

Policy towards Unemployment

The basic finding on unemployment is, therefore: unemployment is primarily influenced by spatial variations in demand coupled with concentrations of specific groups of the population with greater propensities to be unemployed. This suggests that there is little hope of the adoption of a specifically local labour market policy response (see also Mason 1983 for a fuller assessment). Such a view accords with the model of the urban economy and its development in Chapters 3 and 4, in which the critical determinants are the price and income elasticities of demand for the economy's products. Raising national income levels (and hence demand for all output) is thus the key policy response. In order to reduce concentrations of unemployment in certain urban areas, or certain areas of a metropolitan economy, policies must be found which encourage the development of new industries or new technologies with higher income elasticities of demand or lower costs (increased competitiveness); or which encourage greater mobility of the already unemployed (or those at high risk of unemployment) out of the area. We shall look at these two policies in greater detail in the following sections of this chapter. However, neither may result in a reduction in the rate of unemployment for residents of the area, for the reasons we have already suggested.

What is then left is either a policy of labour subsidy or of training schemes. There are, broadly, three types of assistance which have been available: labour subsidies and employment creation schemes, training and work experience schemes, and mobility incentives.

Subsidy and employment creation schemes have very largely been central government-run national schemes aimed at tackling particular problems such as those of young workers, temporary short-time working, job release or job splitting. The fact that these problems have been most pronounced in urban, and particularly inner urban, areas has tended to concentrate the aid, but nothing specifically related to urban labour markets (or making allowance for problems arising from the openness of such labour markets) has been attempted. More recently, the experiment of the pilot Enterprise Allowance scheme and the development of the experimental Community Enterprise Programme into the Community Programme Scheme (with its emphasis on the creation of part-time employment and the encouragement to set up small businesses) have resulted in rather more concentrated aid for urban areas.

In addition, although comprehensive evidence is lacking, local authorities appear not to have used their powers under Section 137 of the Local Government Act (1972) to provide funds for specific labour subsidies to industry. There is in any case considerable confusion surrounding these powers which we shall look at in more detail in Section 7.4 below. Some authorities, which have used their powers more widely, have concentrated their aid into grants to Unemployed Workers' Centres and to Welfare Rights Campaigns aimed at educating the already unemployed.

Training and work experience schemes such as TOPS, those provided by the Industrial Training Boards, in-plant training schemes, and the Youth Opportunities Programme (now the Youth Training Scheme) are all national schemes. However, the close link with the Urban Programme and the reliance on local authorities to help in the selection and administration of such schemes does seem to have given local authorities greater power in the direction, if not the scope and size, of the schemes.

Mobility incentives, such as the job search scheme and employment transfer scheme (which pay potential migrants' expenses), tend to operate in an undirected and fairly arbitrary way. They are of little help in intra-urban situations and, like all mobility schemes, depend on the existence of job opportunities at some locations. Their value during a general recession is much more limited, and will tend to favour the more skilled workers.

In general, therefore, relatively little has been achieved in directing policy at the specific problems of local labour markets. The analysis of unemployment suggests that the pure job creation response to unemployment is in many areas of open labour markets a hopeless task, but, in contrast to the essentially capital and investment measures which we shall look at in Section 7.4, the policy response has been largely undifferentiated according to these specific problems.

7.3 Migration and Commuting

We have noted, both in the general analysis of spatial labour markets and in the discussion of the specific problem of unemployment, that openness in a local labour market is both one of the most critical determinants of its behaviour and response and one of the most difficult to analyse. In this section we aim to set out a fairly simple approach to the nature of this problem and to discuss the results and implications of some recent research.

Both migration and commuting are facets of the same basic problem (choice of workplace and place of residence) and to some extent can be thought of as reflecting, respectively, the long-term and short-term responses to a changing environment. The two principal issues to be faced in attempting to develop a satisfactory analytical approach are the range of influences on both location and movement decisions, and the appropriateness of assuming optimising behaviour and equilibrium in location decisions (Gordon and Vickerman 1982; Vickerman 1984).

The standard economic model for the treatment of migration, which is implicit in many of the treatments of intra-urban location (and hence commuting) decisions, was most clearly presented by Sjaastad (1962). It treated location choice as one aspect of the human capital investment decision. An individual monitors the stream of net benefits accruing in different locations and compares their present values with those perceived at the current location. If the difference in the present value of benefits between the new and the current location exceeds the costs associated with moving, then the individual is better off by moving. At the broader regional level the stream of benefits has essentially been seen as being determined by wages. Migration models in the neoclassical mould, where wage differentials determine migration, lead to a gradual convergence in wages across areas. Within regions it is difficult to find totally convincing evidence about even the pattern of wage differentials. As Table 7.2 shows, there is an Inner London premium for both manual and non-manual workers. The premium for the former is smaller but widening over time, that for the latter considerably larger but tending to narrow slightly, suggesting the differences in the spatial definitions of the labour markets and the locations of such jobs. However, these patterns could be the result of previous movement rather than its cause and, as we shall see when examining the reasons for people changing their residential location, job considerations do not figure largely as a triggering factor, although wage levels and income can prove to be a major constraint.

Table 7.2 Average Earnings for Full-Time Workers in London and the South-east, 1974 and 1982 (£ weekly)

	Males over 21		*Females over 18*	
	Manual	*Non-manual*	*Manual*	*Non-manual*
Greater London				
1974	45.9	63.2	26.1	33.6
1982	146.4	206.8	92.1	123.9
% change	+218.9	+227.2	+252.9	+268.7
Inner London				
1974	46.4	68.3	(25.9)	36.2
1982	149.8	227.1	(95.1)	129.6
% change	+222.8	+232.5	(+267.2)	+258.0
Outer London				
1974	45.9	57.7	–	31.3
1982	144.8	193.5	–	115.7
% change	+215.5	+221.6	–	+269.6
Rest of South-east				
1974	43.8	53.7	23.4	28.5
1982	133.4	178.3	80.2	104.4
% change	+204.6	+232.0	+242.7	+266.3
Inner London Premium (%) over rest of South-east:				
1974	5.9	27.2	(10.7)	27.0
1982	12.3	27.4	(18.6)	24.1
Over Outer London:				
1974	1.1	18.4	–	15.7
1982	3.4	17.4	–	12.0

Source: Department of Employment (1975, 1983) *New Earnings Surveys, 1974, 1982*.
Notes: a) Brackets = figures based on small sample
b) Dash = sample size is too small

A number of attempts have been made to develop and refine the basic model at an intra-urban level and have included more precise specifications of the benefit function. Quigley and Weinberg (1977) developed basic models of employment potential and housing and environmental preferences. Greenwood (1980) used cross-sectional comparisons to relate differential rates of growth to intra-metropolitan location decisions. Weinberg (1979) attempted to introduce commuting accessibility into the specification of the bundle of housing services and recognised the simultaneity of the process in which individuals adjust either residential location to their workplace, or vice versa, as a part of the process of optimising the level of consumption of housing services. Graves and Linneman (1979) attempted to specify the spatial aspects of factors other than employment and housing in the benefit function. On the labour market side Siegel (1975) and Simpson (1980) have attempted to use both industrial and socio-economic classifications to provide a more disaggregated workplace choice decision.

It has been noted (Vickerman 1984) that all these approaches run into problems because they attempt to estimate the behavioural process by observing locations (or changes in locations) as equilibrium states (or moves into equilibrium). A similar concern has been voiced by Linneman and Graves (1983) who note that certain moves may be characterised by changes in equilibrium variables in housing or job markets, whereas others represent adjustments in response to a disequilibrium situation. They still use the idea of moves as fully optimising the situation within a utility framework. Their model aims to estimate the probability of making each of a number of possible responses to such factors as: a change in housing within the same area, a change in the area of residence, a change in job location, or a change in both job and housing or job and area of residence. The model is estimated simultaneously by multinomial logit methods. Whilst it produces generally plausible results, the model includes only a limited range of the factors thought to influence such decisions and does not examine either the process of decision making or the possibility of the various adjustments being made sequentially as a part of a search pattern.

Such factors have been more fully investigated in Vickerman (1984) where the commuting response to the labour market model of Gordon and Lamont (1982) is developed within the framework outlined in Gordon and Vickerman (1982). The basic hypothesis advanced is that observed migration flows are the sum of three different types of household movement response: short distance moves for purely housing reasons (size, quality, etc.); middle distance moves for rather more general housing and environmental quality reasons; and typically longer distance moves motivated by employment factors (see Table 2.6 for some basic data on these for London). In all these the predominant factor influencing the probability of movement is identified as the actual supply of opportunities (housing development, employment growth, etc.) rather than the perceived relative prices which the net benefit approach tends to emphasise. This can also help to explain why similar factors can tend to produce high gross rates of both out-and in-migration in the same area, especially for job-related moves, since new jobs will attract the more mobile (who will also be more inclined to move again in future periods). This is particularly true in a metropolitan situation where younger single workers are attracted into central area jobs and then either move out again completely (e.g. at the end of a training period) or make decentralising moves in response to housing considerations as they move through the family life-cycle.

It is this need to link decisions in a sequential way which requires us also to examine commuting alongside migration and job change patterns. Evidence for London (Vickerman 1984) suggests that although net in-migration to an area reduces net in-commuting, this is by a less than proportional amount; but it appears that at least 30 per cent of in-migrants subsequently move their workplace into their new area of residence. However, if employment in an area expands relative to surrounding areas, about 75 per cent of the differential will be accounted for by changes in commuting patterns.

Factors relating to employment, including problems with journeys to work, do not figure largely in people's stated reasons for wishing to move (Table 7.3). Nevertheless, it appears that access to workplace is an important factor in the choice of a location once the decision to move has been taken although, as Table 7.4 shows, this does not necessarily mean that we observe any particular tendency by movers to reduce journey times to work. Much of this is associated with the decentralising of job opportunities which, although apparently bringing jobs closer to a decentralising population, does not typically improve the accessibility of specific jobs in terms of journey times. This generally poorer accessibility in peripheral areas is a major concern associated with decentralisation; it leads to a fragmentation of labour markets with corresponding difficulties of adjustment for workers (see Vickerman 1983, 1984 for fuller discussion).

Table 7.3 Residents' Reasons for Moving, by Direction of Movement (%)

Reason	*Into Inner London*	*Within Inner London*	*Inner to Outer London*	*London to O.M.A.*	*Other moves*	*Total*
New job	24 (6)	3 (3)	3 (3)	8 (8)	10 (7)	8 (6)
Travel to work problems	12 (12)	1 (1)	– (–)	3 (2)	4 (5)	4 (4)
House too small	18 (12)	28 (17)	15 (13)	29 (18)	25 (21)	25 (19)
House condition	–	17 (11)	4 (9)	– (2)	4 (5)	7 (7)
Health problems	–	14 (13)	9 (6)	3 (3)	4 (3)	7 (5)
Wanting better housing	12 (–)	33 (11)	42 (16)	32 (10)	32 (15)	32 (13)
Plans to buy	–	11 (4)	25 (15)	26 (24)	14 (9)	13 (8)
Housing opportunity	6 (6)	3 (1)	–	–	3 (3)	3 (2)
Eviction	–	11 (8)	2 (–)	–	4 (2)	5 (4)
Other forced move	6 (6)	10 (8)	12 (2)	3 (3)	5 (3)	7 (4)
Household fission	12 (12)	8 (1)	3 (–)	3 (3)	10 (5)	9 (4)
Marriage	17 (17)	1 (–)	–	–	4 (3)	4 (3)
Problems with neighbours	–	11 (10)	4 (2)	11 (5)	4 (4)	6 (5)
Wanting better area	24 (–)	17 (8)	42 (23)	50 (18)	21 (7)	22 (8)
Nearness to relatives	6 (6)	1 (–)	6 (6)	2 (2)	5 (3)	4 (3)
Retirement	6 (6)	1 (1)	–	2 (–)	1 (–)	1 (1)
Other reasons	24 (18)	4 (1)	4 (6)	2 (3)	7 (6)	7 (5)
All reasons	100	100	100	100	100	100

Source: Gordon *et al*. (1983)
Notes: a) O.M.A. = Outer Metropolitan Area
b) Figures in brackets = main reason, among several

Table 7.4 Changes in Travel Times to Work for People Moving both Place of Residence and Workplace (%)

Travel-to-work time after move	*Workplace Unchanged*			*Workplace Changed*				
	Central	*Non-central*	*All*	*From central*	*To central*	*From non-central*	*To non-central*	*All*
Greater	29	24	26	6	27	42	39	36
Same	59	51	54	94	32	28	40	39
Less	13	25	20	0	42	30	21	25
Total	100	100	100	100	100	100	100	100
% with journeys greater than 30 minutes								
Before move	52	26	36	84	38	26	41	41
After move	54	30	39	47	62	28	29	36

Source: Unpublished data from survey material in Gordon *et al*. (1983)

Policy towards Mobility

Much of the spatial change in patterns of residence and workplace which has occurred in all large cities has neither been planned nor understood. It involves a complex process of interaction which has invited the development of sophisticated models of urban development where job markets, housing markets and the transport and land use systems can all interact. The problem with these approaches has been their failure to cope with the essentially disequilibrium nature of the responses. Policy towards such relocation has also failed to comprehend this (Moore and Clark 1980; Quigley 1980; Weinberg 1980). The concern about congestion which we identified over transport has also dominated thinking about the location of households and employment in large cities. Concerted policies of decentralisation through the creation of New Towns and overspill estates in existing towns, the operation of Industrial Development Certificates as a control on industry and the Location of Offices Bureau as an encouragement to the tertiary sector to move out, have clearly all had a destabilising effect on the economies of the large conurbations, particularly London; this is now being felt.

We have noted the way in which various policies still operate to make it easier for new employment to be created in less central areas; and policies towards land release and tenure for new housing development have clearly made the peripheral areas more attractive and more likely to generate the right sort of housing opportunities for those in a position to consider an outward move. Housing policy at both a central and a local level has tended to encourage the trapping of certain groups in inner city areas and has resulted in excessive commuting costs for many of those encouraged to move out. The problem is essentially the failure to plan for a balanced economy at the local level. Too much emphasis seems to have been placed on the achievement of functional regional stability, rather than attempting to break down large metropolitan areas into more self-sufficient market areas with regard to labour, housing and transport. In other words, the problem with policy towards mobility is that it has looked too much towards making mobility easier (to compensate for the inadequacies of other policy measures) and not enough at the fundamental causes of the mobility desires themselves. If sufficient resources had ever been allocated to a pure mobility policy it might have succeeded. But as it is, the very biased and arbitrary way it has worked has only served to make the situation worse and to create new problems of a distributional kind because of the increasing homogeneity of areas. The suggestion here, therefore, is that mobility policy should, if anything, go into reverse as far as the directions of movement are concerned; but for that to succeed requires a fundamental rethink over employment and housing policies in large cities in order to create environmentally acceptable communities at a local level.

Another issue, relating also to the methodological basis of migration models, comes to the fore at the policy level. Most models of migration behaviour are based on extensions of individual preference models. However, it is clear that the residential location decision is one which affects all members of a household, especially in households which have more than one earner (Mincer 1978). It is clear that many households are constrained by this, either in their residential location decision or in the job choice decision of one (or more) members of the household. The availability of more balanced local labour and housing markets could help in this way, too.

7.4 Financing Urban Change

We have noted at several points that, at least in terms of the devotion of funds, aid to industry has been most heavily concentrated through the capital market. The infrastructure of provisions, as part of regional policy, has undergone many detailed changes over the years, including periods of apparent expansion—from 1967 to 1971—and periods of retrenchment—from 1979 onwards. Regional policy measures apply indiscriminately in any part of a designated region and, although attempts have been made to fine-tune the designation to suit specific local variations, this has rarely been successful at less than the sub-regional level. From relatively small and discretionary beginnings the last few years have, however, seen the attempted development of a more comprehensive urban policy, aimed principally at specifically selected urban areas (or parts of conurbations). Although similar types of policy measure have typically been used in this new urban policy, it is interesting to note that the triggering indicator has not been a simple economic one of unemployment, but has usually involved the appearance of much wider social problems. In the early years, urban policy did concentrate on projects involving essentially social or community development. As the problems of urban areas have become more serious, however, it has been recognised that unless the economic problems at the root of these are tackled, there can be no social or community development. Greater reliance has been placed on more traditional types of aid to industrial development, with a major distinction drawn between the Traditional Urban Programme of community projects and the Urban Development Programme aimed at industrial development. We shall contrast the origins of these policies, noting the way in which local initiative has generally been constrained and codified by central government, thus allowing relatively little scope for urban policy to be tailored to specific local needs.

Regional Policy Measures

The present structure of regional policy involves four types of instrument (a fifth, the Industrial Development Certificate, was suspended in 1981) and three broad types of area with different levels of assistance. The three main types of area are designated as

Special Development Areas (SDA), Development Areas (DA) and Intermediate Areas (IA). The latter have generally been regraded in status since July 1979. Most lost IA status, but some became Derelict Land Clearance Areas (DLCA), entitling them to some specific aid. The main policy instrument is still the Regional Development Grant, available at a rate of 15 per cent in DAs and 22 per cent in SDAs for schemes in manufacturing industry involving a minimum outlay. In addition, Regional Selective Assistance concentrates on aid to mining, construction and manufacturing (mainly in IAs), whilst the OSIS scheme for service industries operates in a similar way; both of these involve discretionary grants to firms to safeguard, maintain or expand jobs in an area. Finally, the only demand side measure is the very limited contracts preference scheme for favouring firms in assisted areas in the award of public sector contracts—a scheme which works effectively on a much larger scale in some other countries, for instance in France and Italy.

In addition to these general measures there is a wide range of selective assistance available for individual industries. These concentrate particularly on new industries such as microelectronics, on energy-saving schemes, on research and development activity and on projects in the national interest. There are also grants for derelict land clearance which run at 100 per cent in assisted areas and DLCAs, 75 per cent in National Parks and Areas of Outstanding Natural Beauty and 50 per cent in other areas.

Traditional Urban Programme Measures

Specifically urban policies of what is now known as the 'traditional' programme have developed parallel to the regional policy since 1968 although, until 1978, they concentrated almost entirely on social and cultural projects. Under the Local Government Grants (Social Need) Act, 1979, supplementary grants of up to 75 per cent were made available on approved projects costing up to £140,000 in capital allocation or £40,000 per annum current expenditure. Each local authority could apply for up to a maximum number of permissible projects: ten in 1980. From 1974 onwards, similar financial provision was made for more ambitious Comprehensive Community Programmes in designated areas of special need. From 1978/79 the traditional programme was extended to include environmental, transport and industrial projects.

At the same time, local authorities did have powers to initiate and finance schemes of their own. The Local Authority (Land) Act of 1963 made provision for the granting of mortgages and loans on buildings and land which could be used to aid industrial development in an area. The precise legal powers of local authorities to act in promoting economic development are, however, unspecific and uncodified and this has led to considerable confusion and conflict. Section 137 of the Local Government Act, 1972 gives a general power to all authorities to raise the product of a 2p rate locally to be used for 'local purposes'. What is not clear is whether such expenditure can include the granting of loans or guarantees to industry or, even further, the acquisition of shares in companies or the setting up of local Enterprise Boards, not only to take an equity share in existing firms, but also to promote new developments. Some authorities, notably those with the biggest problems, have taken a maximum involvement and have sought to confirm powers through Local Acts, whilst others have used their powers only to offer business advice centres and to advertise. Central Government has been reluctant to allow a general widening of powers; most of those granted have been so only for limited periods and expire at the end of 1984 at the latest. In February 1982 the Government announced that a more general power would be introduced, but this is not yet in force.

In addition to these broad powers, local authorities can exercise considerable influence through their planning and development control functions, especially through the way in which they are able to ease the path for local firms wishing to expand or to develop new sites (Young 1983). What is clear, however, is that many local authorities have been interested in developing joint schemes with private developers and industry to facilitate local economic development. As Boddy (1983) records, total expenditure on industrial estates and development by local authorities rose from £29 million in 1976/77 to £97 million in 1978/79, and whilst only 5 per cent of authorities had new factory units available in 1971, 57 per cent had built or were building new small units by 1978 and a further 24 per cent were considering doing so. These advance factories were often assisted by various schemes of leaseback and rent sharing to encourage their fuller use. Such policy does, of course, aim typically at smaller firms which may have difficulty in getting both advice and financial assistance from other sources. This type of policy, pursued both directly by councils and indirectly by local Enterprise Boards, has been attacked, notably by the GLC (*Sunday Times*, 28 August 1983), on the ground that small firms are less efficient than large and that job creation is both small scale and possibly short term. On the other hand, it could be argued that the promotion of direct links between an authority and local industry may make an area less vulnerable to random fluctuations in employment—especially where the council secures an equity stake in the enterprise.

The New Urban Programme

In the later 1970s it became clear that the traditional urban programme of central government, topped up by local authorities' essentially random efforts to promote economic development, was quite incapable of coping with the scale of problems manifesting themselves in the large conurbations (especially in their inner areas) and in many of the older industrial towns. Following a 1977 White Paper, 'Policy for the Inner Cities' (Department of the Environment 1977) which marked the turning point in treating urban problems as not just social problems which could be tackled on an *ad hoc* basis but as deep-rooted structural problems in the economy of the city, the Inner Urban Areas Act, 1978 became the basis of an attempt to create a new initiative in urban development. Under the Act designated districts could receive loans and grants for land acquisition and development and for projects involving common ownership or co-operative enterprise. In designated improvement areas there were also loans and grants for improving amenities and converting or improving buildings, based on the premise that jobs would be either saved or created.

The Act established a hierarchy of areas eligible for Urban Programme Grants (UPG) with slightly different statuses (Table 7.5). The most severe cases were designated Inner City Partnership Areas, of which there are seven. The 'Partnership' here was essentially one between central and one or more local government authorities (together with other local organisations) to form an advisory or steering group which would plan a programme of action eligible for 75 per cent grant aid. The ultimate aim was, however, that such money was to be essentially seedcorn investment to encourage a larger flow of private funds into the designated area. A

Table 7.5 Assisted Areas under the Urban Programme

Partnership Areas	*Programme Authority Areas*	*Designated Areas*	*Enterprise Zones*
Birmingham	*Initial list*	*Initial list*	*Initial list*
Hackney/Islington	Bolton	Barnsley	Clydebank (570 acres)
Lambeth	Bradford	Blackburn[1]	Corby (280 acres)
Liverpool	Hammersmith	Brent[1]	Dudley (540 acres)[2]
London Docklands	Hull	Doncaster	Hartlepool (270 acres)
Manchester/Salford	Leeds	Ealing	Isle of Dogs (360 acres)
Newcastle-upon-Tyne/ Gateshead	Leicester	Haringey	Newcastle/Gateshead (1,100 acres)
	Middlesbrough	Hartlepool	
	North Tyneside	Rochdale[1]	Salford/Trafford (870 acres)
	Nottingham	Rotherham	Speke (328 acres)[2]
	Oldham	St. Helens	Swansea (735 acres)
	Sheffield	Sandwell[1]	Wakefield (140 acres)[2]
	South Tyneside	Sefton	Belfast (510 acres)

Sunderland	Wandsworth[1]	*Second round*
Wirral	Wigan	Delyn & Milford Haven (350 acres)
Wolverhampton	Blaenau Gwent	Invergordon
1983 Additions	Cardiff	Londonderry
Blackburn	Newport	Middlesbrough (190 acres)
Brent	Rhondda	N.E. Lancashire (250 acres)[4]
Coventry	Swansea	N.W. Kent (310 acres)[3]
Knowsley	*1983 Additions*	Rotherham (260 acres)
Rochdale	Burnley	Scunthorpe & Glanford (359 acres)
Sandwell	Langbaurgh	Tayside (250 acres)[4]
Tower Hamlets		Telford (250 acres)
Wandsworth		Wellingborough (135 acres)
		West Cumbria (210 acres)

Notes: [1] = promoted to Programme Authority Areas, 1983
[2] = extended in 1983
[3] = over five separate sites
[4] = over seven separate sites

further fifteen areas were designated as Programme Authority Areas with similar terms of grant aiding, but without the special partnership arrangements to encourage schemes: each designated authority had to devise and submit its own programme for approval. This list of fifteen had a further eight areas added in 1983. A final group of nineteen Designated Districts of Special Social Needs was also created, with similar grant-aiding provisions, but essentially for smaller scale projects. Five of these areas were promoted to Programme Authority status in 1983 and two new areas were designated.

It is notable that, of these areas, four Partnership Areas, four of the original Programme Authorities and five of the Designated Districts were in regions which had never previously qualified for regional assistance except under DLCA provisions. Those areas which also qualified for normal regional assistance or for funds from the European Regional Development Fund (ERDF) had the basic 75 per cent grant applied after allowance for this other grant aid. Only marginal extra assistance was thus available to urban areas in DAs and SDAs, recognising again that many of the most severe problems were in urban areas in regions not qualifying for assisted area status. However, the total cost of admitted schemes, inclusive of any ERDF or regional assistance, was to count against the total allocation of UPG. UPG would, however, normally be used instead of grants available for environmental improvements under Housing Action Area or General Improvement Area schemes, capital grants available under TSG, Sports or Arts Council schemes, or grants to voluntary and community centre programmes, all of which are paid at lower rates than available under UPG. Hence a number of joint environmental improvement and transport schemes such as station improvement and refurbishing have been carried out by Partnership Areas in London.

The provisions of the Inner Urban Areas Act, 1978 were reinforced but revised to give central government rather greater control in the Local Government, Planning and Land Act, 1980. This has been the basis of the expansion of central government expenditure on redevelopment since 1980 (Table 7.6). Much greater emphasis has been placed, since the urban riots of July 1981, on the partnership provisions and on the need to use public money only as a catalyst to leverage private investment into areas to which it would otherwise not be ventured. Up to July 1983, ninety-nine

Table 7.6 Expenditure on Urban Programme 1978/79 to 1983/84 (£ million)

	1978–79	*1979–80*	*1980–81*	*1981–82*	*1982–83**	*1983–84**
Urban Programme Grants	49.5	100.0	84.9	104.0	115.0	140.0
Urban Development						
Corporations	–	–	–	37.5	63.5	66.6
London	–	–	–	31.0	39.6	40.5
Merseyside	–	–	–	6.1	23.9	26.1
Current allocation					3.7	9.9
Capital allocation					59.8	56.7

Source: *Supply Estimates* (1978/79 to 1983/84, published annually)
Note: * = Provisional

capital schemes had been authorised for UDG totalling £230 million of which only £45 million was public expenditure and the remaining £185 million private investment. Despite this, there is a great danger that the schemes will not generate a lasting increase in employment, especially the already noted concentration on environmental schemes. This ratio of 1:4 approaches the goal aimed for in an equivalent programme in the United States under the Urban Development Action Grant which has also been criticised for its concentration on prestige environmental or tertiary sector schemes like hotels. The 1980 Act went further, however, by introducing two additional types of special area: Urban Development Areas (UDA) and Enterprise Zones (EZ).

UDAs could be designated in Metropolitan districts or London boroughs and would place the designated areas under the control of Urban Development Corporations (UDC) with powers (modelled largely on those of New Town Corporations) rather wider than those of local authorities. UDCs can acquire and build on land, provide utilities, carry on businesses, etc. and are principally concerned with basic infrastructural provision to attract and consolidate private investment. They also cut across normal local authority land use and planning procedures, are part of the partnership in Partnership Areas, and can apply for Enterprise Zone status. The first two UDCs were established in decayed dockland areas of London and Liverpool and have already aroused considerable interest and controversy over proposals such as the docklands light rapid transit link in London, and the garden festival planned for Liverpool. The principal issue raised is that of the ability of the UDCs to cut through the normal planning and financial constraints which bind local authorities, even those with most favoured status under the urban programme. Whilst this may be good for the two areas mentioned above, it may be less good for urban development generally. We have already noted the way in which development gets dissipated over a wider area in metropolitan areas, and it is certainly not good for local democracy.

Enterprise Zones

If UDCs have been controversial, this is nothing to the amount of criticism which has surrounded Enterprise Zones (see Hall 1982; Harrison 1982; Massey 1982). The creation of EZs was the realisation of a Conservative election pledge in the 1979 election to create zones free from the normal constraints of both legislation and taxation. Rather as the old 1967 idea of Regional Employment Premium had attempted to effect a devaluation through reduced labour costs for lagging regions, so the notion of the EZ was to create, for a ten-year period, similar reductions in capital and administrative costs, but here in a situation rather reminiscent of tax-exempt freeports. The basic provisions for EZs under the 1980 Act were: exemption from local rates on industrial and commercial properties; a much simplified planning procedure to speed up development (in effect, planning permission for permissible activities was deemed given within a designated area); exemption from industrial training levies; and reduced government demands for information. In addition, the 1980 Budget introduced two further measures: exemption from Development Land Tax and 100 per cent capital allowances to offset against income and corporation tax. All of these concessions were to apply to both existing and new firms within the EZ. Local authorities were also empowered to apply for urban development grants for use within an Enterprise Zone.

The procedure for designation was that the Secretary of State would invite applications from local authorities for clearly defined areas—essentially ones available for easy development or redevelopment. A decision would be taken as to the appropriate number and total size of EZs to be allowed and, following acceptance in principle, schemes would be prepared, necessary agreements drawn up to define boundaries, and any necessary rezoning undertaken before final designation which would give effect to the terms of the two Acts. In the first round of eleven designations (see Table 7.5) the zones concerned, although being fairly small and not necessarily single contiguous areas, were nevertheless quite varied in land use terms. It was originally intended to monitor the performance of these 1981-designated areas before taking a further decision, but in 1982 a further group of twelve areas was designated out of a total of fifty-three applications. In the second round, smaller tracts (consisting only of immediately developable land) were requested and the difference in size of these is noted in Table 7.5. This change was mainly effected to reduce the burden of the cost of compensating local authorities for rate loss on existing occupied sites within the zones which had amounted to some £5 million in the first year for the first-round sites. The estimated first-year cost for the second-round zones was about £1 million. To achieve this, however, many of the zones had to be highly fragmented: one had five separate sites and two had as many as seven separate sites spread over quite a large area. This has meant the inclusion of some of the new zones in more than one local authority area. The new North-east Lancashire Enterprise Zone has 250 acres spread over seven sites in four different local authority areas.

The second round was also interesting in that it included three areas which came from outside the traditional industrial urban centres or regional assisted areas: Telford (a new town in the West Midlands); Wellingborough (a small town in the relatively prosperous East Midlands which had experienced considerable job loss because a major local employer vacated a major developable site, but which was close to a first-round EZ at Corby); and North-west Kent (the first area in the South-east outside London to receive any special assistance, related here particularly to the consequences of the closing of the Chatham Naval Dockyard).

The EZ concept has certainly aroused considerable interest, as has a similar scheme in the United States (see Butler 1981). There has also been criticism. The main issue has been the extent to which highly specific and localised benefits will upset the balance of the urban economy as a whole. This is a difficult issue to assess and it is too early to draw any conclusions about experience in either the United Kingdom or the United States. Simply in terms of numbers of businesses and jobs attracted, the British EZs have had very varied experiences. Some, such as Swansea and Clydebank, have had major inflows of both; others, such as Wakefield (initially a very small EZ), have had very little interest shown. Even within an EZ there are contrasts: in the largest one on Tyneside there is a marked difference between the successful regeneration of the Team Valley Trading Estate in Gateshead and the very poor response to derelict areas in Newcastle-upon-Tyne (*Financial Times*, 18 October 1983).

Businesses just outside the designated areas certainly feel aggrieved at the denial of direct benefits to them. But to the extent that most of the designated areas were actually vacant and derelict, the external effects spilling over their boundaries may be more beneficial than otherwise to them. Restrictions on environmentally harmful activities and on retail developments in the EZ should ensure that the environment is improved and that established urban commercial centres are not threatened.

Beyond this, the EZ concept is an act of faith. Traditional aids to industry have not, over a long period, had much lasting effect on either the distribution of industry and employment or, more significantly, on the long-term fortunes of particular regions—if anything, they have actually harmed the non-assisted areas. The cost per job created has been high although, in the more concentrated periods of regional policy (such as 1967–73), the net cost probably became a net benefit. It is argued by some that the rates exemption is the major incentive in an EZ since this will be particularly significant to the small firm which typically benefits little from traditional capital incentives (Botham and Lloyd 1983). The advantage of the EZ, at least as demonstrated by the degree of interest from firms and the competition from local authorities, is that its highly localised status generates much greater, and more focussed local concern than traditional types of assisted area (even under the urban programme). If EZs are a success, it will be as much due to the stimulus they have given to local pride in providing a competitive thrust for new development as to the real value of the incentives offered. What they do not promise is to do anything long-lasting about the structure or distribution of unemployment between urban areas. The total costs of the EZ scheme are difficult to estimate since they depend on the degree of take-up, and on the extent to which new jobs are created rather than existing ones transferred. The cost of the rate remissions is estimated to be of the order of £60 million over ten years and the total cost (including tax relief) anything from £100 million to £200 million or more. This is, however, still small on an annual basis in comparison with the costs of the traditional regional programme or the urban programme as a whole; and these are themselves modest in comparison with total government expenditure.

Local Authority Measures

It can be argued that the urban programme as a whole is another example of the increasing standardisation and centralisation of planning and development functions. Local authority money, under Section 137 of the 1972 Act, may have frequently been replaced by UPGs or other provisions rather than the latter involving new money. On the other hand, there has been considerable criticism of some authorities for squandering money received towards the running of partnership or programme schemes on what are seen as politically-motivated local newspapers and on anti-government propaganda.

It is extremely difficult to get a full picture of total local authority expenditure in this area and we must rely for a lot of information on local studies, such as those reported in Young and Mason (1983). Industrial development expenditure is classified under the Town and Country Planning function of local authorities and trends in this since 1978/79 are detailed in Table 7.7. It is clear that even over this time the rise of alternative aid for capital projects has reduced the capital expenditure on industrial development from over 30 per cent of the capital budget to just 12 per cent, whilst current expenditure has grown slightly from less than 6 per cent to over 7 per cent. Expenditure per head on all development and promotional activity is at a fairly low level (Table 7.8). The highest, in absolute terms, is in the Inner London Boroughs and Metropolitan Districts and, in proportional terms, in some of the Metropolitan Counties which have fewer day-to-day responsibilities.

However, there do appear to be enormous inter-authority variations, with the highest-spending metropolitan authorities such as Camden (£5.48 per head), Barking (£3.40 per head) and Bradford (£3.81 per head) contrasting with Westminster, Waltham Forest and Stockport, all of which had marginally negative net expenditure on this function. Some of the highest per capita expenditures were in non-metropolitan districts, however, including authorities such as Thamesdown and Easington on the one hand (with commitments to industrial development) and Canterbury and Exeter on the other (where general promotional expenditure, particularly on tourism, was high).

Generally, our conclusion must be that direct expenditure by local authorities has been very small and has clearly been squeezed both by the arrival of new money in the form of the urban programme and by government attempts to control total expenditure. We shall look at this problem in the following chapter.

7.5 Distributional Issues in Urban Economies

We have noted at various points how the operation of various urban

Table 7.7 Local Authority Expenditure on Town and Country Planning Functions, 1978/79 to 1981/82 (£ thousands)

	1978–79		*1979–80*		*1980–81*		*1981–82*	
	Revenue	*Capital*	*Revenue*	*Capital*	*Revenue*	*Capital*	*Revenue*	*Capital*
Control of land use	129,346	4,606	147,672	4,907	173,595	11,594	167,430	5,523
Planning implementation	71,494	81,142	98,789	134,855	117,064	147,443	114,653	122,717
Advances to industry	697	5,159	3,472	9,289	5,747	11,190	9,242	8,583
Industrial development	14,911	41,465	16,536	29,088	19,146	22,118	25,104	18,871
Building regulations	37,150	20	49,919	119	48,043	38	40,534	35
Total	253,598	132,392	316,388	178,258	363,595	192,383	356,963	155,729

Source: Department of the Environment, *Local Authority Finance and Expenditure*, published annually.

Table 7.8 Per Capita Expenditures on Planning Functions, 1981/82 (£s)

	Development and promotion	*Other planning functions*	*Total*
Greater London Council	0.49	0.73	1.22
Inner London Boroughs	2.22	6.27	8.49
Outer London Boroughs	0.58	3.58	4.16
Metropolitan Counties	0.55	1.11	1.66
Greater Manchester	0.34	1.12	1.46
Merseyside	1.09	1.27	2.36
South Yorkshire	0.87	1.60	2.47
Tyne and Wear	1.44	1.27	2.71
West Midlands	0.11	0.82	0.93
West Yorkshire	0.28	0.94	1.22
Metropolitan Districts	1.38	3.06	4.42
Non-Metropolitan Counties	0.24	1.40	1.64
Non-Metropolitan Districts	0.80	3.06	3.86

Source: *Local Authority Comparative Statistics* (CIPFA), published annually.

markets leads to important distributional consequences. In transport, both congestion and pricing policies have differential impacts on different groups in the population. In housing, the effects of policy may both favour the better-off in terms of the subsidy paid and lead to problems for the poor by forcing them to consume higher quantities of housing for environmental reasons without adequate compensation. In this chapter we have explored the way the labour market may discriminate against certain skill groups and the way in which both labour and housing markets combine to prevent the spatial adjustments which could overcome such imbalances.

All of these issues relate to aspects of the personal distribution of income, which is itself related to what is normally called the functional distribution: essentially, the way in which the product of economic activity divides between the different factors of production. Typically, economists concentrate on the way in which labour and capital inputs to the production process compete for their shares of the product. As we have seen throughout the discussion of the structure of the urban economy, there is a need to take specific account also of the land input. There is considerable evidence that land availability has been a major constraint on development (whether industrial, commercial or residential) and that much of the profitability of urban activity gets diverted into rent payments because of the spatial immobility of the land input. There is, of course, also some evidence that the benefit of such increased rent accrues more to developers than to original landowners.

From a policy standpoint this fact has been widely recognised and has led to the use of taxes on development gains, although there is increasing evidence that these are potentially not neutral in their incidence and may actually worsen the supply-price problem (Evans 1983; and see the detailed discussion in Chapter 3 above). An alternative prescription could be the public ownership of land. There have been general moves in this direction at certain times, such as the Community Land Act of 1975; and in some cities municipal ownership of land has been quite widespread, stimulated by the need to promote general area development and improvement schemes. Whilst this can provide a mechanism for a local authority to promote development in some instances (Boddy 1983), there is no evidence that even local authorities owning a high proportion of developable land have succeeded in promoting greater efficiency overall in the land market. Indeed, the insistence of some local authorities that their land should only be used for public housing schemes or mixed public–private residential developments may have inhibited the kind of balanced local economies advocated in Section 7.3 of this chapter by creating a shortage of owner-occupied housing of particular types, to the detriment of all groups.

This type of problem is particularly pronounced in terms of inter-urban or inter-authority comparison. In some instances, the development of residential land for owner occupation has been pushed over a boundary into a neighbouring authority's area. Where this is a city pushing development into a suburban or semi-rural area the effect is distorting: the typically low-cost receiving area gains substantial additional rate income, whilst the typically high-cost city receives no income. It still incurs much the same range of costs as before, since the activity center for the residents will remain within the city, and will require much the same infrastructure as if the development had taken place within the city. As we shall see in the following chapter, this has a cumulative twist: the tax rate (rate poundage) in the suburban area can be reduced to produce the same revenue from a larger tax base (rateable value), whilst in the city area the reverse happens. Policy has typically only developed in an attempt to ameliorate the effects of this condition by means of inter-governmental transfers, but has not made any progress towards a means of correcting the imbalances. Even where 'regional' authorities such as Metropolitan Counties have existed they have typically had too little power at the practical (rather than strategic) level to effect any real redistribution. Attempts to go further than exhortation have resulted in inter-authority legal battles of which that over the GLCs 'Fares Fair' scheme is only one example.

Rather more interest has focussed on the inequalities in the personal distribution of income both within and between urban areas. This is associated with two closely related points: the existence of poverty, particularly within inner areas of large cities, and the cumulative concentration of that poverty into what could be termed a ghetto effect.

Poverty is a difficult concept to handle since it involves both absolute and relative effects. In most British cities poverty has essentially been a relative phenomenon: the juxtaposition of people without employment, living in low quality accommodation, next to high concentrations of commercial wealth. In recent years the general downturn in economic activity has pushed a rather higher number of people across the boundary into a state of absolute poverty, where they are unable to maintain a basic existence. Of course, in the presence of a welfare state system of benefits, it becomes an important issue as to whether poverty, relative or absolute, should more accurately be measured including or excluding such benefits.

A more useful approach in trying to measure the incidence of poverty has been to separate various indicators of deprivation and then to categorise individuals according to these, both separately and jointly, in terms of multiple deprivation. The main indicators used relate to unemployment and housing conditions, especially overcrowding and lack of basic amenities. In the most comprehensive analysis of the 1971 Census data, Holterman (1975) has shown how concentrated multiple deprivation is in the conurbations. Using data for Enumeration Districts (EDS) and three indicators (male unemployment; households with more than 1.5 persons per room; and a lack of the exclusive use of all basic amenities) she showed that, although accounting for just 42.9 per cent of EDs, seven conurbations in Britain (excluding South Yorkshire) included 73.2 per cent of the worst 15 per cent of EDs on all three counts. The most deprivation was clearly in Clydeside (with only 4.3 per cent of EDs but 26.6 per cent of the worst deprivation counts) followed by Inner London (with 8.6 per cent of EDs but 18.1 per cent of multiply deprived EDs). In contrast, Outer London had 10.4 per cent of EDs but only 1.4 per cent of the worst cases of deprivation, and the rest of the South-east 14.9 per cent of EDs but only 2.9 per cent of such cases.

It was this concentration of multiple deprivation which led to the setting up of the various Inner Area Studies in the mid-1970s which looked at the social relationships present in a sample of deprived Inner Areas and whose findings were important contributions to the 1977 White Paper on Policy for the Inner Cities. However, documenting the incidence of deprivation and identifying the areas of greatest need does not constitute either an explanation of that concentration or a prescription for policy to overcome it.

One of the major problems is the circular and cumulative causation identified in the discussion of unemployment in this chapter and noted already in the discussion of urban decay in Chapter 4. There is a critical difference between there being concentrations of deprived people in certain areas and people in certain areas being discriminated against as compared with similar people in other locations. In terms of unemployment the critical factors are age, skill and marital status and these seem to lead to similar propensities to be unemployed, regardless of area. However, the recent scale of unemployment has affected two further dimensions of unemployment which may have cumulative effects and which may not be so spatially neutral. The duration of unemployment has come to be regarded as an issue of increasing concern since, at high rates of unemployment, it is not a question of a constant rate of unemployment being associated with a turnover of those actually unemployed but with the growth of a hard-core stock of unemployed people. The length of time spent unemployed has a significant negative influence on the probability of getting re-employed. Secondly, as a result of this, there is developing an increasingly large group of young people who have never been in employment and of increasingly younger mature workers whose chances of re-employment are getting scarcer. There are spatial associations with both of these relating to the market for information which may in the future remove the apparent spatial neutrality of unemployment incidence observed to date.

In the housing market, tenure is one of the critical determinants of deprivation in that high incidences of overcrowding and the lack of amenities have been particularly associated with the private rental sector which has been subject to the process of cumulative degradation discussed in Chapter 4. This is not a sufficient explanation, however, in that it fails to explain why such families are in this sector in the first place. We need to ask questions about access to tenures in which certain groups (principally those who have a high propensity to be unemployed) fail to secure access, not just to owner occupation, but also to the public rental sector by virtue of the points systems which usually determine priorities for the allocation of council housing. There is, in addition, evidence that in carrying out obligations to provide housing for those in need (those who fail to gain access to the private rental sector) local authorities apply discriminatory allocation policies which concentrate problem families on particular estates. This is well documented in studies based in Clydeside (McGregor 1977); and it emerged in a study of migration in London (Gordon *et al.* 1983) where over ten per cent of those actually moving within Inner London (and a higher proportion of those who had failed to move) cited problems with neighbours as a reason for wanting to move. More detailed analysis of responses (talk of wanting to live in a better area) also suggested that this was a very localised concept, relating to the image of the area and the implied image of its residents.

Such evidence is consistent with the ghetto effect which is much more prominent in North American literature on urban problems (Segal 1979). There is a close association of race with the indices of multiple deprivation. Studies of urban unemployment in Britain typically tended to find that unemployment was actually negatively correlated with immigration, but such studies related largely to periods of both lower aggregate unemployment and higher flows of new immigrants who were definitionally more mobile. More recent evidence does suggest that in a more static environment there is a significant positive correlation between race and unemployment (especially in the younger groups). The research on migration in London also found evidence of a significant polarising effect in that, although often disguised, the presence of immigrant groups in an area led to an outflow of traditional residents and an inflow of similar racial groups. This was a further hindrance to the development of well-balanced local economies.

All these issues go right to the heart of the basic economic problems of the urban economy. Most of them are insoluble at a local level since the distributional imbalance is just as much an inter-urban as an intra-urban one. There is insufficient space here to discuss in detail the ways in which policy may be developed to tackle these problems (Cameron 1980a, Chapter 9 gives a good summary of the issues), but such policies do typically concentrate only on the symptoms and rarely attack the essential causes. The lot of the urban poor could be vastly improved by adequate redistributive measures. The urban poor will remain, however, and may well increase in number if they fail to gain access to new opportunities in any upturn in economic activity. In a curious way the cycle of urban development appears to have come full circle, in that both the early and late stages of the urbanisation process are characterised by a large number of urban dwellers in conditions of poverty and deprivation.

Further Reading

Generally, the theoretical discussion of spatial factor markets is rather poor. There is a wealth of evidence about trends and attempted explanations of patterns of unemployment, e.g. Foster and Richardson (1973); Metcalf and Richardson (1976); Corkindale (1980); Evans (1980). For attempts to define labour market areas, see Hall *et al.* (1973); Smart (1974); Ball (1980) and Coombes and Openshaw (1982). Specific studies of unemployment have been discussed in this chapter: useful reviews are contained in Cheshire (1979) and Evans and Richardson (1981). More general analyses can be found in Massey and Meegan (1982) and in the periodic urban and regional assessments of the Cambridge Economic Policy Group (1980, 1982); see also Martin (1982).

Early studies of intra-urban migration are usefully reviewed by Quigley and Weinberg (1977) and a fascinating development of the basic analytical approach is given by David (1974). The volume edited by Moore and Clark (1980) and the earlier one by Brown and Neuberger (1977) contain useful papers extending the present discussion. One important dimension we have only touched on briefly here is the problem occasioned by households with more than one income earner. In addition to the basic analysis by Mincer (1978), see also White (1977), Madden (1980, 1981) and Curran *et al*. (1982).

Whilst there have been many studies of industrial aid at the regional and national levels, the low level of support and the recent change of emphasis towards urban projects means that very few studies are available of urban industrial development *per se*. The best source for an inside view is the volume edited by Young and Mason (1983) which includes both reviews of policy in general and the specific application of certain policies by individual authorities.

8
Local Public Finance

A few years ago the question of urban public finance would not have needed to assume such a central position in our discussion of the urban economy as it must today. We would have been concerned with the general problem of public expenditure analysis and with the difficulty of defining optimal levels of provision in the absence of a market, and also with the variations in the optimal size of an authority implicit in the cost of providing typical urban services. On the revenue side we should have needed to point out the tendency for local governments to rely on property taxation for the bulk of their tax revenue and the problems associated with the specific form of property taxation used in Britain: the rates. We would have pointed out the desirability of some form of redistribution between local authorities in order to deal with problems brought about by various imbalances such as the need to provide certain levels of services on the one hand and the low level of resources available through the mechanism of central government transfers on the other.

The mid-1970s heralded a change. The whole issue of urban public finance became the subject of much wider concern and debate on a political level. In this chapter we shall explore the reasons for this changing role and provide an analysis of the principal issues affecting urban fiscal policy and the principal mechanisms by which policy is implemented. We begin, however, with a more basic discussion of the nature of local public expenditure and revenue.

8.1 Public Expenditure and Revenue

In Chapter 5 we encountered the main arguments for the existence of a local public sector and noted how over time the relative importance of municipal involvement in certain activities declined whilst it increased in others (Table 5.1). In recent years (Table 8.1) local authority expenditure has been dominated by two basic sectors—education and housing—which together account for about 60 per cent of all local authority expenditure.

Expenditure Problems

Although there are clearly differences between local authorities' expenditure levels and varying needs and choices, for any one authority a large proportion of its main items of expenditure is effectively allocated elsewhere. A very high proportion of educational expenditure is accounted for by wages which are determined nationally so that local authorities can only take decisions relating to staffing levels. Similarly, two-thirds of housing expenditure is accounted for by debt charges relating to previous investment decisions and, whilst net expenditure on housing can be influenced by the setting of rent levels, the freedom of manoeuvre of the individual authority is again very limited.

Whilst it is true that education, housing and public transport services are provided in competition with private suppliers, this can be misleading: the publicly provided service is sold in a different market to different people who would otherwise go without. The other urban public services approach more closely the notion of the pure public good for which there is no market test of the 'right' level of provision except that given by the Tiebout-type hypothesis discussed in Chapter 5. In such circumstances, local providers tend to base levels of provision on the application of standards relating to perceived levels of need in the local community. Such standards are typically defined at a national level and can cover such things as the provision of playgrounds and sports fields (on a *per capita* basis) within a certain accessibility range; design parameters for urban roads in terms of average speeds and acceptable delays; and levels of provision of social service personnel *per capita*. These are not necessarily requirements, or even norms, but they almost tend to acquire such a status, especially since, as we shall see, they tend to

Table 8.1 Local Authority Summary Financial Accounts, 1982/83

	(£ *million*)	(%)
Current Account		
Receipts		
Current grants	16,005	47
Rates	12,263	36
Gross Trading Surplus	248	1
Rents	3,218	9
Dividends and interest	812	2
Consumption of non-trading capital	1,419	4
Total	33,965	100
Expenditure		
Education direct expenditure	11,318	33
Other direct expenditure	12,797	38
Subsidies	1,241	4
Grants	1,462	4
Interest	4,218	12
Total current consumption	31,036	91
Surplus	2,929	9
Total	33,965	100
Capital Account		
Receipts		
Current surplus	2,929	88
Capital grants	350	11
Other	44	1
Total	3,323	100
Expenditure		
Fixed capital formation	2,457	74
Transfers to personal sector	509	15
Transfers to public corporations	161	5
Total capital expenditure	3,127	94
Financial surplus	196	6
Total	3,323	100

Source: *Financial Statistics*, Sept. 1983 (HMSO)

be used in assessing expected levels of expenditure for central government grant-aiding purposes.

Whether or not there is any market legitimacy in the level of provision of a given service, there is a further problem (especially in services without user charges) of whether the level of provision is measured by means of outputs or inputs. This applies to a differing extent in many areas of activity, but is particularly pronounced in services such as education, leisure and the personal social services where output is essentially intangible and where a distinction can often be drawn between intermediate and final outputs. Take, for example, the provision of a sports centre or an old people's home. In both cases the final output can only be assessed in terms of the welfare of the participant or the inmate. This is unlikely to be the measure of performance used by either the management or the relevant committee of the responsible council. Output to them is more likely to be measured in terms of throughput and as directly related to the even more easily measured indicator of inputs. Hence performance in the sector is measured by staffing levels and/or total expenditure and changes in productivity are ignored. Even in sectors such as transport (where it is easier to measure output in that it is at least sold) we have already seen in Chapter 6 that input-biased measures such as passenger-kilometres carried are used as targets. It is this confusion of expenditure with output which leads to the type of inefficiency often associated with subsidies (Pucher *et al.* 1983) and particularly with the structure of the bureaucracy where status is measured by the size of the budget administered (see the discussion in Chapter 5).

We shall now turn from these general considerations to the more specific problems of individual authorities. Differences between authorities in *per capita* expenditure will result from both variations in expenditure needs and variations in the cost of provision of a unit of service. These have long been recognised as potential sources of inequity between authorities, and successive schemes for inter-governmental corrective transfers via the Rate Support Grant have attempted to make allowance for this, as we shall see in more detail in Section 8.2. Variations in needs are usually related to specific indicators for an authority's area ranging from numbers of old people and children of specific ages to population density and kilometres of motorway. The present system of Grant Related

Expenditures (GRE) details some sixty-eight indicators grouped into six main blocks. The next step is to associate with each indicator a standard cost of provision, on the assumption that this would be the average cost per unit for a neutral or average authority. The variations in cost between certain classes of authority (mainly between geographical areas) are accounted for by having separate unit cost figures for London (inner and outer), Metropolitan Counties, and English and Welsh Shire Counties (a somewhat different system operates in Scotland). By charging an authority's score on each indicator with the appropriate cost figure, an aggregate GRE for each authority can be derived which represents the cost of providing a standard level of provision in that authority and recognises its particular needs. Table 8.2 illustrates the variations in GRE between authorities in 1983/84, together with other indicators.

If an authority's actual expenditure differs from GRE, this is a reflection of its decision to provide a different level of service (exercising the right of independent choice) or of its inability to provide the service at the presumed unit cost. It does not necessarily mean that the authority is being profligate with public money. It can also mean that the indicators have failed to keep pace with expenditure-related changes within the authority's area. For example, a rapid growth in population, especially where in-moving families have a high proportion of school-age children, may leave the estimated GRE severely underestimating actual expenditure needs.

Whilst GRE is a useful analytical yardstick, there is a danger not only that it may be used as a means of penalising authorities which are seen to be overspending in relation to it (as we shall see in Section 8.2), but also that authorities exercising the opposite choice of spending less than the GRE (or spending, for example, less on a particular service block than the GRE estimate for that block) are open to the charge of neglecting key sections of the community. What this demonstrates is that purely analytical yardsticks or assessments for the basis of grant distribution can rapidly become not just norms but virtually fixed targets removing any local freedom. But before we tackle this issue more fully we need to look at the other side of the local authority accounts—its revenues.

Table 8.2 Variations in Resource, Rates and Expenditure per capita, 1983/84

	Rateable value (April 82) (£)	*Average domestic rate* (*p*)	*Average domestic rate bill* (£)	*Block Grant* (£)	*Grant Related Expenditure* (£)	*Anticipated actual spending* (£)
London						
Inner Boroughs[1]	491.34[2]	171.86	520.08	155[3]	633	1054
Outer Boroughs	186.84	148.21	405.92	189	482	660
Metropolitan areas	126.42	173.58	287.05	227	429	539
Non-metropolitan areas	134.25	139.76	271.06	158	322	423
England	155.32	150.29	301.69	178	411	507

Source: CIPFA, *Finance and General Statistics, 1983/84*

Notes: [1]includes City of London—see notes 2 and 3; otherwise effect is insignificant.
[2]average excluding City is £383.76
[3]average excluding City is £174

Revenue Problems

Local authority revenue comes from three principal sources: local taxation, grants from central government and borrowing. In addition, local authorities' gross expenditure in certain sectors is financed to a greater or lesser extent out of user charges, council house rents, bus fares, admission charges, etc. Our interest here will concentrate on the authority's own tax revenues and we shall defer a discussion of grant income until Section 8.2.

As is clear from Table 8.3, there was a long-term decline in the importance of local tax revenue from rates until the mid-1970s. The reversal of this trend in recent years has in some respects been an artificial one for a number of reasons. First, there was a slow-down in the growth of the local public sector, relative both to public expenditure as a whole and to GNP. Local government expenditure, expressed as a percentage of public expenditure and of GNP at market prices, peaked at about 30 per cent and 13 per cent respectively in the early 1970s and has since shrunk slightly to roughly 25 per cent and 10 per cent respectively. Secondly, although the grant income of authorities continued to rise, albeit at lower rates than hitherto, the ability to borrow became severely limited. Three factors influenced this: one was the downturn in capital activity (as Table 8.3 shows) for which most borrowing was undertaken; the second was the attempt to reduce public sector borrowing in total, coupled with a policy of high interest rates; the third was the danger that local authorities, in trying to avoid these constraints, could themselves run into borrowing difficulties because of their gearing (the relationship between their debt and their assets). Futhermore, the central government imposed a system of grant allocation which not only fixed maximum levels of grant aid relative to expenditure targetted initially in terms of GRE, but later in terms of annual growth as well. It also imposed grant penalties on those authorities going over an expenditure threshold 10 per cent in excess of national GRE *per capita*. Hence some authorities had to rely exclusively on their own revenue-raising to finance expenditure at the desired level.

Let us now look in rather more detail at local authorities' revenue-raising potential through taxation, and specifically at problems associated with rates as a means of taxation. That local authorities need to rely on some form of land or property tax as a

Table 8.3 Trends in Local Authority Expenditure and Finance (%)

	1960	*1970*	*1975*	*1979*	*1980*	*1981*
Expenditure						
Current direct expenditure	66	58	63	70	73	79
Grants and subsidies	7	5	6	8	9	9
Capital formation	31	32	28	18	16	11
Interest net of receipts	−4	5	3	2	2	1
Total expenditure	100	100	100	100	100	100
Finance						
Rates	40	33	27	32	33	39
Current grants from central government	41	44	53	57	55	59
Other, including net borrowing	19	22	19	11	12	2
Total receipts	100	100	100	100	100	100
Local government expenditure as % of:						
Public expenditure	23.7	31.4	29.4	27.3	27.2	25.7
GNP at market prices	7.5	11.2	13.1	10.5	10.9	10.5

Sources: *National Income & Expenditure; Financial Statistics*, published annually.

source of tax revenue is fairly general in many countries. In the United States, for example, some 85 per cent of local tax revenue comes from property tax. However, this is not universal and some countries have a much greater proportion of local revenue coming from income and business taxes. In West Germany, for example, 14 per cent of income tax revenue and 60 per cent of business tax revenue go to local authorities and in 1978 this constituted in total 76.8 per cent of all local tax revenues. Real estate tax provided only

12.3 per cent (Advisory Commission on Intergovernmental Relations 1981).

The arguments for local authorities having a separate source of tax income can be found in the basic theory of taxation. There is a general presumption that different levels of authority do not share a single tax base because of their potential clash of interests. Local authorities are not particularly interested in their taxes being used for stabilisation purposes but if on the other hand they remain free to fix their own rate of, say, local income tax, this may undermine the central government's direct interests. Also, local authority expenditure is less likely to display strong cyclical effects and it is desirable to have a tax base which is more stable over time. These objections carry much less weight than formerly. Central government has been forced to use measures to control local authority spending and even to control freedom in setting tax rates. Furthermore, local authorities have been disadvantaged by having a tax base which fails to change sufficiently quickly over time to reflect changing local circumstances and which is particularly insensitive to changes in a period of inflation.

A further objection to the use of income or sales tax for local purposes (under a system where the local authority sets a tax rate which is added on to a national rate) is that the typical rate would be relatively small and potential changes in that rate would be relatively large. For example, for a local sales tax to replace rates with the same tax yield, the required tax rate was estimated to be 7 per cent; and for local income tax the required rate was 5p in the pound (Cmnd. 8449). Since normal rate changes in these would be likely to involve 1 per cent, or 1p steps, revenue would potentially change by up to 20 per cent for any marginal tax rate change, requiring a complex equalisation account. However, in other systems, such as West Germany's, this is overcome by hypothecating an agreed proportion of total tax revenues thus to enable the local authority sector to finance the bulk of expenditure. Local variations and adjustments can be made via the more finely adjustable locally controlled property tax. This does suggest that it may be very difficult to get away from a tax like rates at a stroke and that a mixed system of revenues may be more appropriate.

Rates

Property taxes can be levied in a number of different ways. The system used in Britain is to set a rate poundage (the tax rate) which is applied to the rateable value of each property (the tax base). Rateable values are based on the gross annual rental value of the property—a figure which is determined by periodic revaluations. The last general revaluation in England and Wales was in 1973. The tax liability of the occupier of property can be reduced by two factors relating to the type of occupation and the economic circumstances of the household. Domestic rate relief is an exchequer grant to local authorities in respect of each property classed as in domestic occupation. It is paid as a flat rate reduction (for a particular type of authority) on the rate poundage charged. Relief to lower-income households from the burden of rate payments comes in the form of rate rebates, paid on a sliding scale according to circumstances and borne principally by direct exchequer grants—only 10 per cent of rate rebates are met out of the rate fund. In addition, rates can be included in housing costs for supplementary benefit claimants. The total cost of these reliefs amounted to around £1,500 million in 1981/82, half of which was domestic rate relief and the rest due in roughly equal proportions to rate rebates and supplementary benefits. This cost amounts to just over 5 per cent of local authorities' current expenditure.

The two principal problems with rates are their cumbersomeness and the lack of horizontal equity. There are also some problems associated with the incidence of non-domestic rates. The difficulty with tax bases for rates is that they depend on an administrative decision, the valuation, which cannot hope to remain current through time, especially during a period of inflation. There are also sometimes charges of unfairness in that differences in valuations as between properties are not readily understood. It is for this reason that alternative systems of valuation, such as capital valuation (which has a market test) or a move to a land tax in the form of site value rating have been suggested. Although the problems involved in determining the tax base may be reduced, there is no indication that such systems would be fairer; and capital valuation does require a fairly regular turnover of similar properties if a system like that for rateable values is not to be necessary.

Horizontal equity is an even more serious issue, both within and between authorities. Essentially, rates fail to treat 'unequals' within an authority in accordance with the usual principles of fairness in taxation; on the other hand, they treat equals in different authority areas unequally (after allowing for any differences in expenditure preferences). The interpersonal equity problem arises because rates are levied on property and not on the residents of that property—the same rates are payable regardless of numbers of residents or their income. To some extent property sizes, and hence rates, do increase with income, but there are particular problems for such groups as retired people in a large family home. Gross rates are, for such reasons, definitely regressive. They range from as much as an average of 10 per cent of income in 1981/2 for those with weekly household incomes of less than £50 per week, to around 3 per cent at £150 per week, and to less than 2 per cent for those with weekly incomes in excess of £300. Taking into account rebates and supplementary benefits does lessen the worst excesses at low levels of income and brings the highest *average* liability down to under 4 per cent. But there is considerable variance at such a low level of income and some still face very high net rate demands because of ineligibility for, or failure to claim, benefits. Over time, rates as a percentage of disposable income have remained fairly stable at around the 3 per cent level, but rises in recent years have started to raise this average somewhat.

Inter-area equity arises because demands on expenditure differ between areas in a way not related to the size of the tax base (the rateable value) of areas. Table 8.2 illustrates the sort of variations which arise in expenditures, rateable values and rate poundages per head. As can be seen, the residents of inner city areas typically have to bear both much higher tax rates and much higher tax bills (given the higher rateable value) than those in less urban areas. This inter-area variation is one of the reasons for needing some form of intergovernmental grant to equalise the burden arising from unequal resource distributions. The basic principle of equalisation has been to try to standardise the tax rate necessary to provide a given level of service. This does leave the problem of unequal distribution of rateable values, however, and hence fails to equalise the total burden of rates.

Non-domestic rates—those imposed on industrial and commercial property—pose additional problems. They have been the source of increasing difficulty for many businesses during a recessionary period because of the absence of the reliefs and rebates which have been allowed to domestic payers. Such difficulties seem particularly to have affected small firms. But rates also operate unequally between industrial sectors. In 1976, for example, a survey showed that rates as a percentage of pre-tax profits averaged about 9 per cent, but that the figure was less than 6 per cent for a typical food or chemical processing firm, and over 18 per cent for firms in distribution or services (Jackman 1978). However, identifying the concern of firms with the burden of rates (and it will be remembered that a key point in the setting up of Enterprise Zones was their freedom from rates) does not adequately assess what the incidence of rates should be. Although it has been suggested that the imposition of rates is an effective tax on the land and capital inputs into business, and that the incidence is therefore on rates of return which are thus distorted between areas, the prevailing view has been that rates are rather like excise taxes and are thus passed on to the consumer in higher prices (Layfield Report 1976). The true incidence of non-domestic rates thus depends on the ability of firms to pass on the rates in higher prices (which will depend on the price elasticity of demand for output) and the share of expenditure on particular goods in final expenditure. Jackman (1978) suggests that the incidence is strongly regressive. Non-domestic rates constitute a fairly constant percentage of household expenditure across the income ranges and hence have an inverse relationship to income. The greatest incidence is in those activities which have the highest liability relative to profits—the service sector, which appears well able to pass on the effects of rates to the consumer.

Alternatives to Rates

All these criticisms of the rating system have been well rehearsed for a long time. There has been both a major enquiry into the system by the Committee of Enquiry into Local Government Finance (Layfield Report 1976), and a government discussion paper on 'Alternatives to Domestic Rates' (Cmnd. 8449, 1981). However, no government has yet been prepared to take the step of either abolishing rates or of introducing an alternative source or sources of revenue to replace them. Proposals have been made for various reforms to the present system: to introduce, variously, local sales, income or poll taxes, or to scrap local taxation altogether and assign an agreed proportion of certain national tax revenues to local authorities as is done in the West German tax-sharing system for income and business taxes. We have already discussed the principal ways in which each of these proposals might meet the usual criticisms of the rating system, but they are themselves not free of objections.

We have already noted the 'lumpiness' problem inherent in 'add-on' rates of sales tax or income tax to the national rate and the potential for conflict between national and local objectives. Sales and income taxes also raise quite formidable logistic problems of administration, assessment and collection unless they can be integrated into the existing work of Customs and Excise and Inland Revenue staffs, in which case some savings could be made on the estimated £120 million which the rating system cost in 1981/82. The principal objections to both sales and income taxes concern the greater geographical arbitrariness which they involve. To the extent that local taxation pays for local services it is sensible to link the taxes paid to the locality in which the services are provided. Most of these services relate to a property and its immediate surroundings and hence rates provide a logical link. But there are problems with properties situated close to an authority boundary or with long-distance commuters who work and enjoy public services in an area to which they pay no taxation, except very indirectly through the equalising grants. Income taxes pose the question of where to register a person for taxation. The Layfield Report logically favoured registration by residence (this still leaves the rates problem as noted above), but this would not easily fit into the existing PAYE system, since the latter operates at the workplace, and would necessitate adding a separate local tax element to each code to reflect different residences. Sales tax poses the reverse problem, since it would operate at the point of supply; typically, therefore, tax revenues would rise in urban centres and fall in others. This suggests either that sales taxes would only be appropriate at larger county levels to minimise this distortion, or that they could only be introduced to complement a residence-based tax.

The problem of cross-border trading is, then, a key issue which no one tax system can avoid. The great advantage of a sales tax is that it can impose some cost on the users of urban services, including tourists and overseas visitors, who otherwise pay nothing except any element of non-domestic rates passed on by shops, hotels, restaurants, etc. An income tax would normally be imposed at the place of residence, but since its collection would typically be made at the workplace, this would give some scope for a more precise imposition of the costs of commuting on individuals rather than indirectly through equalising grants to the authorities. Furthermore, it would make it more possible to adjust the amount of urban public transport costs by imposing, for example, a payroll tax on the users of commuter labour whilst allowing individual commuters to offset some part of their commuting costs against their total tax liability. Such a scheme for the payment of urban transport is one which is rather more common in other European countries and it has some appeal. One means of overcoming many of these border issues (as recognised by both Layfield and the Green Paper on Rates) would be to apply taxation only at higher tiers of local authority. In the Green Paper this was assumed to be borough level in the metropolitan counties, where some of the inequalities and cross-border problems are most prevalent.

A sales tax may well lead to a better distribution of tax revenues in relation to the costs of providing urban services; but if substantial differentials in tax rates emerge (whether or not these are passed on in prices), this may lead to a redistribution of shopping activity which would damage the viability of enterprises in the high tax areas. To the extent that this would lead to a relocation of businesses out of the area there would be a fall in revenue both from sales tax and from any residual rating system (unless rates were charged on empty properties).

The equity implications of the proposed alternative taxes are generally superior to the equity implications of the rating system. They differ in detail between household types according to the number of earners and the total size of the household. Taking a typical couple with one or two children and including one earner, however, on the basis of the 1981/82 figures a sales tax implies a net income gain when their gross income is less than about £210 a week, with a gain of 4 per cent at average income levels in London and the South-east and of 0.7 per cent in the rest of England. The maximum gain would be about 3 per cent of income, and the maximum loss about 1.5 per cent. A local income tax would be rather more sharply progressive and would imply rather lower gains. Only those earning less than about £130 a week would gain (the maximum gain being less than 2 per cent of income). At average income levels there would be a loss of 0.8 per cent, and the maximum loss would approach 3 per cent of income at a gross income level of less than £250 a week.

A further type of tax given quite wide consideration in this context is a poll tax—a simple annual *per capita* levy on residents of an area. The notion here is that the poll tax does represent likely demands on local public expenditure more effectively than any other tax and is relatively neutral in its effects. For the standard family discussed above there is very little effect on net income at any income level, and the only groups more than marginally affected by such a tax are single earners who would typically gain up to 2 per cent, and multiple-earner households who would lose 1 to 2 per cent of net income. Of course, this neutrality does mean that a poll tax would be strongly regressive. It has only been seriously suggested in combination with another source of taxation or with Exchequer grants, as a means of correcting some of the inequities inherent in them and as a means of giving an independent source of taxation to lower tiers of authority.

We have discussed alternative sources of revenue thus far in terms of their advantages over the existing rating systems in producing the same level of revenue and have concluded that a system of central government grants would still be necessary. The Layfield Report went further than this: it came down clearly in favour of a local income tax plus a reformed rating system, believing this to be the right way to generate larger local revenues more fairly and to give local authorities greater independence. It is likely that only an income tax could provide the basis for a major expansion in local revenues, which would of course largely be a diversion of revenues direct to local authorities instead of via central government and Exchequer grants. However, this issue raises again the more general fiscal issue of the role of local authorities and their financing, to which we must now turn.

8.2 The Urban Fiscal Problem

The urban fiscal problem has two primary dimensions: scale and distribution. The demands on local public expenditure have grown very rapidly in recent years without a corresponding increase in the resource base from which such expenditure can be financed. Local authorities would have been unable to meet their expanding commitments without a reform of the local tax system and without an increase by central government in the total grant aid given to them. The primary rationale for central government grants to local authorities has, however, always been one of redistributing the burdens of certain classes of expenditure and attempting to achieve some amelioration of expenditure needs and resource deficiencies outside the control of the individual authority. The original grants were, from the mid-nineteenth century, essentially hypothecated grants for specific services, responsibility for which had been delegated to local authorities. From 1929, however, the most important element in grants has been an unhypothecated block grant aimed at a distributional objective. The emphasis placed on what later came to be known as resource and needs elements changed somewhat over the years, as did the preferred method of attempting to achieve both redistribution and equalisation. We cannot hope to discuss the full history of this issue here (for a detailed discussion of both the theory and the practice of grant, see Foster *et al.* 1980), but we do need to discuss some basic elements of principle in order to understand the present system and the disagreements concerning its operation.

Basic Principles of Equalising Grants

We have noted how the main sources of inequality between authorities arise from discrepancies in either or both the demands placed on expenditure and the resources available as a tax base to finance that expenditure. It is insufficient just to look at expenditure levels per head (or rate poundages) since variations in these might reflect elements of choice being exercised by the local population through its elected representatives. An authority which chooses to have low fares on its public transport and low rents in its council houses, whilst paying its employees at above national rates, will typically have above-average levels of expenditure and rates; it should not be subsidised by tax-payers in other areas (through a central government transfer) for this.

There are, therefore, two guiding principles in any equalising formula. First, we need to establish a standard level of expenditure per head for an agreed range of services and the standard tax rate associated with this. Secondly, we need to devise a formula for grant payments which is both closed, in that the government can determine the total figure available for redistribution in advance (and not have the expenditure or tax rate plans of local authorities affect this), and does not allow the individual local authority to control the size of its own grant receipts (see LeGrand 1975).

There is a third element which needs consideration. Do redistribution and equalisation imply that there should simply be a movement of resources between authorities so that 'rich' authorities subsidise 'poor' ones, or is the basic aim just to assist poor authorities to reach some base-line level of ability to pay without any 'taxation' of rich authorities? In the latter case, redistribution comes out of general taxation funds, which means that richer tax-payers in both rich and poor authorities pay to support poorer authorities. But if the local tax rate remains higher in poor authorities, both poor and rich tax-payers in poor authorities will pay higher total (national plus local) taxes than an equivalent tax payer in a rich authority for the same standard of service. This problem raises all the issues introduced in Chapter 5 about the means of expressing collective preferences. If the wishes of the authority reflect the wishes of the median voter, who effectively controls the balance of power, then we also need to know something about the distribution of expenditures and of rateable values. It is very unlikely that the median voter is either an average recipient or tax-payer in this context and this is the source of further non-equalisation.

Rate Support Grant in Practice

The system of rate support grants (RSG) which developed from 1947 onwards has been based on the principle of equalising rate poundages necessary to provide an equal level of service. This has generally been achieved by considering the two elements of needs and resources separately.

Equalisation of resources has meant compensating authorities with a rateable value per head below some target level. Until 1974 the national average was used as the target and those below it received sufficient grant to compensate them up to that level. Those above it received no grant under this head, but also no penalty, and hence there was only a partial equalisation. From 1974, the target was an arbitrarily set standard rateable value per head. This standard was set at a rather higher level than the average, so that most authorities qualified for grant—this achieved greater equalisation but at the cost of a much higher total level of grant. Authorities with a rateable value per head above standard were not taxed on this directly, except that those in London (which accounted for 19 out of the 27 above-standard authorities in 1978/79) suffered a clawback out of their needs element.

The resources element has two principal drawbacks. First, since it compensates an authority directly and completely for any deficiency in rateable value, the authority has no incentive to encourage any development which increases the rateable value per head. A successful economic development would reduce a resources element grant by the amount of rates it generated. Only the eight authorities receiving no grant and no clawback would stand to gain. Secondly, since the amount of the grant actually paid is equal to the deficient rateable value multiplied by the current rate poundage (i.e. it is the deficiency in income which is made up in full) a high-spending authority can control the amount of grant it receives. Hence the resources element has tended to undermine the basic principle of equalisation.

The needs element relates to differences in expenditure per head arising from the different level of needs or differences in the unit costs of providing services which are outside the control of the authority. This requires assessment both of needs and of the cost weighting to be applied to them to arrive at a definition of standard expenditure. The method evolved for this was to use regression analysis to relate actual authority expenditures to a series of indicators. The systematic relationship between these would be identified in the regression equations coefficients, and could be held to be the involuntary variation in expenditure which required compensation, whilst the unaccounted-for stochastic errors would be the voluntary variations which were not to be compensated for. The regression method does suffer from a number of problems, however, not the least of which is its lack of simplicity. The main difficulties arise from the method itself, since any correlation between the indicators can lead to bias in estimates of the coefficient which are used as the implicit expenditure weights. Secondly, re-estimation of the equation year by year can lead to large variations in these estimates which could produce considerable year-by-year swings in actual grant levels for an authority. Furthermore, since a given year's grant depends on a previous year's expenditure, there is a problem both of open-endedness (no upper limit on the total level of grant) and of redistribution towards higher-spending authorities.

In the 1970s these problems became acute, so that it was necessary to introduce a damping mechanism. It related part of a given year's grant to the basis on which the previous year's was paid and provided a safety net to limit the reduction in total grant paid year on year. At the same time, the share of needs elements in RSG going to London and the metropolitan districts went up from 41.8 per cent in 1974/75 to 48.1 per cent in 1978/79.

The problems associated with this approach were well known, but were reiterated in the Layfield Report which advocated a move to unitary grant (see also Cripps and Godley 1976; Cambridge Economic Policy Group 1980). The principle of a unitary grant is that it attemps to return to the basic notion of equalising to a standard tax rate for the provision of a standard level of expenditure and paying grant on the difference between expenditure and the proceeds of the standard rate. The theoretical principles underlying such a grant system are quite clear-cut and can produce a fair and equitable distribution which conforms more readily to any total level of grant which the government lays down. This does not necessarily cut more deeply into some authorities' independence than others'. It does provide the government with a much stronger weapon to influence and control both the total level of expenditure and specific expenditures by individual authorities.

The Block Grant System in Practice

The Local Government Act, 1980 introduced a new basis for RSG calculations which replaced separate needs and resources elements. The new system of block grants requires the government to fix the total level of RSG settlement for a year in advance (although this figure can be modified upwards or downwards in the light of experience). Secondly, the government fixes the level of grant-related expenditure (GRE) on the basis of indicators and *per capita* standard unit costs. The indicators and the allowable unit expenditures are published for each class of authority and then aggregated to give an aggregate GRE for each authority. A grant-related poundage is then established as the effective standard rate for an authority at the average GRE in such a way as to determine the correct level of total grant. Of course, this poundage has to vary as GRE varies from the average for the class of authority. Hence there is a poundage schedule which specifies the rate at which the poundage must change as GRE for the authority deviates from the standard level. The grant-related poundage schedule specifies the effective price (in terms of the local tax rate) for marginal expenditure. It is fixed by the government and for 1981/82 the figure was 0.6p, so that the appropriate GRP for expenditure could be calculated as

$$\text{GRP} = \text{GRP}^* + 0.6\ \frac{\text{Total Expenditure} - \text{GRE}}{\text{Population}} \tag{8.1}$$

where GRP* is the poundage for expenditure equal to the GRE (149.29p for English authorities in 1981/82 and 167.31p in 1982/83). Having calculated GRP for the authority, the total amount of grant is given as

$$\text{Grant} = \text{Total Expenditure} - \text{RV} \times \text{GRP} \tag{8.2}$$

Hence the grant increases with expenditure, and this requires two adjustments. First, the transition from RSG calculated on the old basis to the new Block Grant could produce some major changes in grant which does not reflect the distribution of rateable values and hence could produce some big changes in effective rate burdens. For this reason a multiplier could be applied to certain authorities' GRP to correct for this. Typically, multipliers greater than one were applied to high rateable value London boroughs, and less than one to some shire counties which would otherwise have lost a considerable share of grant. These were envisaged as temporary measures but, as we shall see, they have increasingly been used for other purposes.

The second adjustment is to prevent authorities over-exceeding GRE. For this a threshold equal to 10 per cent of the GRE for that class of authority is set, above which level the GRP schedule is steeper by 25 per cent (i.e. the poundage must increase by 0.75p for every pound of marginal expenditure above the threshold). This steepening of the GRP schedule means that authorities lose grant at an increasing rate. Authorities particularly likely to suffer are those with both a high rateable value and a high GRP (resulting from spending above the threshold—essentially central city authorities) although even some very high rateable value authorities below the threshold could still finish up with a negative grant on the basis of equation 8.2.

The major problem of this approach is that the GRE becomes not a guideline but a norm or absolute target, variations from which, specially upwards, are construed as overspending. This has particularly been the case in the 1980s. The government has been motivated to control not only its own expenditure on local authority services through the level of RSG, but also to control total local expenditure as part of the wider bid to cut aggregate public expenditure. In an ideal system, deviations of actual expenditure from the standard level set could be made self-financing over all authorities by adjusting the appropriate standard rate poundage. As long as the standard expenditure reflects the estimated cost of providing the average range and standard of services rather than a government-controlled norm (Moore and Rhodes 1976), variations in expenditure from the standard can be financed by local variations in rate levels; but the marginal cost of such variations would be uniform over authorities (Cripps and Godley 1976).

The effect of the switch to the Block Grant system has been to distort quite widely the marginal cost of additional spending to domestic ratepayers between authorities, particularly between those in London and those elsewhere. Table 8.4 summarises calculations by Foster and Jackman (1982) of these marginal costs for 1980/81 under the old RSG system and for 1981/82 under the new Block Grant system. Here it is quite clear that whilst ratepayers in most authorities are marginally better off at levels of expenditure below the threshold, at levels above the threshold they have to bear a rather larger share than previously in the form of increased rates. However, in Central London the loss of some of the inbuilt advantages which the old formulae gave to such authorities has led to a doubling (or more) of the burden falling on ratepayers even at expenditure levels below the threshold.

However, the failure to exercise sufficient control on aggregate expenditure levels has led successively to three further government measures: control of expenditure growth; additional use of multipliers for specific authorities; and the control of local autonomy on fixing rate levels (rate capping). The measures to control expenditure growth introduced for 1982/83 put a ceiling on the allowable year-on-year rises in aggregate expenditure. Spending above this expenditure guidance target would result in grant deductions unless the target was below GRE, in which case expenditure up to the GRE level would be allowed without penalty.

Table 8.4 Percentage Contributions by Ratepayers to Marginal Expenditure

	1980/81 Rate Support Grant	*1981/82 Block Grant*	
		Below threshold	*Above threshold*
London			
Camden	24.3	47.4	59.3
Kensington and Chelsea	51.3	102.9	128.6
Westminster	16.0	97.6	122.0
Barnet	67.4	67.3	84.1
Bexley	48.6	43.1	53.9
Greater London Council	38.4	48.7	60.9
Metropolitan Areas			
Birmingham	41.0	38.0	47.5
Kirklees	23.6	23.2	29.0
Liverpool	33.3	31.4	39.3
Manchester	34.1	28.2	35.3
Newcastle	34.0	31.8	39.8
South Yorkshire	27.8	26.1	32.6
West Midlands	42.1	41.3	51.6
Non-Metropolitan Areas			
Nottingham	34.0	31.8	39.8
Avon	37.5	34.9	43.6
Surrey	57.1	52.4	65.5
Warwickshire	44.8	44.7	55.9

Source: Foster and Jackman (1982)

This target was tightened even further for the 1983/84 settlement. In the revised estimates for 1982/83 and provisional estimates for 1983/84 the government announced its intention to protect, with full grant aiding, authorities with expenditure less than the level of GRE, and to provide partial protection for those with expenditure less than 5 per cent in excess of either GRE or the expenditure guidance (whichever was higher). Above this target level there would be penal multipliers (which for metropolitan districts were set at .8075p) for the first and second one per cent of

Table 8.5 Planned Expenditure, Targets and GRE, 1983/84

	Guidance target (*£ million*)	*Planned overspend* (*%*)	*GRE assessment* (*£ million*)	*Planned overspend* (*%*)	*Block Grant anticipated entitlement* (*£ million*)
London					
Inner Boroughs	898	6.4	695	37.5	318
Outer Boroughs	1,719	2.1	1,616	8.7	752
GLC	566	53.2	480	80.7	0
ILEA	761	12.8	517	65.9	138[1]
Metropolitan Police Area	346	0.0	346	0.0	
Metropolitan Areas					
Districts	4,056	1.5	3,891	5.8	2,090
Counties	1,104	6.5	927	26.8	473
Non-Metropolitan Areas					
Districts	1,446	−0.1	1,472	−1.8	755
Counties	9,237	1.6	9,287	1.0	4,587
Total	20,133	3.8	19,231	8.7	9,113

Source: CIPFA, *Finance and General Statistics, 1983/84*
Note: [1]This is the anticipated total entitlement of all precepting authorities in Greater London; most of it goes to the Metropolitan Police Area.

overspend, and multipliers of five times this value for each additional one per cent of overspend (i.e. 4.0375p for metropolitan districts).

It is these cash targets which for many authorities have now become the key to grant assessments rather than the more logical assessments of GRE based on the services which need to be covered. Table 8.5 shows the relationship between spending on the basis of targets and that on the basis of GRE assessments together with the planned overspend associated with each (Smith 1983). The marginal grant rate associated with such overspending is, however, not always predictable, nor is the response to it in terms of fixing rate increases. Some of the highest negative marginal grant rates (the percentage of a marginal pound of expenditure met by grant) are found in Outer London boroughs and shire counties with relatively low rates of planned overspend, although it is true that only those authorities aiming to hit or fall short of target can actually get a positive marginal grant rate. Many of the highest overspenders do enjoy quite high *per capita* rateable values which must provide a cushion, although this does not imply a neutral change in rate levels. The biggest changes in rate poundages have come from both wider-target and over-target authorities. For example, between 1982/83 and 1983/84 Wandsworth had a planned underspend of 2.22 per cent against target, a marginal grant rate of 32.4 per cent, but a rate poundage increase of 159.3 per cent. In contrast, Islington planned to overspend by 9.37 per cent, faced a massive negative marginal grant rate of −162.7 per cent, but imposed a rate poundage rise of 84.4 per cent. A number of councils met the situation by reducing balances substantially.

Since councils do ultimately have the power to pay for expenditure out of rate income it is logical that this should have become the target for a further government effort to control local authority spending. In a White Paper (August 1983, Cmnd. 9008) the Government proposed to select a small number of councils which were deemed to be responsible for most of the overspending. In 1983–84, 75 per cent of the overspend on target is accounted for by about sixteen authorities, according to the Government. The power sought is that the Government can set a legal maximum rate level for each council, although it aims to exclude councils with annual budgets of less than £10 million. This will apply initially for the 1985–86 year on the basis of budget estimates, though the actual selection of authorities who will then have ceilings imposed on their rate poundages is not determined by any objective formulae. As Table 8.6 shows, some very different lists could be drawn up on the basis of different indicators: cash overspending by the largest councils; percentage overspending—a rather different list whether based on guidance targets or on GRE (only five out of ten appear in both lists); percentage change in rate poundages produces yet another list. This last list is interesting since it includes five authorities which have clearly tried to follow the Government's edicts on spending. It is not clear, therefore, that the high spenders have been those seeking to burden their own ratepayers; and hence controls on rate levels are a curious response to the inability to

Table 8.6 Rankings of Authorities by Alternative Criteria of Overspending

Cash overspend (£ million)		*Overspend on expenditure guidance target %*		*Overspend on GRE assessment %*		*Increase in rate poundage 1982/83–1983/84 %*	
GLC	300.6	GLC	53.1	City of London	229.7	Wandsworth	159.3
ILEA	95.4	Greenwich	20.7	Thamesdown	86.1	Broxbourne	112.9
West Midlands	16.9	Southwark	16.6	GLC	80.6	Islington	84.4
Greater		Crawley	13.5	Sedgefield	77.5	Greenwich	81.0
Manchester	15.9	Leicester	12.7	South Yorkshire	76.0	Epsom & Ewell	79.8
Avon	15.5	ILEA	12.5	Harlow	72.5	Lewisham	68.9
Southwark	14.3	Basildon	10.4	Crawley	72.2	Southwark	60.2
Sheffield	14.2	Lambeth	9.5	ILEA	65.9	Westminster	56.6
Merseyside	13.6	Islington	9.3	Camden	64.7	Lambeth	49.5
Derbyshire	12.9	Harlow	9.2	Greenwich	62.9	Richmond	46.1
Humberside	11.7						

Source: CIPFA, *Finance and General Statistics, 1983/84*, after D. Walker, *New Society*, 21 July 1983, p. 95.

control via other means. It is unlikely, therefore, that rate capping is at all beneficial to rate payers.

What is certainly clear is that a carefully devised system of assessing local authority spending needs based on GRE assessments as a means of distributing grants in the most neutral way has essentially been destroyed for the short-term aim of controlling aggregate local authority expenditure. This implies a redistribution of grant between authorities in an essentially random way, bearing little relationship to either needs or resources. Whilst it can be argued that the reduction in local authority spending in total is an essential part of national economic strategy, there is little evidence that there has been any real reduction in aggregate expenditure. Budgets for 1983–84 suggest a 4 per cent rise in real terms since 1978-79 and even the Government's plan is for an identical level to that of 1978–79. Level of expenditure in real terms implies a rising share of output in such a period of recession. There has been little real gain from the exercise.

This is not to argue that GRE is a perfect system. Many of the indicators need refinement and some of them can themselves cause unplanned shifts of grant between authorities. Nevertheless, if these refinements can be made and if GREs can come to be regarded as standards rather than norms or targets, they do have the advantage of being objective measures which provide the basis for a rational system of grant distribution.

8.3 The Future of Urban Public Finance

The recent history of the system of local public finance in Britain is essentially one of cumulative failure. This fiscal situation requires us to pose two questions which provide the key to any future reform. First, in the absence of penalties, how far can the existing grant system and any reform of the rating system achieve an equitable redistribution of resources and tax effort between authorities? Secondly, is there any sense in which the structure of local government is incompatible with any workable system of local finance and grant-based redistribution?

It is clear that, following a period in which the structure of the RSG system occasioned quite a major shift of resources towards the more highly urban areas, the last two or three years have seen a stabilising of the proportion of grant going to these areas. Reductions in grant entitlement in London and the metropolitan counties have typically occurred because of the poundage schedule and its taper, specific penalty withholding of grant and the reduction in total grant payable rather than any bias in the system of needs assessment. In fact, most such authorities would gain substantially from the GRE system of assessment, particularly in relation to the housing indicators (especially HRA deficits) and social service provision indicators. Although they score rather less heavily in unit terms on education indicators, the density and weight given to these makes education expenditure a major element in redistribution (Bramley 1983).

There are two conclusions to be drawn from this. One is that such authorities are continuing to exercise their right of choice in spending at above GRE; and that this cost should rightly fall on the local electorate as increased rates. Alternatively it could be argued that although GRE does appear to redistribute in favour of such areas (when compared with assessed spending needs under the old RSG system) it fails to do so sufficiently and to adjust sufficiently quickly to changing circumstances, especially in that it can produce quite different effects for authorities with different resource levels. This highlights the danger of regarding the GRE assessment as a norm or target for a class of authority and of imposing a grant penalty which assumes that GRE is neutral in its treatment of authorities. This latter conclusion seems more likely to fit the facts, and it is a matter of concern that, having introduced a new basis for grant assessment (which quite desirably overcomes the erstwhile problem of local authorities collectively being able to influence the scale and distribution of RSG), central government has been prepared to manipulate the system with regard only to the size of the total grant and not to its distributional impact.

There is of course a genuine concern (we have discussed previously the way in which subsidies may influence both the prices and the costs of provision of specific services) that grants in themselves may be a source of high expenditure and inefficiency in local government. Where the full marginal cost of additional expenditure does not fall directly on the electors, there is less control exercised by them. Such a finding may be partly contradicted by the recognition that the very high spending authorities have recently had negative marginal grant rates, so that each additional pound of expenditure requires the finding of more than one pound from rate income. However, the system of rate rebates to low income households, directly underwritten by central government, shifts the true incidence of the increased rate bills not only between individuals within a local authority area, but, more importantly, between local authority areas.

We have so far indicated that the trade-off available to a local authority is one between grants and rates, but this is not the only source of revenue. Many of the services provided by local authorities are traded and the pricing policy for these is a critical determinant of the amount of rate fund subsidy needed. Some evidence has been forthcoming that, especially where matching grants are involved, the existence of grants can reduce the degree of optimisation in pricing policy for certain services (Gibson 1980, 1982). Also, a survey of pricing practices has suggested that there is considerable scope for improvement in the pricing of a wide range of services (Coopers and Lybrand 1981). We have already considered in some detail the specific issues surrounding transport and housing charges and the same principles apply to other local public services. Since this issue does raise a considerable amount of political concern it is important to bear in mind that optimal pricing does not necessarily mean higher prices, but rather a better correspondence between prices and output levels, so that the marginal return on the subsidy paid is increased.

Discussion of more commercial practices in the pricing of public services does, of course, also raise the currently topical issue of privatisation, either by the selling-off of assets, or by contracting out certain services such as refuse collection or street sweeping to private sector firms. Typically the latter approach has been used by those councils following such a policy, and all that happens is that the contractors are paid by the council out of the rate fund for the work done. This fails to establish the direct relationship between the value of the service to the final consumer and the cost of its provision necessary for an optimal pricing policy to work effectively. The danger in fragmenting local public services in this way, however, is that they fail to maintain a coherence, and fail to include the merit and public good qualities established as a rationale for a local public sector in the first place.

An optimal system of local public provision and its finance does, however, require an optimal structure of local government authorities. As we suggested in Chapter 5, there is no totally obvious way of defining an optimal structure of local government in relation to the economics of the functions it controls. The system of counties divided into urban or rural districts, with most large towns having county borough status, lasted from 1888 until the reorganisations of 1964 in London and 1974 in the rest of England and Wales. The 1974 reorganisation followed a Royal Commission, but failed to accept the main findings of that Commission's Report. The main effect of the reorganisation was to downgrade the role of traditionally independent larger urban centres, as well as to group together the main conurbations under the umbrella of the metropolitan counties (which would, however, have rather lesser powers than non-metropolitan counties in the day-to-day running of certain services, especially of education).

The metropolitan counties have in many respects an impossible task: they have to provide the strategic framework for planning within their areas, but have only a small number of direct instruments available to effect their policies. Control of police, fire or refuse disposal can hardly be used as an instrument of economic policy and the possibility of direct economic intervention is severely limited by central government. Only transport provides any opportunities for direct policy measures. Assertion of a county role comes about more typically through the very limited scope for support of the arts and for general propaganda of social, economic and political types. The current proposal to abolish the metropolitan counties and the Greater London Council has as its primary motive the curbing of what is seen as excessive and uncontrolled expenditure by these authorities. Their functions will either be transferred to the constituent boroughs or replaced by *ad hoc* joint boards.

The proposal has been widely criticised, principally because it removes the one set of elected authorities given a general power to oversee complete functional regions. Those functions, such as transport or police and fire (which would remain at county level), would be transferred to non-directly elected boards which, being constituted from the various district authorities, could find themselves in the position of being unable to act, given the potential disagreements. In London, the proposal to treat transport differently yet again, with a board directly responsible to the Department of Transport, creates another dimension of confusion.

Despite these arguments, the continuance of metropolitan counties in their present form seems difficult to defend on economic grounds. To be effective they would need to be larger in terms of their responsibilities and would need to take on a number of functions devolved from central government to make genuine regional government possible. This might mean that some of the authorities would have to be larger in area and would have to have their own internal redistributive equalisation fund. This in turn could make urban economic policy and development in the major urban areas a real possibility. Otherwise, it would seem sensible to remove this tier of government —though with rather more thought and consultation than is embraced in the current proposals.

Any wider attempt to reform the system of local government must include provisions to create further local financial autonomy through the power to levy a locally-determined tax. Once again, we are thrown back on the need to reform and supplement the rating system as an absolute precondition for any real progress in this area.

Further Reading

The most useful single further source of information on all aspects of local authority finance and expenditure, including information on both theoretical and historical aspects, is Foster *et al.* (1980). A useful comparison on the issues raised in other systems such as the federal state is that of Oates (1972). The main issues in the debate over rates are summarised quite well in the Government Green Paper, *Alternatives to Domestic Rates* (Cmnd. 8449) but many of the papers prepared for, and evidence submitted to, the Layfield Committee on Local Government Finance (1976) are well worth reading. Although much of the debate has been over domestic rates, there is considerable concern over non-domestic rates both in terms of actual incidence and the distribution of the burden; the papers in the report edited by Jackman (1978) clarify many of the issues involved.

The question of rate support grant assessments and central government control has grown in importance but many of the assessments of these are not totally objective. Useful studies include those of Burgess and Travers (1982) and Bennett (1982), and up-to-date analyses are contained in the Chartered Institute of Public Finance and Accountancy's journal, *Public Money*, (see, for example, the article by Smith 1983). We have not discussed in detail the systems of assessing grant-related expenditure indicators, but for some examples see Bebbington and Davies (1980). On the distributional implications of changing fiscal bases and grants, see Jackson *et al.* (1982).

9
The Future of Urban Policy

In the previous four chapters we have explored the application of a fairly traditional view of the rationale for public sector intervention in an urban economy. The existence of externalities and goods with merit and public good characteristics leads to the need for a public sector. The size of that sector is envisaged as being determined to some extent at least by public voting, either through the ballot box or through migration to and from areas with particular patterns or levels of provision—the so-called voice or exit options for revealing preferences. We have also seen how the particular methods of policy implementation used have largely led to a situation in which the primary economic objectives for the policies are not achieved and how the existence of externally imposed constraints (for example, by central government on local government) has led to distortions both within and between sectors. In recent years there has additionally been a gradual loss of independence by local authorities, occasioned both by statutory limitations on local authority powers upheld through the courts so that the apparent will of a majority of voters can be checked through legal action by a minority, and by the fact that the local authority no longer receives the major part of current revenue from its locally controlled taxation.

In this final chapter we shall make some assessment of the current position in the light of the implications of the analytical framework established, and evaluate the possibilities for a rather different approach to urban economic policy in the future. There are two principal aspects to this discussion: the level of urban economic policy making, and the process of policy implementation and monitoring.

The Level of Urban Policy Making

We have on a number of occasions encountered difficulties with the most appropriate level of policy making for urban areas. This occurs in theoretical terms when considering the relevant level for collective choice decisions and in practical terms in all the dimensions of policy we have considered. Principally, it raises the question of whether we are more interested in the welfare of the urban part of the national economy as a whole, or in the promotion of the individual interests of the various urban economies—in the belief that they know what is best for themselves and, moreover, that in a free market the ensuing competition would produce the best overall outcome. However, such a simplistic view of the alternatives ignores the way in which the urban economies all interrelate with each other, and the way in which an established framework of inter-governmental transfers places a constraint on individual local governmental freedom, largely because of the difficulty of devising a system of transfers which is neither open-ended nor manipulable by the recipient. There are two practical issues which we do need to comment on: the most appropriate size and structure of local authority areas, and the most appropriate level at which to organise particular urban policies.

The size of local authority areas depends on a number of relevant factors. First, there is the economics of producing the publicly provided goods and services. We have seen how this typically gives us very little in the way of clear evidence for optimal sizes of either cities or their controlling authorities. What it does show is that different functions may be more efficiently carried out by differently sized authorities. It suggests that a tiered system of authorities could provide the best way of ensuring that a particular function is carried out by the most appropriately sized authority. As an alternative, a case could be made for a completely separate regionalism for different functions currently provided by a standard system of local government authorities. Such a pattern already exists in Britain for nationalised utilities such as gas, electricity and water and in health care through the Area Health Authorities, all functions originally carried out in most areas by local authorities.

Secondly, there is the question of public choice and accountability. The public provision of goods and services requires that some form of expression of public preference is possible, especially where the financing of that provision is through some form of taxation. The conventional wisdom following Tiebout is that the most effective form of local authority autonomy occurs when authority areas are as homogeneous as possible in terms of the characteristics of the population. However, this does ignore many of the economic realities. At the most basic level it ignores the possibility of producing the goods with only a single, homogeneous type of labour. It also ignores problems such as high concentrations of unemployment and the severe imbalances in the size of tax bases which would arise. Such a view would tend to defend the notion of larger authorities and the existence, in particular, of umbrella authorities for large metropolitan regions. Accountability is a question of making the authority responsible and responsive to the wishes of the community. There has been a feeling in Britain that since the reorganisation of local government into larger units much of this directness has been lost. This argument has been applied particularly in the case of the larger Metropolitan and Greater London Councils which have rate precepting powers on the lower tier of authority but, as we have noted on a number of occasions, have relatively little direct responsibility for the provision of services, except for transport, police, fire, and refuse disposal. Their functions have beyond this been largely strategic and cultural. All of these have also been areas of considerable conflict over the philosophy of policy.

Thirdly, related to size, there is the question of the relationships between different authorities and between local and central government. Smaller authorities clearly give rise to greater cross-border spillovers and a blurring of the direct link between tax levels and service provision. Smaller authorities are also likely to be more vulnerable to central government pressure and control on their level and range of spending. And they are less likely to be able to provide the infrastructure for such services as transport without the need to resort to some form of inter-authority co-operation. Before reorganisation, joint boards of local authorities were quite common, especially in conurbation areas, as a means of providing transport services. Indeed, the initial establishment of Passenger Transport Authorities perpetuated this type of arrangement with nominated members from relevant local authorities. This form of organisation seems to be the one favoured by the Government in its present plans to abolish the metropolitan county authorities. Since the joint boards can call on member authorities for financial support, there is the possibility for conflict without any hope of direct resolution through voting by the actual tax payer who remains one stage removed. The alternative would be a directly elected authority for each service, with the power to demand revenues from the local authorities, or even to raise its own, as do water authorities. The problem here is that, although it would enable the size of relevant authorities to be tailored to the needs of particular services, it could also lead to a proliferation of elected bodies.

In discussing size, we have also needed to introduce the rather different relationships implied by different types of locally provided services. There is a more general question about the level of control of urban policy, however. Urban policy as an infrastructure within which specific services are provided, and which aims to ensure the best use of private resources, can be conceived as being either a local or a national responsibility. Whilst local authorities may be seen as the most appropriate level at which the 'self-determination' of the residents of that area can take place, it is also clear that the problems of large cities in particular are much wider than just the city boundaries, and much deeper than city resources can cope with. This leads to the notion of a national urban policy which deals with the way in which national resources are distributed between areas. The problem with the growth of a national urban policy is that to be effective it has to take control out of the hands of the locally elected representatives to avoid the clash of conflicting policies.

Our conclusion on the level of urban policy making must, therefore, be that there is no clear over-riding consideration which argues for one size or one structure for a local authority or an urban policy making process. The final outcome involves a balance of issues and a weighting of priorities, but this brings us back to the basic issue of public choice and political control: who should take the decisions about who takes the decisions? Whilst the current proposals to reform big city government and to control local financial independence may meet some of the objections to the present system, they clearly raise new problems which require wider discussion and more thought.

Policy Implementation and Monitoring

We have concentrated in this book on establishing economic principles on which policy can be based and on defining objectives and the relative merits of alternative policy instruments. However, there is much more to successful policy intervention than the definition of optimal prices, subsidy levels or levels of rate support grant. It could be argued that one of the main problems of urban policy in recent years has been the failure to turn theoretical solutions into working policies and, even more, the failure to monitor and control the effects of such policies in operation. We noted, for example, the way in which different aspects of housing policy have been contradictory and the way in which traditional regional policy has been counter-productive, from the urban standpoint. It is perhaps too early to assess the impact of the new urban programmes, but even there we have noted the possibilities of contradictions and the expansion of policies such as Enterprise Zones without due consideration for the lessons to be learned from the first round of zones and the implications of having as many as 23 zones in competition with each other.

The general philosophy in interventionist policy of all types has in recent years tended to be one of examining and attempting to reduce total costs, or cost per unit of objective (where the latter is not evaluated) and not one of maximising the net benefit per unit cost of intervention. Thus, for example, much of the discussion on policy towards industrial location has been on the basis of the cost per job saved or created, rather than the total net welfare resulting from this. It is clear that such costs are typically very large when measured against the specific job directly affected, with no second round or induced effects. It is also clear that such a measure does not discriminate between types of jobs, levels of productivity or levels of output. A similar approach has been discussed and criticised in Chapter 7 in connection with transport subsidies. There has in all cases been very little attempt to provide *ex post facto* evaluations of the total effectiveness of policies.

A further problem has been the way in which unconnected policy measures may have unexpected or unconsidered effects on urban affairs. Attempts to stimulate urban economies directly by investment aid can be undermined by national economic policies which keep interest rates high and demand depressed. Most studies of unemployment in local economies have come to the conclusion that the most effective way of reducing unemployment and narrowing at least the absolute differentials between areas in unemployment rates is by stimulating the general level of demand in the economy as a whole. This type of interconnectedness has been quite widely recognised in the United States, where series of 'impact analyses' are required for federal policies, most notably on environmental impact, but also on urban impact and other areas of policy interest. Similarly, the EEC has introduced the notion of a regional impact assessment for non-regional policies of the Community to ensure greater coherence of policy as a whole.

Coherence of policy both between sectors and between different levels of government does, however, raise yet again the question of the distribution of weights to the objectives and the views of the different sectors and authorities. At the moment, conflicts are resolved by legal means to the extent that all public authorities are governed by statutes which delimit their powers. However, central government remains in the strongest position since it has the final say in changing the statutory powers of other authorities. We see this happening over the proposal to limit local authority independence in rate levels. If we are to see a proliferation of *ad hoc* authorities, the possibilities for conflict become even greater and are likely to require a more formal (and possibly expensive) system for arbitrating inter-authority disputes.

There is also a much wider issue. Urban policy in general, and urban economic policy in particular, can no longer be seen just as a purely local matter of ensuring efficiency in the provision of certain services and ensuring some form of compensation to authorities with either below-standard levels of resources or above-standard levels of demand on their services. The growth and efficiency of urban economies within a country contributes vitally to the overall performance of the national economy, and vice versa. Urban policy, therefore, needs to figure much more strongly in the deliberations of government at the national and international level. The danger of seeing urban economic policy in a purely restricted role is that the potential harm done to the national economy by imposing severe constraints on levels and types of intervention is also ignored. A strong and positive urban economic policy may serve as a vital, intrinsic part of any general economic policy. At the moment, no such coherent view is emerging. This book has aimed to provide a firmer foundation for understanding at least a part of the debate.

Bibliography

Advisory Commission on Intergovernmental Relations (1981) *Studies in Comparative Federalism: West Germany*, ACIR, Washington, D.C.

Alonso, W. (1964) *Location and Land Use*, Harvard University Press.

Anas, A. (1976) 'Short run dynamics in the spatial housing market', in G.J. Papageorgiou (ed.), *Mathematical Land Use Theory*, Lexington Books.

Armstrong, H. and Taylor, J. (1978) *Regional Economic Policy and its Analysis*, Philip Allan.

Arnott, R.J. and Stiglitz, J.E. (1979) 'Aggregate land rents, expenditure on public goods and optimal city size', *Quarterly Journal of Economics*, 93, pp. 471–500.

Austen-Smith, D. (1982) 'Non-profit organisations under uncertainty: a model of subsidized repertory theatre', unpublished paper, University of York.

Ball, R.M. (1980) 'The use and definition of travel to work areas in Great Britain: some problems', *Regional Studies*, 14, pp. 125–139.

Bartels, C.P.A. and van Duijn, J.J. (1982) 'Regional economic policy in a changed labour market', *Papers of the Regional Science Association*, 49, pp. 97–111.

Baum, H. (1973) 'Free public transport', *Journal of Transport Economics and Policy*, 7, pp. 3–19.

Baumol, W.J. (1967) 'Macroeconomics of unbalanced growth: the anatomy of urban crisis', *American Economic Review*, 57, pp. 415–426.

Baumol, W.J. and Bradford, D.F. (1970) 'Optimal departures from marginal cost pricing', *American Economic Review*, 60, pp. 265–283.

Bebbington, A. and Davies, B. (1980) 'Territorial needs indicators: a new approach', *Journal of Social Policy*, 9, pp. 145–168, 433–462.

Becker, G.S. (1965) 'A theory of the allocation of time', *Economic Journal*, 75, pp. 493–517.

Beesley, M.E. (1972) 'Economic criteria for the maintenance, modification, or creation of public transport services which may not necessarily be profitable', in *Fourth International Symposium on Theory and Practice in Transport Economics*, European Conference of Ministers of Transport, Paris, reprinted in Beesley (1973).

Beesley, M.E. (1973) *Urban Transport: Studies in Economic Policy*, Butterworth.

Beesley, M.E. (1974) *Economic Criteria for the Maintenance, Modification or Creation of Public Urban and Suburban Transport Services*, Round Table 24, European Conference of Ministers of Transport, Paris.

Beesley, M.E., Gist, P. and Glaister, S. (1983) 'Cost–benefit analysis and London's transport policies', *Progress in Planning*, 19, pp. 169–269.

Beesley, M.E. and Walters, A.A. (1970) 'Some problems in the evaluation of urban road investments', *Applied Economics*, 1, pp. 241–260.

Bennett, R.J. (1982) *Central Grants to Local Government: the Political and Economic Impact of the Rate Support Grant in England and Wales*, Cambridge University Press.

Bishop, K.C. and Simpson, C.E. (1972) 'Components of change analysis: problems of alternative approaches to industrial structure', *Regional Studies*, 6, pp. 59–68.

Boddy, M. (1983) 'Changing public–private sector relationships in the industrial development process', in K. Young and C. Mason (eds), *Urban Economic Development*, Macmillan.

Borts, G.H. and Stein, J.L. (1964) *Economic Growth in a Free Market*, Columbia University Press.

Botham, R. and Lloyd, G. (1983) 'The political economy of Enterprise Zones', *National Westminster Bank Quarterly Review*, May.

Bradbury, K., Engle, R., Owen, I. and Rothenberg, J. (1977) 'Simultaneous estimation of the supply and demand for housing location in a multizoned metropolitan area', in G.K. Ingram (ed.), *Residential Location and Urban Housing Markets*, NBER, New York.

Bramley, G. (1983) 'Grant related expenditure and the inner city', unpublished paper, School for Advanced Urban Studies, Bristol.

Brechling, F. (1967) 'Trends and cycles in British regional unemployment', *Oxford Economic Papers*, 19, pp. 1–21.

Breton, A. (1974) *The Economic Theory of Representative Government*, Aldine.

Broadbent, T.A. (1977) *Planning and Profit in the Urban Economy*, Methuen.

Brown, A.A. and Neuberger, E. (eds) (1977) *Internal Migration: A Comparative Perspective*, Academic Press.

Brown, A.J. (1972) *The Framework of Regional Economics in the U.K.*, Cambridge University Press.

Buchanan, J.M. (1965) 'An economic theory of clubs', *Economica*, 32, pp. 1–14.

Buchanan, J.M. and Goetz, C. (1972) 'Efficiency limits of fiscal mobility: an assessment of the Tiebout model', *Journal of Public Economics*, 1, pp. 25–43.

Buchanan, J.M. and Stubblebine, W.C. (1962) 'Externality', *Economica*, 29, pp. 371–84.

Burgess, E.W. (1925) 'The growth of a city', in R.E. Park, E.W. Burgess and R.D. Mackenzie (eds), *The City*, Chicago University Press.

Burgess, T. and Travers, T. (1980) *Ten Billion Pounds: Whitehall's Takeover of the Town Halls*, Grant McIntyre.

Burridge, P. and Gordon, I.R. (1981) 'Unemployment in the British metropolitan labour areas', *Oxford Economic Papers*, 33, pp. 274–297.

Butler, S.M. (1982) *Enterprise Zones: Greenlining the Inner Cities*, Heinemann.

Button, K.J. (1982) *Transport Economics*, Heinemann.

Cambridge Economic Policy Group (1980) *Cambridge Economic Policy Review*, vol. 6, no. 2, Gower.

Cambridge Economic Policy Group (1982) *Cambridge Economic Policy Review*, vol. 8, no. 2, Gower.

Cameron, G.C. (1973) 'Intra-urban location and the new plant', *Papers and Proceedings of the Regional Science Association*, 31, pp. 125–143.

Cameron, G.C. (ed.) (1980a) *The Future of the British Conurbations*, Longman.

Cameron, G.C. (1980b) 'The inner city—new plant incubator?', in A. Evans and D. Eversley (eds), *The Inner City: Employment and Industry*, Heinemann.

Cameron, G.C. and Johnson, K.M. (1969) 'Comprehensive urban renewal and industrial relocation—the Glasgow case', in S.C. Orr and J.B. Cullingworth (eds), *Regional and Urban Studies*, Allen & Unwin.

Cameron, G.C. and Wingo, L. (eds) (1973) *Cities, Regions and Public Policy*, Oliver and Boyd.

Carlino, G.A. (1982) 'Manufacturing agglomeration economies as returns to scale: a production function approach', *Papers of the Regional Science Association*, 50, pp. 95–108.

Cheshire, P. (1973) 'Regional unemployment differences in Great Britain', in NIESR, *Regional Papers 2*, Cambridge University Press.

Cheshire, P. (1979) 'Inner Areas as spatial labour markets: a critique of the Inner Area Studies', *Urban Studies*, 16, pp. 29–43.

Chisholm, M. (1971) 'Freight transport costs, industrial location and regional development', in M. Chisholm and G. Manners (eds), *Spatial Policy Problems of the British Economy*, Cambridge University Press.

Christaller, W. (1966) *Central Places in Southern Germany*, transl. C.W. Baskin, Prentice Hall.

Collins, M.F. and Pharoah, T.M. (1974) *Transport Organisation in a Great City: The Case of London*, Allen and Unwin.

Congdon, P. (1983) 'A model for the interaction of migration and commuting', *Urban Studies*, 20, pp. 185–195.

Coombes, M.G. and Openshaw, S. (1982) 'The use and definition of travel to work areas in Great Britain: some comments', *Regional Studies*, 16, pp. 141–149.

Coopers and Lybrand Associates (1981) *Service Provision and Pricing in Local Government*, HMSO.

Corkindale, J.T. (1980) 'Employment trends in the conurbations', in A. Evans and D. Eversley (eds), *The Inner City: Employment and Industry*, Heinemann.

Cripps, T.F. and Godley, W.A.H. (1976) *Local Government Finance and Its Reform: A Critique of the Layfield Committee's Report*, Department of Applied Economics, Cambridge.

Curran, C., Carlson, L.A. and Ford, D.A. (1982) 'A theory of residential location decisions in two-worker households', *Journal of Urban Economics*, 12, pp. 102–114.

Danson, M.W., Lever, W.F. and Malcolm, J.F. (1980) 'The inner city employment problem in Great Britain, 1952–76: a shift-share approach', *Urban Studies*, 17, pp. 193–210.

David, P.A. (1974) 'Fortune, risk and the microeconomics of migration', in P.A. David and M.W. Reder (eds), *Nations and Households in Economic Growth*, Academic Press.

Dear, M. and Scott, A.J. (1981) *Urbanization and Urban Planning in a Capitalist Society*, Methuen.

Dennis, R. (1978) 'The decline of manufacturing employment in Greater London: 1966–74', *Urban Studies*, 15, pp. 63–73.

Dixit, A. (1973) 'The optimal factory town', *Bell Journal of Economics and Management Science*, 4, pp. 637–651.

Dixon, R.J. and Thirlwall, A.P. (1975a) 'A model of regional growth rate differentials on Kaldorian lines', *Oxford Economic Papers*, 27, pp. 201–214.

Dixon, R.J. and Thirlwall, A.P. (1975b) *Regional Growth and Unemployment in the United Kingdom*, Macmillan.

Dixon, R.J. and Thirlwall, A.P. (1979) 'An export-led growth model with a balance of payments constraint', in J.K. Bowers (ed.), *Inflation, Development and Integration: Essays in Honour of A.J. Brown*, University of Leeds Press.

Domencich, T.A. and McFadden, D. (1975) *Urban Travel Demand: A Behavioral Analysis*, North-Holland.

Donnison, D. and Ungerson, C. (1982) *Housing Policy*, Penguin Books.

Downs, A. (1957) *An Economic Theory of Democracy*, Harper & Row.

Downs, A. (1967) *Inside Bureaucracy*, Little, Brown.

Dunleavy, P. (1980) *Urban Political Analysis: The Politics of Collective Consumption*, Macmillan.

Eaton, B.C. and Lipsey, R.G. (1977) 'The introduction of space into the neoclassical model of value theory', in M.J. Artis and A.R. Nobay (eds), *Studies in Modern Economics*, Basil Blackwell.

Eaton, B.C. and Lipsey, R.G. (1978) 'Freedom of entry and the existence of pure profit', *Economic Journal*, 88, pp. 455–469.

Edel, M. and Sclar, E. (1974) 'Taxes, spending and property values: supply adjustment in a Tiebout–Oates model', *Journal of Political Economy*, 82, pp. 941–954.

Edwards, S.L. (1970) 'Transport costs in British industry', *Journal of Transport Economics and Policy*, 4, pp. 65–83.

Edwards, S.L. (1975) 'Regional variations in freight costs', *Journal of Transport Economics and Policy*, 9, pp. 115–126.

Edwards, S.L. and Bayliss, B.T. (1971) *Operating Costs in Road Freight Transport*, Department of the Environment, London.

Environment, Dept of (1976) *Report of Committee of Inquiry into Local Government Finance* (Chairman, F. Layfield), Cmnd. 6453, HMSO.

Environment, Dept of (1976) *Transport Policy: A Consultative Document*, HMSO.

Environment, Dept of (1977) *Housing Policy: A Consultative Document*, HMSO.

Environment, Dept of (1977) *Policy for the Inner Cities*, Cmnd. 6845, HMSO.

Environment, Dept of (1981) *Alternatives to Domestic Rates*, Cmnd. 8449, HMSO.

Environment, Dept of (1983a) *Streamlining the Cities: Government Proposals for Reorganising Local Government in Greater London and the Metropolitan Counties*, Cmnd. 9063, HMSO.

Environment, Dept of (1983b) *Rates: Proposals for Rate Limitation and Reform of the Rating System*, Cmnd. 9008, HMSO.

Evans, A.W. (1972) 'The pure theory of city size in an industrial economy', *Urban Studies*, 9, pp. 49–77.

Evans, A.W. (1973) *The Economics of Residential Location*, Macmillan.

Evans, A.W. (1975) 'Rents and housing in a theory of urban growth', *Journal of Regional Science*, 15, pp. 113–125.

Evans, A.W. (1980) 'A portrait of the London labour market', in A. Evans and D. Eversley (eds), *The Inner City: Employment and Industry*, Heinemann.

Evans, A.W. (1982) 'The neutrality of a development gains tax', *Public Finance/Finances Publiques*, 37, pp. 59–66.

Evans, A.W. (1983) 'The determination of the price of land', *Urban Studies*, 20, pp. 119–129.

Evans, A.W. and Richardson, R. (1981) 'Urban unemployment: interpretation and additional evidence', *Scottish Journal of Political Economy*, 28, pp. 107–124.

Eversley, D.E.C. (1972) 'Rising costs and static incomes: some economic consequences of regional planning in London', *Urban Studies*, 9, pp. 347–368.

Ewers, H.J. and Wettmann, R.W. (1980) 'Innovation-oriented regional policy', *Regional Studies*, 14, pp. 161–179.

Fagg, J. (1980) 'A re-examination of the incubator hypothesis: a case study of Greater Leicester', *Urban Studies*, 17, pp. 35–44.

Foster, C.D. and Glaister, S. (1975) 'The anatomy of the development value tax', *Urban Studies*, 12, pp. 213–218.

Foster, C.D., Jackman, R.A. and Perlman, M. (1980) *Local Government Finance in a Unitary State*, Allen and Unwin.

Foster, C.D. and Jackman, R.A. (1982) 'Accountability and the control of local spending', *Public Money*, 2, pp. 11–14.

Foster, C.D. and Joy, S. (1967) 'Railway track costs in Britain', in *Development of Railway Traffic Engineering*, Institute of Civil Engineers, London.

Foster, C.D. and Richardson, R. (1973) 'Employment trends in London in the 1960s and their relevance for the future', in D. Donnison and D. Eversley (eds), *London: Urban Patterns, Problems and Policies*, Heinemann.

Fothergill, S. and Gudgin, G. (1979a) 'In defence of shift-share', *Urban Studies*, 16, pp. 309–319.

Fothergill, S. and Gudgin, G. (1979b) 'Regional employment change: a sub-regional explanation', *Progress in Planning*, 12, pp. 155–219.

Fothergill, S. and Gudgin, G. (1982) *Unequal Growth*, Heinemann.

Frankena, M. (1975) 'Alternative models of rent control', *Urban Studies*, 12, pp. 303–308.

Frankena, M. (1983) 'Public transport objectives and subsidy formulas', *Journal of Transport Economics and Policy*, 17, pp. 67–76.

Gibson, J.G. (1980) 'The effect of matching grants on local authority user charges', *Public Finance/Finances Publiques*, 35, pp. 372–379.

Gibson, J.G. (1982) 'The Block and Target Grant System and local authority expenditure—theory and evidence', *Local Government Studies*, 8, pp. 15–31.

Glaister, S. (1974) 'Generalised consumer surplus and public transport pricing', *Economic Journal*, 84, pp. 849–867.

Glaister, S. (1976) 'Transport pricing policies and efficient urban growth', *Journal of Public Economics*, 5, pp. 103–117.

Glaister, S. (1981) *Fundamentals of Transport Economics*, Basil Blackwell.

Glaister, S. (1984) 'Allocation of urban public transport subsidy', in J. LeGrand and R. Robinson (eds), *Privatisation and the Welfare State*, Allen and Unwin.

Glaister, S. and Collings, J.J. (1978) 'Maximisation of passenger miles in theory and practice', *Journal of Transport Economics and Policy*, 12, pp. 305–321.

Glaister, S. and Lewis, D. (1978) 'An integrated fares policy for transport in Greater London', *Journal of Public Economics*, 9, pp. 341–355.

Gordon, I.R. (1977) 'Regional interdependence in the United Kingdom economy', in W.W. Leontief (ed.), *Structure, System and Economic Policy*, Cambridge University Press.

Gordon, I.R. and Lamont, D.W. (1982) 'A model of labour market interdependencies in the London region', *Environment and Planning A*, 14, pp. 237–264.

Gordon, I.R. and Vickerman, R.W. (1982) 'Opportunity, preference and constraint: an approach to the analysis of metropolitan migration', *Urban Studies*, 19, pp. 247–261.

Gordon, I.R., Vickerman, R.W., Lamont, D.W. and Thomas, A.M. (1983) *Opportunities, Preferences and Constraints on Population Movement in the London Region*, Urban and Regional Studies Unit, University of Kent.

Graves, P.E. and Linneman, P.D. (1979) 'Household migration: theoretical and empirical results', *Journal of Urban Economics*, 6, pp. 383–404.

Greenhut, M.L. (1956) *Plant Location in Theory and Practice*, University of North Carolina Press.

Greenhut, M.L. (1963) *Microeconomics and the Space Economy*, Scott Foresman, Chicago.

Greenhut, M.L. and Ohta, H. (1975) *Theory of Spatial Pricing and Market Areas*, Duke University Press.

Greenwood, M.J. (1980) 'Metropolitan growth and the intrametropolitan location of employment, housing and labour force', *Review of Economics and Statistics*, 62, pp. 491–501.

Grigsby, W. (1963) *Housing Markets and Public Policy*, University of Pennsylvania Press.

Gripaios, P. (1977) 'The closure of firms in the inner city: the south-east London case, 1970–75', *Regional Studies*, 11, pp. 1–6.

Gudgin, G. (1978) *Industrial Location Processes and Regional Employment Growth*, Saxon House.

Gwilliam, K.M. (1979) 'Transport infrastructure investments and regional development', in J.K. Bowers (ed.), *Inflation, Development and Integration—Essays in Honour of A.J. Brown*, Leeds University Press.

Gwilliam, K.M. and Nash, C.A. (1972) 'Evaluation of urban road improvements—a comment', *Applied Economics*, 4, pp. 307–315.

Hägerstrand, T. (1967) *Innovation Diffusion as a Spatial Process*, transl. A.R. Pred, Chicago University Press.

Hall, P. (1982) 'Enterprise Zones: a justification', *International Journal of Urban and Regional Research*, 6, pp. 416–421.

Hall, P. and Hay, D. (1980) *Growth Centres in the European Urban System*, Heinemann.

Hall, P., Thomas, R., Gracey, H. and Drewett, R. (1973) *The Containment of Urban England*, (2 vols), Allen and Unwin.

Harloe, M. (ed.) (1977) *Captive Cities*, Wiley.

Harris, R.I.D. (1983) 'The measurement of capital services in production for U.K. regions, 1968–78', *Regional Studies*, 17, pp. 169–180.

Harrison, B. (1982) 'The politics and economics of the urban Enterprise Zone proposal: a critique', *International Journal of Urban and Regional Research*, 6, pp. 422–428.

Hensher, D.A. and Dalvi, M.Q. (eds) (1978) *The Determinants of Travel Choice*, Saxon House.

Hirsch, W.Z. (1973) *Urban Economic Analysis*, McGraw-Hill.

Hoch, I. (1972) 'Income and city size', *Urban Studies*, 9, pp. 299–328.

Hoch, I. (1977) 'Variations in the quality of life among cities and regions', in L. Wingo and A. Evans (eds), *Public Economics and the Quality of Life*, Johns Hopkins University Press.

Holland, S. (1976) *Capital vs. the Regions*, Macmillan.

Holterman, S.E. (1975) 'Areas of urban deprivation in Great Britain: an analysis of 1971 Census data', *Social Trends*, 6, pp. 33–47.

Hotelling, H. (1929) 'Stability in competition', *Economic Journal*, 39, pp. 41–57.

House of Commons Expenditure Committee (1972) *Urban Transport Planning*, HC57 (1972/73), HMSO.

House of Commons Transport Committee (1982) *Transport in London*, HC127 (1981/82), HMSO.

Hoyt, H. (1939) *Structure and Growth of Residential Neighbourhoods in American Cities*, Federal Housing Administration, Washington, D.C.

Hughes, G. (1979) 'Housing income and subsidies', *Fiscal Studies*, 1, pp. 20–38.

Hurd, R.M. (1903) *Principles of City Land Values*, The Record and Guide, New York.

Isard, W. (1956) *Location and the Space Economy*, MIT Press.

Issaev, B., Nijkamp, P., Rietveld, P. and Snickars, F. (eds) (1982) *Multiregional Economic Modelling: Practice and Prospect*, Studies in Regional Science and Urban Economics, 9, North-Holland.

Jackman, R.A. (ed.) (1978) *The Impact of Rates on Industry and Commerce*, CES Policy Series 5, Centre for Environmental Studies, London.

Jackson, P.M. (1982) *The Political Economy of Bureaucracy*, Philip Allan.

Jackson, P., Meadows, J. and Taylor, A. (1982) 'Urban fiscal decay in U.K. cities', *Local Government Studies*, 8, pp. 23–43.

Jones, J.T. (1981) 'Industrial development and economic divergence', in M. Hodges and W. Wallace (eds), *Economic Divergence in the European Community*, Allen and Unwin.

Kaldor, N. (1970) 'The case for regional policies', *Scottish Journal of Political Economy*, 17, pp. 337–347.

Kaldor, N. (1972) 'The irrelevance of equilibrium economics', *Economic Journal*, 82, pp. 1,237–1,255.

Keeble, D. (1966) *Industrial Growth in North West London: A Geographical Analysis*, Ph.D. thesis, University of Cambridge.

Keeble, D. (1976) *Industrial Location and Planning in the United Kingdom*, Methuen.

Keeble, D. (1980) 'Industrial decline, regional policy and the urban–rural manufacturing shift in the United Kingdom', *Environment and Planning A*, 12, pp. 945–962.

King, M. (1980) 'An econometric model of tenure choice and demand for housing as a joint decision', *Journal of Public Economics*, 14, pp. 137–159.

King, M. and Atkinson, A.B. (1980) 'Housing policy, taxation and reform', *Midland Bank Review*, Spring.

Klaassen, L.H., Bourdrez, J.A. and Volmuller, J. (1981) *Transport and Reurbanisation*, Gower.

Lancaster, K. (1966) 'A new approach to consumer theory', *Journal of Political Economy*, 74, pp. 132–157.

Lee, N. and Steedman, I.W. (1970) 'Economies of scale in bus transport I: some British municipal results', *Journal of Transport Economics and Policy*, 4, pp. 15–28.

LeGrand, J. (1975) 'Fiscal equity and central government grants to local authorities', *Economic Journal*, 85, pp. 531–547.

Leone, R.A. and Struyk, R. (1976) 'The incubator hypothesis: evidence from five SMSAs', *Urban Studies*, 13, pp. 325–331.

Lerner, A.P. and Singer, H.W. (1939) 'Some notes on duopoly and spatial competition', *Journal of Political Economy*, 45, pp. 145–186.

Lever, W.F. (1972) 'Industrial movement, spatial association and functional linkages', *Regional Studies*, 6, pp. 371–384.

Lever, W.F. (1974) 'Regional multipliers and demand leakages at establishment level', *Scottish Journal of Political Economy*, 21, pp. 111–122.

Lever, W.F. (1978) 'Company dominated labour markets: the British case', *Tijdschrift voor Economische en Sociale Geografie*, 69, pp. 306–311.

Lever, W.F. (1979) 'Industry and labour markets in Great Britain', in F.E.I. Hamilton and G.J.R. Lüge (eds) *Spatial Analysis, Industry and the Industrial Environment*, Wiley.

Lever, W.F. (1980) 'The operation of local labour markets in Great Britain', *Papers of the Regional Science Association*, 44, pp. 37–55.

Lever, W.F. (1981) 'The measurement and implications of employment concentration ratios in British local labour markets', *Papers of the Regional Science Association*, 47, pp. 139–154.

Lewis, J. Parry (1979) *Urban Economics—A Set Approach*, Arnold.

Linneman, P. and Graves, P.E. (1983) 'Migration and job change—a multinomial logit approach', *Journal of Urban Economics*, 14, pp. 263–279.

Lloyd, P. (1979) 'Components of industrial change for Merseyside', *Urban Studies*, 16, pp. 45–60.

Lloyd, P.E. and Dicken, P. (1977) *Location in Space*, 2nd ed., Harper and Row.

Lösch, A. (1954) *The Economics of Location*, Yale University Press.

MacDonald, J.F. (1979) *Economic Analysis of an Urban Housing Market*, Academic Press.

McGregor, A. (1977) 'Intra-urban variations in unemployment duration: a case study', *Urban Studies*, 14, pp. 303–313.

McKay, D.H. and Cox, A.W. (1979) *The Politics of Urban Change*, Croom Helm.

Mackie, P.J. and Garton, P.M. (1979) *The Financing of Local Transport*, Working Paper No. 117, Institute for Transport Studies, University of Leeds.

Maclennan, D. (1982) *Housing Economics*, Longman.

Madden, J.F. (1980) 'Urban land use and the growth in two earner households', *American Economic Review*, 70, pp. 191–197.

Madden, J.F. (1981) 'Why women work closer to home', *Urban Studies*, 18, pp. 181–194.

Madden, M. and Batery, P.W.J. (1983) 'Linked population and economic models: some methodological issues in forecasting, analysis and policy optimisation', *Journal of Regional Science*, 23, pp. 141–164.

Martin, R.L. (1982) 'Job loss and the regional incidence of redundancies in the current recession', *Cambridge Journal of Economics*, 6, pp. 375–395.

Mason, C. (1983) 'Labour market policy', in K. Young and C. Mason (eds) *Urban Economic Development*, Macmillan.

Massey, D. (1982) 'Enterprise Zones: a political issue', *International Journal of Urban and Regional Research*, 6, pp. 429–434.

Massey, D. and Meegan, R. (1982) *The Anatomy of Job Loss*, Methuen.

Metcalf, D. (1975) 'Urban unemployment in England', *Economic Journal*, 85, pp. 578–589.

Metcalf, D. and Richardson, R. (1976) 'Unemployment in London', in G.D.N. Worswick (ed.) *The Concept and Measurement of Involuntary Unemployment*, Allen and Unwin.

Miernyk, W. (1965) *Elements of Input–Output Economics*, Random House.

Mills, E.S. and de Ferranti, D.M. (1971) 'Market choices and optimum city size', *American Economic Review, Papers and Proceedings*, 61, pp. 340–345.

Mincer, J. (1978) 'Family migration decisions', *Journal of Political Economy*, 86, pp. 749–773.

Mirrlees, J.A. (1972) 'The optimum town', *Swedish Journal of Economics*, 74, pp. 114–135.

Mogridge, M.J.H. (1979) 'Changing spatial patterns in the journey to work: a comparison of the 1966 and 1971 census data in London', *Urban Studies*, 16, pp. 179–190.

Mohring, H. (1972) 'Optimisation and scale economies in urban bus transportation', *American Economic Review*, 62, pp. 591–604.

Monopolies and Mergers Commission (1982) *Bristol Omnibus Co. Ltd, Cheltenham District Traction Co., City of Cardiff District Council, Trent Motor Traction Co. Ltd, and West Midlands P.T.E. A Report on Stage Carriage Services supplied by the Undertakings*, HC442 (1981/82), HMSO.

Moore, B. and Rhodes, J. (1976) 'The relative needs of local authorities', in *Evidence to Committee of Inquiry into Local Government Finance* (Layfield Committee) Vol. 7, HMSO.

Moore, E.G. and Clark, W.A.V. (1980) 'The policy context for mobility research', in E.G. Moore and W.A.V. Clark (eds) *Residential Mobility and Public Policy*, Sage.

Moore, E.G. and Clark, W.A.V. (eds) (1980) *Residential Mobility and Public Policy*, Sage.

Morris, D. and Jepson, D. (1981) 'Coventry and the motor-vehicle industry', *National Westminster Bank Review*, May.

Morrison, W.I. (1973) 'The development of an urban inter-industry model', *Environment and Planning A*, 5, pp. 369–383, pp. 433–460, pp. 545–554.

Moses, L.N. (1958) 'Location and the theory of production', *Quarterly Journal of Economics*, 72, pp. 259–272.

Mueller, D.C. (1979) *Public Choice*, Cambridge University Press.

Muth, R.F. (1969) *Cities and Housing*, Chicago University Press.

Muth, R.F. (1976) 'A vintage model with housing production', in G.J. Papageorgiou (ed.) *Mathematical Land Use Theory*, Lexington Books.

Myrdal, G. (1957) *Economic Theory and Underdeveloped Regions*, Duckworth.

Nash, C.A. (1978) 'Management objectives in bus transport', *Journal of Transport Economics and Policy*, 12, pp. 70–85.

Nash, C.A. (1982) *Economics of Public Transport*, Longman.

Neutze, M. (1974) 'The development value tax: a comment', *Urban Studies*, 11, pp. 91–92.

Nicholson, B.M., Brinkley, I. and Evans, A.W. (1981) 'The role of the inner city in the development of manufacturing industry', *Urban Studies*, 18, pp. 57–71.

Nicholson, R.J. and Topham, N. (1971) 'The determinants of investment in housing by local authorities: an econometric approach', *Journal of the Royal Statistical Society A*, 134, pp. 273–303.

Niskanen, W.A. Jr. (1971) *Bureaucracy and Representative Government*, Aldine-Atherton.

Oates, W.E. (1969) 'The effects of property taxes and local spending on property values: an empirical study of tax capitalisation and the Tiebout hypothesis', *Journal of Political Economy*, 77, pp. 957–971.

Oates, W.E. (1972) *Fiscal Federalism*, Harcourt Brace Jovanovich.

Oates, W.E., Howrey, E.P. and Baumol, W.J. (1971) 'The analysis of public policy in dynamic urban models', *Journal of Political Economy*, 79, pp. 142–153.

Paelinck, J.H.P. (1982) *Formal Spatial Economic Analysis*, Gower.

Papageorgiou, G.J. (ed.) (1976) *Mathematical Land Use Theory*, Lexington Books.

Park, R.E., Burgess, E.W. and MacKenzie, R.D. (eds) (1925) *The City*, Chicago University Press.

Pauly, M.V. (1967) 'Clubs, commonality and the Core: an integration of game theory and the theory of public goods', *Economica*, 35, pp. 314–324.

Pauly, M.V. (1970) 'Cores and Clubs', *Public Choice*, 9, pp. 53–65.

Pearce, D.W. (1976) *Environmental Economics*, Longman.

Perroux, F. (1955) 'Note sur la notion de pôles de croissance', *Economie Appliquée*, 7, pp. 307–320.

Pestieau, P. (1983) 'Fiscal mobility and local public goods. A survey of the empirical and theoretical studies of the Tiebout model', in J.F. Thisse and H.G. Zoller (eds) *Locational Analysis of Public Facilities*, North-Holland.

Pines, D. (1976) 'Dynamic aspects of land use patterns in a growing city', in G.J. Papageorgiou (ed.) *Mathematical Land Use Theory*, Lexington Books.

Prebisch, R. (1950) *The Economic Development of Latin America and its Principal Problems*, U.N. Economic Commission for Latin America, New York.

Predöhl, A. (1928) 'The theory of location in its relation to general economics', *Journal of Political Economy*, 36, pp. 371–390.

Pucher, J., Markstedt, A. and Hirschmann, I. (1983) 'Impacts of subsidies on the costs of urban public transport', *Journal of Transport Economics and Policy*, 17, pp. 155–176.

Pullen, M.J. and Proops, J.L.R. (1983) 'The North Staffordshire regional economy: an Input–Output assessment', *Regional Studies*, 17, pp. 191–200.

Quigley, J.M. (1980) 'Local residential mobility and local government policy', in E.G. Moore and W.A.V. Clark (eds) *Residential Mobility and Public Policy*, Sage.

Quigley, J.M. and Weinberg, D.H. (1977) 'Intra-urban residential mobility: a review and synthesis', *International Regional Science Review*, 2, pp. 1–66.

Ratcliffe, R.U. (1949) *Urban Land Economics*, McGraw-Hill.

Rees, R. (1976) *Public Enterprise Economics*, Weidenfeld and Nicolson.

Renaud, B. (1981) *National Urbanization Policy in Developing Countries*, Oxford University Press.

Richardson, H.W. (1972) *Input–Output and Regional Economics*, Weidenfeld and Nicolson.

Richardson, H.W. (1973a) *Regional Growth Theory*, Macmillan.

Richardson, H.W. (1973b) *The Economics of Urban Size*, Saxon House.

Richardson, H.W. (1977) *The New Urban Economics: and Alternatives*, Pion, London.

Richardson, H.W. (1978) *Regional and Urban Economics*, Penguin Books.

Richardson, H.W. (1981) 'National urban development strategies in developing countries', *Urban Studies*, 18, pp. 267–283.

Richardson, R. (1980) 'Unemployment', in G.C. Cameron (ed.) *The Future of the British Conurbations*, Longman.

Robinson, R. (1979) *Housing Economics and Public Policy*, Macmillan.

Rose, L.A. (1973) 'The development value tax', *Urban Studies*, 10, pp. 271–285.

Samuelson, P.A. (1954) 'The pure theory of public expenditure', *Review of Economics and Statistics*, 36, pp. 386–389.

Samuelson, P.A. (1983) 'Thünen at Two Hundred', *Journal of Economic Literature*, 21, pp. 1,468–1,488.

Sant, M. (1975) *Industrial Movement and Regional Development: the British Case*, Pergamon.

Saunders, P.R. (1979) *Urban Politics: A Sociological Interpretation*, Hutchinson.

Seers, D. (1962) 'A model of comparative rates of growth in the world economy', *Economic Journal*, 72, pp. 45–78.

Segal, D. (1976) 'Are there returns to scale in city size?', *Review of Economics and Statistics*, 58, pp. 339–350.

Segal, D. (1977) *Urban Economics*, Irwin.

Segal, D. (ed.) (1979) *The Economics of Neighbourhood*, Academic Press.

Sharp, C. (1980) 'Transport and regional development with special reference to Britain', *Transport Policy and Decision Making*, 1, pp. 1–11.

Shefer, D. (1973) 'Localization economies in SMSAs: a production function analysis', *Journal of Regional Science*, 13, pp. 55–64.

Siegel, J. (1975) 'Intrametropolitan migration: a simultaneous model of employment and residential location of white and black households', *Journal of Urban Economics*, 2, pp. 29–47.

Simpson, W. (1980) 'A simultaneous model of workplace and residential location incorporating job search', *Journal of Urban Economics*, 8, pp. 330–349.

Sinclair, M.T. and Sutcliffe, C.M.S. (1978) 'The first round of the Keynesian income multiplier', *Scottish Journal of Political Economy*, 25, pp. 177–186.

Sinclair, M.T. and Sutcliffe, C.M.S. (1982) 'Keynesian income multipliers with first and second round effects: an application to tourist expenditures', *Oxford Bulletin of Economics and Statistics*, 44, pp. 321–338.

Sjaastad, L.A. (1962) 'The costs and returns of human migration', *Journal of Political Economy*, 70, pp. 80–93.

Smart, M.W. (1974) 'Labour market areas: uses and definition', *Progress in Planning*, 2.

Smith, C.T.B., Clifton, R., Makeham, P., Creigh, S.W. and Burn, R.W. (1978) *Strikes in Britain*, HMSO.

Smith, D.M. (1971) *Industrial Location: an Economic Geographical Analysis*, Wiley.

Smith, P. (1983) 'Local authority budgets 1983: no reduction of services', *Public Money*, 4, pp. 47–53.

Smithies, A. (1941) 'Optimal location in spatial competition', *Journal of Political Economy*, 49, pp. 423–439.

Solow, R.M. (1973) 'Congestion costs and the use of land for streets', *Bell Journal of Economics and Management Science*, 4, pp. 602–618.

Steinnes, D. (1977) 'Causality and intra-urban location', *Journal of Urban Economics*, 4, pp. 67–79.

Steinnes, D. (1982) 'Do "people follow jobs" or do "jobs follow people"? A causality issue in urban economics', *Urban Studies*, 19, pp. 187–192.

Stiglitz, J.E. (1977) 'The theory of local public goods', in M. Feldstein and R.P. Inman (eds), *The Economics of Public Services*, Macmillan.

Stiglitz, J.E. (1983) 'Public goods in open economies with heterogeneous individuals', in J.F. Thisse and H.G. Zoller (eds), *Locational Analysis of Public Facilities*, North-Holland.

Storey, D.J. (1982) *Entrepreneurship and the New Firm*, Croom Helm.

Struyk, R.J. and James, F.J. (1975) *Intrametropolitan Industrial Location: The Pattern and Process of Change*, Lexington Books.

Sugden, R. (1981) *The Political Economy of Public Choice*, Martin Robertson.

Sveikausas, L. (1975) 'The productivity of cities', *Quarterly Journal of Economics*, 89, pp. 393–413.

Thirlwall, A.P. (1966) 'Regional unemployment as a cyclical phenomenon', *Scottish Journal of Political Economy*, 13, pp. 205–219.

Thirlwall, A.P. (1969) 'Types of unemployment: with special reference to "non-demand-deficient" unemployment in the U.K.', *Scottish Journal of Political Economy*, 16, pp. 20–49.

Thirlwall, A.P. (1974) 'Types of unemployment in the regions of Great Britain', *Manchester School*, 42, pp. 325–339.

Thirlwall, A.P. (1980a) *Balance of Payments Theory and the U.K. Experience*, Macmillan.

Thirlwall, A.P. (1980b) 'Regional problems are "balance-of-payments" problems', *Regional Studies*, 14, pp. 419–425.

Thomson, J.M. (1974) *Modern Transport Economics*, Penguin Books.

Thomson, J.M. (1978) *Great Cities and their Traffic*, Penguin Books.

Thünen, J.H. von (1966) *The Isolated State*, Pergamon.

Thwaites, A.T. (1982) 'Some evidence of regional variations in the introduction and diffusion of industrial products and processes within British manufacturing industry', *Regional Studies*, 16, pp. 371–381.

Tiebout, C.M. (1956) 'A pure theory of local expenditures', *Journal of Political Economy*, 64, pp. 416–424.

Townroe, P.M. (1973) 'The supply of mobile industry: a cross sectional analysis', *Regional and Urban Economics*, 2, pp. 371–386.

Trade and Industry, Dept of (1973) 'Memorandum on the inquiry into location attitudes and experience', in House of Commons Expenditure Committee, *Regional Development Incentives*, HC85 (1973/74), HMSO.

Transport, Dept of (1979) *Report of the Independent Committee of Inquiry into Road Haulage Operators Licensing* (Chairman, C.D. Foster) HMSO.

Transport, Dept of (1980) *Report of the Inquiry into Lorries, People and the Environment* (Chairman, Sir Arthur Armitage), HMSO.

Transport, Dept of (1982) *Public Transport Subsidy in Cities*, Cmnd. 8735, HMSO.

Transport, Dept of (1983) *Public Transport in London*, Cmnd. 9004, HMSO.

Tullock, G. (1965) *The Politics of Bureaucracy*, Public Affairs Press, New York.

Ullman, E.L. (1962) 'The nature of cities reconsidered', *Papers and Proceedings of the Regional Science Association*, 9, pp. 7–23.

Vickerman, R.W. (1979) 'The evaluation of urban change: equilibrium and adaptive approaches', *Urban Studies*, 16, pp. 81–93.

Vickerman, R.W. (1980) *Spatial Economic Behaviour*, Macmillan.

Vickerman, R.W. (1983) 'Transport, residential satisfaction and the decision to move', in *Interpreting and Valuing Transport's Role in Social Well-Being*, Ministry of Transport and Public Works, The Hague.

Vickerman, R.W. (1984) 'Urban and regional change, migration and commuting—the dynamics of workplace, residence and transport choice', *Urban Studies*, 21, pp. 15–29.

Vipond, J. (1974) 'City size and unemployment', *Urban Studies*, 11, pp. 39–46.

Wabe, J.S. and Coles, O.B. (1975) 'The peak and off-peak demand for bus transport: a cross-sectional analysis of British municipal operations', *Applied Economics*, 7, pp. 25–30.

Walters, A.A. (1961) 'The theory and measurement of private and social cost of highway congestion', *Econometrica*, 29, pp. 676–697.

Walters, A.A. (1982) 'Externalities in urban buses', *Journal of Urban Economics*, 11, pp. 60–72.

Watkins, A.J. (1980) *The Practice of Urban Economics*, Sage.

Weber, A. (1929) *Theory of the Location of Industries*, transl. C.J. Friedrich, University of Chicago Press.

Weinberg, D.H. (1979) 'The determinants of intra-urban household mobility', *Regional Science and Urban Economics*, 9, pp. 219–246.

Weinberg, D.H. (1980) 'Mobility and housing change: the housing allowance demand experiment', in E.G. Moore and W.A.V. Clark (eds), *Residential Mobility and Public Policy*, Sage.

White, M.J. (1977) 'A model of residential location choice and commuting by men and women workers', *Journal of Regional Science*, 17, pp. 41–52.

Whiting, A. (ed.) (1976) *The Economics of Industrial Subsidies*, HMSO.

Whitman, M. von N. (1972) 'Place prosperity and people prosperity: the delineation of optimal policy areas', in M. Perlman, C.L. Leven and B.Chinitz (eds), *Spatial, Regional and Population Economics: Essays in Honor of Edgar M. Hoover*, Gordon and Breach.

Wingo, L. Jr. (1961) *Transportation and Urban Land*, Resources for the Future, Washington, D.C.

Young, K. (1983) 'The problems of economic strategy', in K. Young and C. Mason (eds), *Urban Economic Development*, Macmillan.

Young, K. and Mason C. (eds) (1983) *Urban Economic Development: New Roles and Relationships*, Macmillan.

Zipf, G.K. (1949) *Human Behaviour and the Principle of Least Effort*, Addison-Wesley.

Author Index

Subject Index